Rare Collection

Superb Recipes by The
Junior League of Galveston County

Published by
JLGC Publications

The Junior League
of Galveston County, Inc.

210 Kempner Street • Galveston, Texas 77550

The Junior League of Galveston County, Inc. is an organization of women committed to promoting voluntarism and to improving the community through the effective action and leadership of trained volunteers. Its purpose is exclusively educational and charitable.

ISBN: 0-96137790-9
The Junior League of Galveston County, Inc.
Library of Congress Card Catalog 84-081639

Copies of Rare Collection may be obtained from the
Junior League of Galveston County, Inc.
210 Kempner
Galveston, Texas 77550
409-765-7646
or by mailing an order blank from the back
of the book to the above address.

Proceeds from the sale of *Rare Collection* will go to support the many worthwhile projects sponsored by the Junior League of Galveston County, Inc. including Ronald McDonald House, Scholarships, Family Literacy, Project Casa (Casa de Esperanza de los Ninos), Books Alive!, and Community Assistance Fund.

Art work designed by Robin Shaw, Alvin, Texas.
Nutritional revisions by Mary Ann Schaper, R. D., L. D., Texas City, Texas.

First Printing, May 1985, 10,000 copies
Second Printing, October 1985, 10,000 copies
Third Printing, May 1988, 10,000 copies
Fourth Printing, August 1990, 10,000 copies
Fifth Printing, October 1992, 10,000 copies

Printed in the USA by
WIMMER BROTHERS
A Wimmer Company
Memphis • Dallas

COOKBOOK COMMITTEE
1990-91

Past Chairman ....Meredith Zalesak
Chairman ....Monica Ott
Co-Chairman ....Liz Jackson
Wholesale Chairman ....Mary Maxwell
   Assistant ....Amy Rodysill
Retail Chairman ....Susan Brossman
Marketing Chairman ....Debby Molloy
Subcommittee ....Ellen Mosher

Brenda Carlile
Rene Salvato
Kristy Christensen
Karen Owen

Sustainer Advisor ....Tonka Lane
Executive Board Liasons ....Paula Roberts

Anne Henderson

STEERING COMMITTEE
1984-85

Chairman..Sue Langston
Editing and Production
   Co-Chairman...Kathy Albright
   Assistant .... Peggy Rapp
Printing and Design
   Co-Chairman.. Kitty Potter
   Assistant ....Pamela Lawder
Testing
   Co-Chairman.. Jean Honey
   Assistant .... Ellen Druss
Marketing
   Co-Chairman...Pamela Lawder
   Wholesale Assistant... Debby Citti
   Retail Assistant...Raney Ritter
   Media Assistant .... Jane Micks
Kick Off Party
   Co-Chairman.. Kitty Potter
   Assistant ....Stevie Jo Brown
Sustainer Advisor .... Marcia Lee Hutchings

CONTRIBUTORS

The Cookbook Committee expresses grateful appreciation to League members and friends who contributed recipes to Rare Collection. Each recipe has been tested for accuracy and excellence. We regret that we were unable to include many recipes which were submitted, due to similarity or availability of space.

Carolyn Haynes Adams
Kathy Heyel Albright
Jean C. Alston
Sue Douglas Anderson
Vandy Anderson
Winifred Bean Ansell
Linda Lanier Ansell
Sue Krueger Anthony
Irene Johnson Ayers
Pat Romero Beach
Louise Touchstone Bell
G. Shari Ladanyi Blackwell
Marjorie Willits Blum
Karolyn Kucera Bowles
Lawren Ethridge Bradford
Susan Real Broll
Juanita Brookshire
Mary Partridge Brown
Marjorie McCullough Brown
Lou Ann Wright Brudner
Betsy Henderson Bryant
Betty Gentry Bunce
Lynn McCright Burkhardt
Barry Burkhardt
Robyn Russell Bushong
Viva Waite Butler
Kay Ellis Byrd
Mary Jones Cain
Connie Spinosa Campbell
Jo Wadler Capito
Kathleen Mann Carney
Trish Severance Carr
Gwen Stratten Charpentier
Barbara Potter Christa
Debby McIlroy Citti
Carolyn Smith Clyburn
Rosemary Giles Coleman
Marie English Collins
Franka Dawson Correia
Nancy Cothron
Dorothy Reading Cross
Harriett Baron Furhop

Dorothy Peek Currie
Cynthia D'Ascenzo-Davis
Leah Ellis D'Ascenzo
Virginia Willrich Dalehite
Susie Lee Davis
Margaret Carter Denton
Peggy Godard Dietel
Betty Walton Dodge
Weez Gilley Doherty
Mary Ellen Hipp Doyle
Kathleen Dresso
Ellen Fisk Druss
Gayle Fierce Dupree
Wallice A. O'Quin Durbin
Helen Cox Duval
Susan Shirley Eckel
Doris Dickinson Ethridge
Rose A. Dominey Farmer
Evelyn Montagne Farmer
Katy Nutt Farmer
Janet Russell Farmer
Sidney C. Farmer III
Debra Faubion
Susan Trice Fieglein
Elizabeth Peterson Files
Carolyn Lanterman Foutch
Katherine Wakefield Fowler
Allan Fradkin
Linda Toubin Fradkin
Pat Martin Fradkin
Margie Gibbs Frantz
Linda Wander Fredrickson
Sally McCullough Futch
Carolyn Torregrossa Gaido
Mary Kay Gallagher Gaido
Mary Waterman Gajewski
Carolyn Allbritton Garrison
Dorothy Gill
Jeannie Watson Gillespie
Ella McNiel Gilman
Sara Lillian Ater Glenn
William Glenn

June Nunez Godard
Joan Frenkel Golden
Rhonda Gonzales
Debra Barnes Gorman
Molly George Granagham
H. Ross Grief
Seal Seinsheimer Grief
Ruby Kelley Grimes
Augustine Watts Grimes
Lucia Hart Gurley
Camille Ellis Haglund
Jane Hines Hamilton
Kitty Haner
Helen Reynolds Harloe
John Harloe
June Bricksom Harris
Betty Keneipp Harris
Koreen Shelstad Harstad
Lucy Spink Hays
Dorothy Whitehurst Heard
Doris Durbin Heard
Esther Cutrer Hebert
Diana K. Hempy
Marguerite Stechman Hendrickson
Linda Russell Henkel
Marcia Miller Herndon
B. J. Ravel Herz
Susan Ellis Hesley
Peggy O'Donnell Heyel
Penny Cady Heyel
Ruby Boling Hitzfeld
Ruth Holzschuh
Jean Hampton Honey
Anne B. Hooser
Gerry Levin Hornstein
Marilyn Burlington Howard
Sissy Shelton Howell
Susan Kalinke Huffman
Myrtle Hunter
Brenda Levy Hutchings
Marcia Lee Hagleman Hutchings
Joan Neal Hyatt
Meredith Brick Ippolito
Sidney Halverton Jackson
David James
Kathy McWilliams James
Joe Keene
Miki Bailey Keene
Francey Russell Kelso
Kate Murray Kelso
Margy Runge Kelso
Peaches Towler Kempner
Mary Ann Churchill Kent

Patricia Kelley Kilborn
Pieri Kitchen
Cecilia Kunc Kouns
Joyce Kay Lain
Curtis W. Lambert
Tonka Milicich Lane
Carolyn Hays Langston
Laura Ann Langston
Sue Hays Langston
Holly Hawke Larson
Pam Bradley Lawder
Susan Keyes Lawson
Joann Goode Lee
Tia Tyler Leslie
Edna Seinsheimer Levin
Bob Lewis
Mary Haynes Lewis
Vicki Walker Lewis
Imp Pettigrew Lightner
Suzanne Guyette Little
Janie Larscheid Loomis
Mike Loomis, Jr.
Betty Hooser Lord
Dixie Deer Louis
Mary Margaret Nagle Love
Claire Tsuhako Lutey
Caroline Giacchino Mallory
Barbra Hebert Markey
Pat Mullins McCloy
Lola Haden McDaniel
Marilyn Levy McFatridge
Joan Williams McLeod
Debi Nottingham McNabb
Joan Gobroski Mcgna
Olivia Thomas Meyer
Jane Ryan Micks
Linda LaMounit Mignerey
Dana Yarbrough Miller
Julie Basanda Mills
Phyllis Schwartz Milstein
Caron Caffal Miser
Gayle Monroe
Gayle Monsour Monsour
Mary Lee Moore
Colleen Warren Moore
Ida Jo Tabaracci Morse
Judith Youngblood Muller
Moore Murray
Linda Zindler Nathan
Bill Nicol
Cleta Iverson Norcross
Becky Oswalt Norman
Carmen N. Filidei Norris

5

Virginia Daly Olsan
Ellen Nunnally Owens
Suzanne Parrott
Betty Knox Passmore
Maureen Mezzino Patton
Mary Lou Hooser Pawlowski
Stella Kaminski Pawlowski
"Liz" Trench Payer
Karen Landureth Payne
Elaine Listwan Pendergast
Lori Reese Pepper
Ursa Keneipp Pierce
Lena Fontana Piperi
"Cici" Lonabough Posey
Kitty Owens Potter
Connie Vincent Powel
Pat Curran Presnall
Carol Marr Rankin
Diana Casey Rasmussen
Dianne Kouns Rasmussen
Arlene Button Redrow
Karen Tyner Redrow
Mary Ellen Wolf Reinarz
Gail Passmore Rider
Livie Rios
Margaret Lucas Ritter
"Raney" Ritter
Susan Henderson Ritter
Sally Sue Robinson
Franie Clark Rochkind
Eva Vonchovsky Roden
Mary Jane Steding Rogers
Sara Perrott Rose
Ethel Lucas Runge
Chloe Dell Sanders
Pamela Oyston Schadt
Marilyn Geller Schaffer
Laurie Londrigan Schaper
Alicia Mendez Schwager
Marilyn Cohn Schwartz
Betty Hodgson Shirley
Tosha Blackwell Short
Sue Perrott Siferd
Ann Terrell Singleton
Ellen Wommack Smith
Suzi Domel Smith
Marty Harrison Smith
Lara Hooper Smith
Diane Bergstrom Smith
Trudy Jackson Smither

Margaret Snipes
Verita Melancon Stansfield
Celeste Rochkind Stein
Susan Wilson Stevens
Charlene Stewart
Sally Menefee Stiernberg
Gloria Egbert Stratton
Kim Purrington Strauss
Ann Gipson Stubbs
Bernice Gustafson Sullivan
Cindy Lightner Sullivan
Susanne Hooser Sullivan
Andrea Pieri Sunseri
Lana Walker Swift
Maria Mancuso Tabaracci
Nonie Kempner Thompson
Mary Lou Sneyd Torregrossa
Hetta Jockusch Towler
Mary Hardwicke Townsend
Mary Ann Trevino
Dana Lain Tulloch
Leota Butler Tyner
Alma Wells Uher
Mary Rose Perrett Uher
John G. Unbehagen
Phyllis Grimes Vaughn
Stephanie Thiem Verkin
Kris Konugres Vogelpohl
Kay Benge Vroman
Carla Jensen Wahler
Lorna Walker
Sally John Wallace
Melva Wear
Marjorie Weaver
Leslie Herman Welch
Lois Wetzel Werner
Fran Chausse White
Evangeline Loessin Whorton
Shyrll L. Shaefer Williams
Elizabeth Manly Wilson
Susan Stampfli Wilson
Mary Suttles Woodward
Susan Turner Worthen
Alice Voorhees Yanasak
Ida Purjet Yankee
Carol Urbani Yarbrough
Barbara Woolford Yoder
Cindy Zaunbrecher Young
Judy Sandy Young
Michelle Dufilho Zaunbrecher

6

INTRODUCTION

From the sand and surf of Galveston Island comes a new selection of culinary delights that we know will excite your families and guests. A *Rare Collection* is as its title implies—a collection of recipes that are not found in every magazine or cookbook, but are success-proven recipes that after three years of collecting and testing have been carefully gathered for your enjoyment. Only those recipes that received an excellent rating consistently throughout the testing period have been included. One of the many goals of a *Rare Collection* is for you to feel assured that the book may be opened to any page — a recipe prepared — and that the finished result will be attractive and prompt compliments to the chef.

It is the wish of the Junior League of Galveston County, Inc. that all your dining adventures, from family meals, picnics, luncheons, to formal dinner parties — be enhanced by a *Rare Collection* delicacy.

Cookbook Committee

 We have used a shell to signify those recipes that we consider truly exceptional.

 We have used a heart to signify those recipes that have been revised to be Heart Healthy.

TABLE OF CONTENTS

SCALLOPS

Most people identify the scallop as one of the most tempting seafoods; however it also deserves to be recognized because of the interesting shell. The clever little scallop rapidly opens and closes its shell while swimming through the water and is able, therefore, to adroitly dodge its enemies.

Appetizers & Beverages

WON TON DELIGHTS

Yields: **2½-3 dozen**
Preparation Time: 20-30 minutes

½   **pound fresh crabmeat,
drained and flaked**
1   **8-ounce package cream
cheese, softened**
½   **teaspoon A-1 sauce**
½   **teaspoon garlic powder**
2½-3 **dozen won ton wrappers**
1   **egg yolk, well beaten
oil for deep frying**

1. Combine first four ingredients and blend into a paste. Place heaping teaspoons of mixture on each won ton wrapper.
2. Gather four corners at top. Brush edges with egg yolk and pinch or twist together gently to seal.
3. Heat oil in wok, deep fryer or heavy skillet to 375°. Fry until golden brown, about 3 minutes.
4. Drain on paper towel and serve with Chinese Mustard Sauce or other favorite sauce.

NUTTY CRABMEAT SPREAD

Yields: **16 servings**
Preparation Time: 20 minutes

2   **8-ounce packages cream
cheese, softened**
2   **tablespoons milk**
2   **tablespoons Worcestershire
sauce**
2   **cups fresh crabmeat (or two
7½-ounce cans of crabmeat)**
¼   **cup green onions, finely
chopped**
6   **tablespoons toasted almonds**

1. Using an electric mixer or food processor, combine cream cheese, milk, and Worcestershire sauce.
2. Drain and flake crabmeat. Add to cream cheese mixture. Add green onions and mix thoroughly by hand.
3. Turn into two 8-inch pie plates and top with toasted almonds. Bake for 15 minutes or until heated through. Keep warm on warming tray.
4. Serve with triscuits or other wheat cracker.

Temperature: **350 °**
Time: 15 minutes

CRUNCHY COCKTAIL MEATBALLS

*Yields: **50 meatballs***
Preparation Time: 10 minutes

1   *pound ground chuck*
1   *pound package regular bulk sausage*
½   *teaspoon garlic powder*
½   *teaspoon onion powder*
½   *cup water chestnuts*
1   *18-ounce bottle hickory smoked barbecue sauce*

1. Combine ground chuck, sausage, garlic powder and onion powder. Mix thoroughly.
2. Finely chop water chestnuts. Add to meat mixture and mix well.
3. Form into small balls. Bake on cookie sheet in 350° oven until well done (approximately 20 minutes).
4. Heat barbecue sauce. Add meatballs to sauce. Simmer 10 minutes. Serve warm in chafing dish.

*Temperature: **350** °*
Time: 20 minutes

Can be made ahead and frozen.

JALAPEÑO MUSHROOMS

Make 24 Hours Ahead Of Time

*Yields: **30***
Preparation Time: 20 minutes

1   *pound small fresh mushrooms*
1   *11-ounce can whole jalapeños with juice*
½   *cup tarragon vinegar*
1   *cup water*
1   *clove garlic, crushed*

1. In medium saucepan, bring water to rolling boil. Add whole mushrooms and continue boiling 15 minutes or until mushrooms turn grayish.
2. Drain and rinse with cool water. When cool, place in container with lid.
3. Mix remaining ingredients; add to mushrooms, covering completely with this mixture.
4. More water may be added if less jalapeño flavor is desired. Marinate at least overnight.

SMOKED OYSTER DIP

*Yields: **20 servings***
Preparation Time: 10 minutes plus
30 minutes set time

1   *8-ounce package cream cheese, softened*
1½   *cups good quality mayonnaise*
4   *drops Tabasco*
1   *tablespoon lemon juice*
1   *4¼-ounce can chopped black olives*
1   *3.66-ounce can smoked oysters, drained and chopped*

1. Combine cream cheese and mayonnaise with electric mixer or food processor. Add rest of ingredients. Blend thoroughly.
2. Chill for 30 minutes or more if desired.
3. Serve with crackers.

TOASTED SAVORIES

*Yields: **2 cups***
Preparation Time: 20 minutes

2   *egg whites*
2   *cups unsalted pecans*
1   *teaspoon salt*
1   *teaspoon dry mustard*
1   *teaspoon garlic powder*

1. Cover baking sheet with foil and butter it. Set aside.
2. Beat whites until foamy. Drop pecans into whites and stir to coat. Lift with fork to drain. Place pecans on foil.
3. Mix salt, dry mustard, and garlic powder. Pour into empty salt shaker. Sprinkle on pecans.
4. Bake in 350° oven for 25 minutes or until coating is set.
5. Lift foil to loosen nuts and break them apart. Cool. Store in airtight container or freeze.

*Temperature: **350 °***
Time: 25 minutes

Pecans will keep no longer than 1 week in refrigerator or 3 weeks in freezer.

SALMON STUFFED EGGS

*Yields: **4 servings***
Preparation Time: 10 minutes

4   *eggs, hard boiled*
½   *cup smoked salmon, mashed*
3   *tablespoons good quality*
     mayonnaise
8   *strips anchovy fillets,*
     optional
     capers
     dill

1. Half eggs lengthwise. Remove yolks and mash.
2. Combine yolks with salmon and mayonnaise.
3. Fill egg whites with mixture, mounding it.
4. Garnish each egg with 2 thin strips of anchovy fillets (crossed), capers, and dill.

CRAB SPREAD ON MUFFINS

*Yields: **48 Pieces***
Preparation Time: 10 minutes

"So Simple, Yet So Good"

1   *cup fresh white crabmeat or*
     one 7-ounce can
¼   *cup butter, softened*
1   *3¼-ounce jar Old English*
     Cheese Spread
½   *teaspoon garlic salt*
1½   *teaspoons mayonnaise*
     cayenne to taste
     paprika
4   *English muffins, split*

1. Drain crabmeat and remove any cartilage.
2. Combine crabmeat, butter, cheese, garlic, and mayonnaise. Mix thoroughly using a mixer or food processor. Add cayenne to taste.
3. Spread mixture on muffin halves. Cut muffins into sixths.
4. Place muffin pieces on cookie sheet. Sprinkle with paprika.
5. Broil until lightly brown.

Temperature: Broil
Time: 5 minutes

Can be frozen after spreading; when ready to serve, cut into sixths and pop under the broiler.

ANGELS ON HORSEBACK
"There's never enough"

Yields: 6 servings
Preparation Time: 10 minutes

1	*pint large fresh oysters*
12	*slices bacon, cut in half*
½	*teaspoon salt*
⅛	*teaspoon black pepper*
⅛	*teaspoon paprika*
2	*tablespoons fresh parsley, chopped*

1. Drain oysters. Lay an oyster across ½ slice of bacon. Sprinkle each oyster with seasonings and parsley.
2. Roll entire strip of bacon around oyster and fasten with toothpicks.
3. Place oyster on a rack in a shallow baking dish. Bake in 450° oven for 10 minutes or until bacon is crisp. Remove toothpicks and serve.

Temperature: 450°
Time: 10 minutes

SHRIMP MOUSSE
Must Make Ahead Of Time

Yields: 5½ cups mold
Preparation Time: 1 hour

2	*pounds shrimp, cooked, cleaned, and chopped*
1	*8-ounce package cream cheese*
1	*10½-ounce can tomato soup*
2	*envelopes unflavored gelatin*
½	*cup water*
1	*cup good quality mayonnaise*
½	*cup celery, chopped*
½	*cup pimiento, chopped*
¼	*cup onion, chopped*

1. Crumble cream cheese in large bowl.
2. Heat soup without diluting until hot and bubbly. Pour over cheese.
3. Dissolve gelatin in ½ cup water. Pour into mixture, mixing well. Add remaining ingredients and blend thoroughly.
4. Turn into a 5½-cup buttered mold. Refrigerate overnight.
5. To remove, go around edge of mold with sharp knife; then immerse outside of mold in warm water 10 seconds. Turn onto platter lined with lettuce leaves.

Wonderful on crackers or for lunch or as a salad.

JALAPEÑO CHEESE BALL

Yields: **16-20 servings**
Preparation Time: 20 minutes

½   **pound mild Cheddar cheese, grated**
1   **8-ounce package cream cheese, softened**
½   **cup olives (optional)**
2   **large pickled jalapeños, finely chopped**
2   **cloves garlic, finely minced**
3   **tablespoons jalapeño pepper juice**
1   **cup pecans**

1. In a medium size mixing bowl, combine cheeses, olives, jalapeños, garlic, and pepper juice. Mix into a ball.
2. Roll ball mixture in chopped pecans.
3. Serve with crackers.

DEVONSHIRE TIDBITS
"Melt In Your Mouth"

Yields: **48 pieces**
Preparation Time: 15 minutes
plus set time

6   **English muffins**
1½   **cups green onions, finely chopped**
1½   **cups black and green olives, finely chopped**
1   **teaspoon salt**
1   **teaspoon black pepper**
1   **cup good quality mayonnaise**
3   **cups sharp Cheddar cheese, shredded**

1. Split English muffins into halves.
2. Mix ingredients in order given and spread thickly on muffin halves.
3. Cut each muffin half into four pie shaped pieces. Freeze on cookie sheet until hard. Store in plastic bag.
4. Bake frozen in 350° oven for 10-15 minutes.

Temperature: **350 °**
Time: **10-15 minutes**

The great thing about these is that you bake them frozen and you can always keep them on hand in the freezer for unexpected company.

PICKLED SHRIMP
Make 24 Hours Ahead Of Time

Yields: **8-12 servings**
Preparation Time: 1 hour

2½   pounds fresh shrimp
½   cup celery tops
3¼   teaspoons salt
¼   cup crab boil
4   small white onions, sliced in
      rings
7-8   bay leaves
¾   cup vegetable oil
¼   cup olive oil
1   cup white vinegar
1½   teaspoons salt
2½   tablespoons capers and juice
      dash Tabasco sauce
2½   teaspoons celery seed

1. In a large saucepan, place unpeeled shrimp and add water to cover. Add celery tops, salt, and crab boil. Bring to a boil. Reduce heat and cook shrimp 8-10 minutes.
2. Drain shrimp and cool under running cold water.
3. When shrimp are sufficiently cool, peel and devein.
4. In a 9" × 13" flat serving dish, alternate cleaned shrimp and sliced onion rings.
5. Add bay leaves. Combine other ingredients and pour over shrimp.
6. Cover and refrigerate 24 hours. Serve with crackers.

TERIYAKI
Make 24 Hours Ahead Of Time

Yields: **10 servings**
Preparation Time: 15 minutes

½   cup Soy sauce
¼-½   cup dry white wine
1   tablespoon cider vinegar
1   tablespoon sugar
1   clove garlic, crushed
½   teaspoon ground ginger
1½   pounds top sirloin, cut in
        thin slices about 2-inches
        long

1. Combine Soy sauce, wine, vinegar, sugar, garlic and ginger in a jar. Shake well.
2. Pour marinade over sliced meat in a shallow baking dish. Cover and refrigerate 8 hours or overnight.
3. About 10-15 minutes before serving, remove meat from marinade pan. Broil 5-7 minutes turning once. Remove to chafing dish.
4. Serve on French bread, party rye or heavy cracker.

Temperature: Broil
Time: 5-7 minutes

CRUNCHY SPINACH DIP

Yields: **6-8**
Preparation Time: 20 minutes

Must Make Ahead Of Time

1   *10½-ounce package frozen spinach, chopped, thawed with juice squeezed out thoroughly*
1   *package Knorr vegetable soup mix*
¼   *cup green onions, chopped*
1   *cup water chestnuts, chopped*
1   *cup good quality mayonnaise*
1   *cup sour cream*
    lemon juice to taste
    Tabasco to taste

1. In large bowl, combine all ingredients. Mix thoroughly.
2. Chill well in refrigerator before serving.
3. Very pretty served in a round of pull apart bread with chunks of bread or crackers on the side.

SALMON MOUSSE

Yields: **10-12 servings**
Preparation Time: 20 minutes
plus set time

Must Make Ahead of Time

1   *package unflavored gelatin*
½   *cup hot chicken broth*
1   *15-ounce can red salmon, skinned and boned*
½   *cup good quality mayonnaise*
⅛   *teaspoon cayenne pepper*
1   *tablespoon parsley, chopped*
¼   *teaspoon dill weed*
½   *onion*
½   *cup heavy cream*

1. Dissolve gelatin in hot broth.
2. Place all ingredients, except cream, in blender or food processor and process until blended.
3. In a stream, add cream and blend ten more seconds.
4. Pour into a well-greased 3 cup fish mold and refrigerate until firm.
5. Unmold on lettuce leaves.
6. Serve with rye bread and pickle slices.

MARY MARGARET'S CHEESE BALL

Yields: **1 cheese ball**
Preparation Time: 15 minutes plus 1 hour set time

1	8-ounce package cream cheese, softened
4	tablespoons Marie's Bleu Cheese Salad Dressing
	Dash of garlic salt
3/4	cup Cheddar cheese, grated
1	teaspoon good quality mayonnaise
1	cup nuts, chopped (or)
1	cup fresh parsley, chopped

1. Mix all ingredients well and form into a ball.
2. Roll in parsley or nuts. Chill for an hour before serving.

May be made 2-3 days in advance.

MEXICAN DIP
Must Make Ahead Of Time

Yields: **10 servings**
Preparation Time: 15 minutes

2	10½-ounce cans jalapeño bean dip
3	medium avocados
2	tablespoons lemon juice
½	teaspoon salt
¼	teaspoon black pepper
½	cup good quality mayonnaise
1	cup sour cream
1	package taco seasoning mix
1	large bunch green onions, chopped
3	tomatoes, cored, halved, seeded & chopped
2	3½-ounce cans chopped black olives
1	8 to 10-ounce package Cheddar cheese, grated

1. In a 9″ × 13″ glass dish, spread the bean dip in order to cover the bottom of the dish.
2. In a separate small bowl, peel avocados. Remove pit. Mash avocados with lemon juice and season with salt and pepper. Spread over the bean dip.
3. Combine mayonnaise, sour cream, and taco seasoning. Spread over the avocados.
4. Layer green onions, tomatoes, and olives on top of casserole. Top with Cheddar cheese.
5. Cover and refrigerate until serving. Serve with large corn chips or tortilla chips.

PLAINS SPECIAL CHEESE RING

Must Make Ahead Of Time

*Yields: **10-20 servings***
Preparation Time: 20 minutes

1	*pound medium Cheddar cheese, grated*
1	*cup good quality mayonnaise*
1	*cup nuts, chopped*
1	*small onion, grated*
	dash black and red pepper
	stawberry preserves

1. In a large bowl, combine cheese, mayonnaise, nuts, and onion. Mix well. Add seasonings.
2. Mold with hands into a ring.
3. Place in refrigerator until chilled, preferably overnight.
4. Before serving, fill center with strawberry preserves.
5. Serve with crackers, spreading cheese on crackers and preserves on cheese.

Use either mild or medium Cheddar cheese.

SMOKED OYSTER MOLD

Make 24 Hours Ahead Of Time

*Yields: **3½ cup mold***
Preparation Time: 30 minutes plus set time

2	*envelopes unflavored gelatin*
½	*cup cold water*
1	*8-ounce package cream cheese*
1	*cup good quality mayonnaise*
2	*3.66-ounce can smoked oysters, drained and chopped*
3	*tablespoons parsley, chopped*
1	*tablespoon Worcestershire sauce*
½	*teaspoon garlic powder*
¼	*teaspoon Tabasco sauce*

1. Soften gelatin in water and set aside.
2. In a 2-quart saucepan, combine cream cheese and mayonnaise. Cook over low heat, stirring constantly until cheese melts and mixture is smooth. Remove from heat.
3. Add gelatin to cream cheese mixture. Stir in rest of ingredients. Mix thoroughly. Spoon into a greased 3½-cup mold. Chill overnight.
4. When ready to serve, unmold onto a bed of lettuce and serve with crackers.

TEXAS CAVIAR

Must Make Ahead Of Time

*Yields: **10 servings***
Preparation Time: 30 minutes

1	3-ounce can green chiles, chopped
1	3¼-ounce can chopped black olives
1	bunch green onions, finely chopped
1-2	tomatoes, peeled, seeded and finely chopped
3	tablespoons olive oil
1½	tablespoons red wine vinegar

1. Combine all ingredients and set overnight in refrigerator.
2. Serve with king size corn chips to dip.

FRESH CAULIFLOWER ANTIPASTO

*Yields: **4-6 servings***
Preparation Time: 20 minutes

1	medium head fresh cauliflower
1	cup carrots, sliced diagonally
1	cup celery, sliced diagonally
1	cup small green olives
½	cup wine vinegar
½	cup vegetable oil
¼	cup lemon juice
¼	cup water
2	tablespoons sugar
1	teaspoon salt
½	teaspoon basil leaves, crushed

1. Slice cauliflower into flowerets.
2. Combine with remaining ingredients in large skillet.
3. Bring to boil. Reduce heat. Simmer exactly 3 minutes.
4. Cool and store in refrigerator in tightly sealed jar.
5. Drain and serve cold.

Will keep for several days in the refrigerator.

SUPER SIMPLE SALMON SPREAD

Yields: **10-15 servings**
Preparation Time: 15 minutes

2	*3-ounce packages smoked salmon, chopped*
2	*8-ounce packages cream cheese, softened*
1	*16-ounce container sour cream*
6	*green onions, tops and bottoms included, chopped*
1	*3¼-ounce jar of capers, drained*
⅛-¼	*teaspoon black pepper*
1	*whole lemon, sliced round parsley (optional)*

1. Combine all ingredients except lemon. Mix thoroughly.
2. Transfer to serving plate. Garnish with lemon rounds and parsley.

Serve with crackers.

STEAK TARTARE
Must Make Ahead Of Time

Yields: **10 servings**
Preparation Time: 15 minutes

2	*pounds ground sirloin, put through grinder twice*
1	*medium onion, finely chopped*
2	*tablespoons Dijon mustard*
1	*raw egg, beaten*
1	*teaspoon Worcestershire sauce*
	Salt - to taste
¼	*cup Cognac*
2	*tablespoons green peppers, finely chopped (optional)*
	capers or parsley for garnish

1. Blend all ingredients into meat, one at a time. Mix thoroughly.
2. Place in refrigerator until chilled - preferably overnight.
3. Garnish with capers or parsley if desired.

Great served on small pumpernickel rounds or crackers.

CRAB STUFFED EGGS

*Yields: **24 egg halves***
Preparation Time: 30 minutes
plus 1 hour set time

1   dozen hard-boiled eggs, peeled
¾   cup fresh white crabmeat
½   cup celery, chopped fine
1   teaspoon dry mustard
½   teaspoon salt
⅓   cup good quality mayonnaise
     paprika for garnish

1. Cut eggs in half lengthwise. Remove yolks and mash.
2. Drain and flake crabmeat, carefully removing any cartilage from crabmeat. Cut crabmeat into small pieces.
3. Combine crabmeat, egg yolks, celery, mustard, salt, and mayonnaise. Mix thoroughly.
4. Stuff egg whites with crabmeat mixture. Sprinkle with paprika.
5. Chill for at least an hour before serving.

NINFA'S AVOCADO SAUCE

*Yields: **1 cup***
Preparation Time: 10 minutes
plus 1 hour set time

1   ripe avocado
¼   cup sour cream
¼   cup whole milk
1   teaspoon minced onion
1   clove garlic, mashed (with)
½   teaspoon salt
¼   teaspoon dried cilantro
½   teaspoon hot pepper sauce
2   tablespoons fresh lemon juice
     Tortilla chips

1. Peel avocado and mash to a smooth pulp.
2. Add sour cream, milk, onion, garlic, salt, cilantro, pepper sauce, and lemon juice. Blend well with wire whisk.
3. Let stand at least 1 hour before serving. Serve with tortilla chips.

The use of a food processor makes this a real snap.

CAVIAR AND EGG HORS D'OEUVRES

Yields: **8-10 servings**
Preparation Time: 30 minutes

Make 24 Hours Ahead Of Time

6	hard-boiled eggs, peeled and chopped fine
1/2	cup butter, softened
1/4	cup good quality mayonnaise
1/3	cup onion, finely chopped
1/2	teaspoon lemon juice
	salt, if desired
1/8	teaspoon black pepper
1	8-ounce container sour cream
1	3½-ounce jar white fish caviar

1. In a small bowl, combine egg, butter, mayonnaise, and onion. Add lemon juice, salt, and pepper. Mix thoroughly.
2. Line a medium size bowl with aluminum foil. Firmly pack egg mixture into foil-lined bowl. Chill in refrigerator overnight.
3. When ready to serve, invert onto serving plate. Remove foil.
4. Frost with sour cream. Spoon caviar around this mixture.
5. Serve crackers on the side.

CRAB VEGETABLE DIP

Yields: **8-10 servings**
Preparation Time: 10 minutes

Must Make Ahead Of Time

1	cup sour cream
1	cup good quality mayonnaise
1/2	teaspoon Worcestershire sauce
1/2	teaspoon lemon juice
1/4	teaspoon garlic salt
1/4	teaspoon onion salt
3	shakes Tabasco sauce
1/4	teaspoon dry mustard
8	ounces Cheddar cheese, shredded
1	pound fresh white crabmeat
	fresh cauliflower
	fresh carrot sticks

1. Combine sour cream and mayonnaise. Add Worcestershire, lemon juice, garlic salt, onion salt, Tabasco, and mustard. Add Cheddar cheese. Mix thoroughly.
2. Drain and flake crabmeat, carefully removing any cartilage. Fold into cheese mixture.
3. Chill thoroughly, preferably overnight. Serve surrounded by cauliflower and carrot sticks.

MARINATED BROCCOLI WITH CURRY DIP

Yields: 6-8 Servings
Preparation Time: 30 minutes

Make 24 Hours Ahead Of Time

1   large bunch fresh broccoli
¼   cup cider or wine vinegar
¾   cup vegetable oil
2   cloves garlic, coarsely
     chopped
1   teaspoon sugar
2   teaspoons dill seed

Curry Dip

2   cups good quality
     mayonnaise
1½   teaspoons curry powder
1   tablespoon ketchup
¼   teaspoon Worcestershire
     sauce

1. Wash and cut broccoli into small bite size pieces.
2. Place broccoli in large plastic bag. Set aside.
3. Combine vinegar, oil, garlic, sugar, and dill seed. Mix thoroughly. Pour marinade over broccoli and seal bag. Shake bag to make sure marinade coats all broccoli pieces. Refrigerate overnight.
4. Combine ingredients for curry dip. Drain marinade from broccoli.
5. Serve broccoli with curry dip.

JOANNE'S SHRIMP DIP

Yields: 12 servings
Preparation Time: 30 minutes

30-40 medium shrimp
1   8-ounce package cream
     cheese, softened
½   cup good quality mayonnaise
2   tablespoons ketchup
1   tablespoon Worcestershire
     sauce
1   tablespoon lemon juice
½   teaspoon Tabasco
1   teaspoon garlic powder
2   tablespoons onion, minced
     salt and pepper to taste

1. Cook shrimp in boiling water for 5 minutes. Drain well. Clean and devein shrimp and chop fine. Let cool.
2. Blend cream cheese and salad dressing thoroughly. Add shrimp and remaining ingredients. Serve cold with chips or crackers.

MUSHROOM TARTS PASHA

Yields: **75 pieces**
Preparation Time: 45 minutes

Must Make Ahead Of Time

1	cup butter or margarine
1	8-ounce package cream cheese
2	cups flour
½	cup butter or margarine, melted
2	large green onions, minced
¾	pound fresh mushrooms, sliced
½	teaspoon salt
⅛	teaspoon black pepper
2-3	tablespoons flour
1	tablespoon chives, chopped
1	tablespoon parsley, chopped
1	tablespoon lemon juice
4	tablespoons sherry
½	cup sour cream

1. Cream 1 cup of butter and cream cheese. Blend in 2 cups of flour. Mix thoroughly. Wrap in wax paper and refrigerate overnight.
2. Sauté onions in melted butter until golden. Add mushrooms, salt, and pepper. Cook 5 minutes, covered. Add flour to make roux.
3. Add chives, parsley, lemon juice, and sherry. Cook 1 minute, until thickened. Add sour cream and just heat through.
4. Roll out dough thinly and cut into 3" rounds. Fill each round with ¼-½ teaspoon of filling and fold over. Pinch ends together and prick with a fork.
5. Bake in 400° oven for 20 minutes on a lightly greased cookie sheet.

Temperature: **400 °**
Time: 20 minutes

You may freeze before cooking. Thaw a few minutes before baking.

HUMUS

Yields: **10-15 servings**
Preparation Time: 10 minutes

2	cups chick peas
1½	teaspoons salt
3	cloves garlic, finely chopped
¼-½	cup vegetable oil
¼	cup lemon juice

1. Put all ingredients in a blender. Purée to desired consistency.
2. Serve on flat Arabic bread (Pita bread).

MUSHROOM SPREAD

Yields: 2½-3 cups
Preparation Time: 30 minutes

6   slices bacon
1   8-ounce package, fresh
    mushrooms, sliced thin (stems
    removed)
1   medium onion, finely
    chopped
1   clove garlic, minced
2   tablespoons flour
¼   teaspoon salt
⅛   teaspoon black pepper
1   8-ounce package cream
    cheese, softened
2   teaspoons Worcestershire
    sauce
1   teaspoon Soy sauce
½   cup sour cream
    rye bread rounds or crackers

1. In a medium skillet, fry bacon until crisp. Drain well and crumble. (May use microwave to cook bacon). Set aside. Reserve 2 tablespoons of bacon drippings in skillet.
2. Sauté mushrooms, onion, and garlic in drippings until tender and most of the liquid has evaporated.
3. Stir in flour, salt, and pepper.
4. Add softened cream cheese, Worcestershire sauce, and Soy sauce. Heat and stir until cheese is melted. Stir in sour cream and crumbled bacon.
5. Heat thoroughly. Do not boil.
6. Serve warm on rye bread rounds or crackers.

May be made ahead and reheated on *low* heat.

MINI QUICHES

Yields: 24 quiches
Preparation Time: 30 minutes

1   8-ounce tube butterflake
    rolls
8-10 strips bacon, cooked and
    crumbled
4   ounces Swiss cheese, grated
1   egg, beaten
¼   cup light cream
2   tablespoons onion, minced

1. Grease 24 miniature muffin cups.
2. Divide each roll into halves and press each into a muffin cup to make a shell.
3. Distribute bacon and cheese evenly in shells.
4. Mix egg, cream, and onion. Place one teaspoon of mixture in each shell.
5. Bake in 350° oven for 20 minutes. Serve warm.

Temperature: 350 °
Time: 20 minutes

CURRIED CRAB DIP

Yields: **3 cups**
Preparation Time: 10 minutes

1   8-ounce package cream
     cheese, softened
1   tablespoon crab juice
¼   teaspoon curry powder
4   tablespoons lemon juice
2   cups fresh lump crabmeat,
     drained, reserve juice

1. Place softened cream cheese, crab juice, curry powder, and lemon juice in a 1½-quart casserole. Mix thoroughly.
2. Gently fold in crabmeat. Bake in 325° oven for 30 minutes.
3. Serve hot with crackers or melba toast. (May use chafing dish or electric fondue pot to keep warm).

Temperature: **325** °
Time: 30 minutes

HAWAIIAN CHICKEN WINGS

Yields: **8-10 servings**
Preparation Time: 20 minutes

3-4   pounds chicken wings
1   teaspoon salt
⅛   teaspoon black pepper
⅛   teaspoon garlic powder
1   tablespoon lemon juice
3   tablespoons dark brown
     sugar
¼   cup Soy sauce
5   tablespoons honey
6   peppercorns
1   cup hot water

1. Cut wings in half. Discard tips. Rinse and pat dry. Place side by side in 11″ × 14″ baking dish.
2. Add salt, pepper and garlic powder.
3. Mix rest of ingredients. Pour over wings. Cover pan with foil. Bake in 350° oven for 2 hours.
4. Remove foil. Bake in 300° oven for 30 minutes more. Baste 3-4 times while cooking. Serve hot or cold.

Temperature: **350** °
Time: 2 hours
Temperature: **300** °
Time: 30 minutes

BACON CRISPS

Yields: **10-15 servings**
Preparation Time: 30 minutes

½   **teaspoon dry mustard**
½   **teaspoon cayenne pepper**
3   **teaspoons cider vinegar**
3   **eggs, well beaten**
1   **pound bacon, cut in thirds**
2-3   **cups coarse ground saltine cracker crumbs for dipping bacon**

1. Make a paste of first three ingredients. Add eggs and mix well.
2. Dip bacon pieces in egg mixture and roll in cracker crumbs. Lay bacon on large cookie sheet with sides.
3. Bake in 350° oven for 15-18 minutes. Drain and pour off grease before cooking second batch. Serve warm.

Temperature: **350 °**
Time: 15-18 minutes.

May be frozen after baking. When ready to serve, warm in 250° oven for 10-15 minutes.

KING ARTHUR'S OYSTERS

Yields: **6 servings (4 each)**
Preparation Time: 30 minutes

"There is never enough"

2   **tablespoons butter, melted**
¼   **cup lemon juice**
½   **cup dry sherry**
1   **cup A-1 steak sauce**
2   **tablespoons flour**
3   **tablespoons water**
2   **dozen oysters**
     salt
     pepper

1. In medium size saucepan, combine butter, lemon juice, sherry, and steak sauce. Cook over low heat.
2. Blend flour and water together. Slowly stir into sauce being careful not to let boil.
3. Add oysters to sauce and heat for 1 minute. Adjust seasonings to taste with salt and pepper.
4. Transfer to chafing dish to keep warm. If oysters are to be eaten immediately they can be placed in a shallow baking or serving dish.

HOT CLAM DIP

Yields: 2 cups
Preparation Time: 15 minutes

1   6½-ounce can minced clams
    (save juice)
2   8-ounce packages cream
    cheese, softened
1   tablespoon onion, minced
    cayenne pepper to taste
    salt to taste

Serve with crackers.

1. Soften cream cheese. Add other ingredients, using only enough juice to make mixture spread easily.
2. Heat in chafing dish over hot water.

CHICKEN LIVER BOATS
"Something Different"

Yields: 10-12 servings
Preparation Time: 35 minutes

1   pound chicken livers
4   tablespoons flour
4   tablespoons butter or
     margarine
4   tablespoons onion, finely
     chopped
1   teaspoon steak sauce
½   teaspoon salt
     dash black pepper
½   cup light cream
½   cup fresh Parmesan cheese,
     grated
1   pie crust recipe (any that you
     normally use)
     paprika (optional)

1. Coat chicken livers with flour. Cook in melted butter with onions and steak sauce for 10 minutes.
2. Add salt and pepper and mash well. Stir in cream. Set aside.
3. Prepare pie crust and roll out. Cut in 2¼-inch rounds. Place 1 teaspoon of chicken liver mixture on each round. Pinch ends to form boats. Sprinkle with Parmesan cheese.
4. Bake on ungreased cookie sheet in 425° oven for 10 minutes. Sprinkle with paprika before serving if desired.

Temperature: 425 °
Time: 10 minutes

GARLIC SHRIMP

Yields: **16 servings**
Preparation Time: 15 minutes

1	cup butter, melted
2	cloves garlic, minced
1/3	cup parsley, chopped
1/2	teaspoon paprika
1/8	teaspoon cayenne pepper
2/3	cup cooking sherry
2	cups soft bread crumbs
5-6	cups shrimp, cooked and cleaned (4 pounds in shell)

1. Combine butter, garlic, parsley, paprika, cayenne, and sherry. Mix well. Add bread crumbs and toss lightly.
2. Place shrimp in 11" × 7" baking dish. Spoon butter mixture over shrimp.
3. Bake in 325° oven for 20-25 minutes.

Temperature: **325 °**
Time: 20-25 minutes

This may easily be used as a main dish for 8-10 people.

ZUCCHINI DELIGHTS

Yields: **4 dozen**
Preparation Time: 30 minutes

3	cups zucchini, unpared and thinly sliced (about 4 small zucchini)
1	cup Bisquick mix
1/2	cup onion, chopped
3/4	cup Parmesan cheese, grated
2	tablespoons parsley flakes
1/2	teaspoon salt
1/2	teaspoon seasoned salt
1/2	teaspoon dried oregano leaves
	dash pepper
1/2	teaspoon garlic powder
1/2	cup vegetable oil
4	eggs, beaten

1. In a large mixing bowl, combine all ingredients. Mix thoroughly.
2. Spread in a greased 9" × 13" baking dish.
3. Bake in 350° oven for 25 minutes, or until golden brown. Cut into squares.

Temperature: **350 °**
Time: 25 minutes

Freezes well.

CHEESY ARTICHOKE SQUARES

Yields: **36 squares**
Preparation Time: **15 minutes**

2	*6-ounce jars marinated artichoke hearts*
1	*small onion, finely chopped*
1	*clove garlic, minced*
4	*eggs, beaten*
¼	*cup dry bread crumbs*
½	*teaspoon salt*
⅛	*teaspoon black pepper*
¼	*teaspoon dried oregano leaves*
1	*cup sharp Cheddar cheese, grated*
1	*cup Gruyere or Parmesan cheese, grated*
2	*tablespoons fresh parsley, minced*
1	*pimiento, finely diced*

1. In a medium skillet, heat marinade from one jar of artichokes. Discard marinade from other jar. Chop artichokes and set aside.
2. Add onion and garlic to marinade in skillet. Sauté about 5 minutes.
3. In a separate bowl, combine eggs, bread crumbs, salt, pepper, and oregano. Fold in cheeses. Add parsley and pimiento and mix well.
4. Add artichokes, onion, garlic and marinade to cheese mixture. Pour artichoke mixture into well greased 9-inch square baking dish.
5. Bake in 325° oven for 30 minutes. Cool slightly before cutting into 1½-inch squares.

Temperature: **325 °**
Time: **30 minutes**

May be made 1-2 days ahead of time.

CHUTNEY CHEESE BALL
"Great Flavor"

Yields: **1 medium cheese ball**
Preparation Time: **15 minutes**

2	*8-ounce packages cream cheese, softened*
½	*cup chutney and juice*
2	*teaspoons curry powder*
½	*teaspoon dry mustard*
1	*cup dried parsley flakes*
½	*cup nuts, chopped*

1. Combine all ingredients in medium size mixing bowl. Blend thoroughly with electric mixer on medium speed.
2. Form into ball. Roll in dried parsley flakes and nuts.
3. Refrigerate until ready to serve.

May be made ahead of time and frozen.

SAUSAGE CHEESE DIP

Yields: **25 servings**
Preparation Time: 30 minutes

1	pound ground chuck
1	1-pound package hot bulk sausage
1	onion, chopped
1	tablespoon Worcestershire sauce
1	1-pound box Velveeta cheese, cubed
1	10-ounce can Rotel tomatoes
1	teaspoon garlic powder
2	tablespoons chili powder
1	tablespoon white vinegar
1	10¾-ounce can cream of mushroom soup

1. Brown ground chuck and sausage. Drain off fat. Add onion and brown. Transfer to large pot or crockpot.
2. Add rest of ingredients. Mix thoroughly. Simmer until cheese is melted.
3. Serve with tortilla chips.

CRAB STUFFED MUSHROOMS

Yields: **2 dozen**
Preparation Time: 20 minutes

2	dozen large mushrooms
2	tablespoons fresh Parmesan cheese, grated
1	8-ounce package cream cheese, softened
½	cup fresh white crabmeat, drained and flaked
2½	tablespoons olive oil
2	tablespoons fresh parsley, chopped
1½	tablespoons plain bread crumbs
2	tablespoons fresh lemon juice
1½	teaspoons green onion, minced
1½	teaspoons Cognac
½	teaspoon Dijon mustard
1	teaspoon salt
½	teaspoon black pepper, freshly ground

1. Remove mushroom stems. Clean caps and set aside to drain. Discard stems or save for another recipe.
2. In a medium size bowl, combine all ingredients except mushrooms. Mix thoroughly with mixer on medium low speed then medium speed.
3. Stuff mushroom caps with plentiful amount of mixture. Lightly grease a baking sheet and place mushrooms on it.
4. Bake in 425° oven for 10-15 minutes.

Temperature: **425 °**
Time: **10-15 minutes**

SEAGULLS

Everyone who visits Galveston is captivated by the antics of the seagulls flying overhead. Many people try to get a close-up view of the engaging creatures b tossing up breadcrumbs to the birds in flight. Seagulls are web-footed birds wit sturdy bodies and heavy, hooked bills who make their homes on coastlines and i inland waterways and wet areas.

SAVORY BEEF DIP

Yields: **8-10 servings**
Preparation Time: 30 minutes

1	2½-ounce jar dried beef, finely chopped
1	8-ounce package cream cheese, softened
½	cup green pepper, chopped
2	tablespoons milk
1	cup sour cream
¾	cup pecans, chopped
¼	teaspoon white pepper
½	teaspoon garlic powder
2	tablespoons dried onion flakes

1. In large bowl, combine all ingredients. Mix thoroughly with electric mixer or food processor.
2. Transfer mixture to baking dish. Bake in 350° oven for 20 minutes.
3. Serve with wheat crackers.
4. Best if made day before and heated just before serving.

Temperature: **350 °**
Time: 20 minutes

MUSHROOMS FLORENTINE

Yields: **20 mushrooms**
Preparation Time: 15 minutes

1	10-ounce package frozen chopped spinach
3	green onions, chopped
¼	cup sour cream
	salt
	pepper
20	large mushrooms
2	tablespoons butter
	melted butter

1. Prepare spinach according to package directions. Drain thoroughly.
2. In a medium size bowl, combine spinach, onions, and sour cream. Add salt and pepper to taste.
3. Wash mushrooms and remove stems. Sauté in butter for about 8 minutes. Remove from pan.
4. Stuff each mushroom with spinach mixture. Place in a 9″ × 13″ ovenproof dish. Drizzle melted butter over all and sprinkle with pepper.
5. Heat under broiler just before serving until piping hot.

Temperature: Broil
Time: 2-3 minutes

To keep mushrooms from turning dark, cook them for 30 seconds in boiling water to which 2 tablespoons of lemon juice have been added. Drain and dry; then proceed with recipe.

ESCARGOT
"So Elegant"

*Yields: **2 dozen***
Preparation Time: 15 minutes

½   cup butter (Do Not
     Substitute)
3   large garlic cloves, crushed
4   tablespoons fresh parsley,
     chopped
     salt and pepper to taste
2   dozen escargot and shells

1. Cream butter by beating with a wooden spoon until fluffy. Add garlic and parsley. Season with salt and pepper to taste. Mix well.
2. Place ¼ teaspoon butter mixture into each shell. Add escargot. Place another ¼ teaspoon of butter mixture on top.
3. Bake in 450° oven for 10 minutes. Serve piping hot with French bread on the side.

*Temperature: **450 ***°
Time: 10 minutes

SAUSAGE BALLS IN BLANKETS
Must Make Ahead Of Time

*Yields: **3-4 dozen***
Preparation Time: 1 hour

1½   cups flour, sifted
2   teaspoons curry powder
1   teaspoon paprika
¼   teaspoon salt
2   cups sharp Cheddar cheese,
     shredded
½   cup butter or margarine
1   1-pound package regular
     bulk sausage
     toothpicks

1. Up to one week before, mix first five ingredients. With pastry blender, cut in butter until mixture resembles coarse lumps.
2. With your hands, shape mixture into large ball. Cover and refrigerate.
3. Meanwhile shape heaping teaspoons of sausage into small balls and fry until brown in a skillet. Drain on paper towel.
4. Divide dough into same number as sausage balls and shape dough around balls, wrap and freeze.
5. To serve, bake in 400° oven for 12-15 minutes or until golden brown.

*Temperature: **400 ***°
Time: 15 minutes

PECAN KISSES

Yields: **20 servings**
Preparation Time: 15 minutes

6   slices bacon
1   6-ounce package whole pecan
     halves
     decorated toothpicks

1. Cut bacon slices into small strips, about 1-inch wide.
2. Wrap pecan with bacon and hold with toothpick. Place on pie plate and bake in 375° oven for 10-15 minutes.
3. Serve hot.

Temperature: **375 °**
Time: 10-15 minutes

DAIQUIRITAS

Yields: **6 servings**
Preparation Time: 10 minutes

     lime wedge
     salt
1   12-ounce can frozen limeade
     concentrate, undiluted
¾   cup cold water
¾   cup light rum
⅓   cup tequila
     lime slices

1. Rub rim of six cocktail glasses with wedge of lime.
2. Spin rim of each glass in saucepan of salt.
3. Combine limeade, water, rum, and tequila in blender with ice.
4. Process quickly on high. Pour in prepared glasses. Garnish with lime slices.

MOLLY HOGANS
"Great For A Brunch"

Yields: **12 servings**
Preparation Time: 20 minutes plus 1 hour set time

6   eggs
1   tablespoon vanilla
1   12-ounce can frozen orange
     juice
1   6-ounce can frozen limeade
1   cup sugar
1   quart gin
1   32-ounce bottle of Seven-Up

1. Put the eggs in a blender. Add sugar, vanilla, and juices a little at a time. Blend well. Pour into a large container and add gin. Let stand at least 1 hour.
2. Using large glasses, pour two ounces of the gin mixture into the glasses. Fill with ice and Seven-Up.

BANANA-ORANGE PUNCH

Yields: **20 servings**
Preparation Time: overnight to freeze

6   *cups water*
3   *cups sugar*
1   *46-ounce can pineapple-grapefruit juice*
1   *12-ounce can frozen orange juice*
4   *bananas, mashed*
2   *quarts gingerale, chilled*

1. Heat water and sugar, stirring until dissolved. Mix in pineapple-grapefruit juice. Add frozen orange juice and mashed bananas.
2. Stir and pour into 4 pint containers to freeze until completely solid.
3. When ready to serve, let thaw 4 hours and pour into punch bowl. Add 1 quart chilled gingerale to a quart of mixture.

Dash of dark rum or vodka may be added for taste.

CAPPUCCINO BRANIFF

Yields: **1 serving**
Preparation Time: 5 minutes

3   *teaspoons Nestle's Quick*
1   *jigger Kahlua (or other coffee liqueur)*
2   *teaspoons instant coffee*
    heavy cream, whipped
    boiling water enough to fill cup ¾ full

1. Place Nestle's Quick, Kahlua, and instant coffee in coffee mug or Irish coffee glass.
2. Fill with boiling water and stir well.
3. Top with a dollop of whipped cream.

EGG NOG

Yields: **6-8 servings**
Preparation Time: 15 minutes

1   *dozen eggs, separated*
1   *cup sugar, divided*
½   *cup rum*
1   *cup bourbon*
1   *pint heavy cream, whipped*
    nutmeg

1. Beat yolks until light. Gradually add ½ sugar.
2. Blend rum and bourbon, then slowly add to mixture.
3. Beat egg whites until stiff, slowly adding other ½ cup sugar. Fold white mixture carefully into yolk mixture.
4. Beat whipping cream until stiff. Add to egg mixture. Sprinkle top with nutmeg.

MILK PUNCH
Must Make Ahead Of Time

Yields: 8 servings
Preparation Time: 5 minutes

1½ cups bourbon
1½ pints light cream
1   teaspoon vanilla
2½ teaspoons powdered sugar
½   cup heavy cream, whipped
     nutmeg

1. Combine first three ingredients. Stir in sugar until dissolved.
2. Cover and refrigerate several hours until very chilled.
3. Pour bourbon mixture into punch bowl. Spoon whipped cream on top. Sprinkle with nutmeg.

SPECIAL HOLIDAY PUNCH

Yields: 45 servings
Preparation Time: Overnight

1   fresh pineapple
6   lemons
3   cups bar-type sugar
1   quart strong green tea
1   bottle cognac
1   pint light rum
1   bottle peach or apricot
     brandy
4   quarts champagne
2   quarts sparkling soda water
1   jar cherries

1. Core, peel, and dice pineapple.
2. Slice lemons thinly and place in bowl with pineapple. Add sugar and cognac, let stand overnight.
3. Four hours before serving, add tea, rum, and brandy. Pour over block of ice in punch bowl.
4. Just before serving, pour in champagne and soda water. Add cherries. Stir gently and serve.

STRAWBERRY DAIQUIRI

Yields: 4 servings
Preparation Time: 5 minutes

1   cup fresh strained lemon
     juice
½   cup sugar
1   cup light rum
1   10-ounce package frozen
     strawberries
     ice

1. Combine ingredients in blender. Blend on high speed until mixed thoroughly (30-45 seconds).
2. Pour into chilled glasses.

CAFE DIABLO

Yields: **1 serving**
Preparation Time: 15 minutes

1½   ounces brandy
1½   ounces Kahlua
2   whole cloves
1   teaspoon brown sugar
1   1½-inch strip of orange peel
1   8-ounce cup of coffee
     lemon juice
     granulated sugar
     heavy cream, whipped

1. In a small saucepan, combine brandy, Kahlua, cloves, brown sugar, and orange peel.
2. Ignite with match to burn off alcohol (approximately 10 minutes).
3. Add coffee and boil 1 minute. Dip glass into lemon juice and then sugar and hold over flame to crystallize.
4. Pour mixture into glass. Top with a dollop of whipped cream.

SPICED TEA

Yields: **12 servings**
Preparation Time: 10 minutes

1¼   cups Lipton sweetened, with lemon, instant tea
2   cups Tang
1   teaspoon cinnamon
½   teaspoon ground cloves

1. Combine all ingredients well.
2. Store in airtight container.
3. Use 3 teaspoons of mix in 8 ounces of hot water. Stir well.

TOMATO FRAPPÉ

Yields: **10-12 servings**
Preparation Time: 40 minutes

1   46-ounce can of V-8 juice
2   12-ounce cans of tomato juice
2   lemons (juice of)
2   tablespoons Worcestershire sauce
     Tabasco sauce to taste
     seasoned salt to taste
     celery sticks, optional

1. Mix all ingredients.
2. Freeze until a mushy consistency.
3. Serve in old-fashion glasses with celery stick garnish.

Great non-alcoholic Bloody Mary.

HOT BUTTERED RUM

*Yields: **4 servings***
Preparation Time: 30 minutes
(plus 30 minutes storage
time in freezer)

1   *pound dark brown sugar*
1   *cup butter, softened*
1   *pint vanilla ice cream*
½   *teaspoon cinnamon*
½   *teaspoon allspice*
½   *teaspoon nutmeg*
     rum
     boiling water
     cinnamon stick (optional)

1. Mix all ingredients except rum in a bowl. Mix until smooth.
2. Store in freezer for 30 minutes.
3. To prepare each drink, put one heaping tablespoon of the mixture and 1½ ounces of rum into each 8-ounce mug.
4. Fill mug with boiling water. Stir well.
5. Add cinnamon stick, if desired.

BORDER BUTTERMILK

*Yields: **4-6 servings***
Preparation Time: 5 minutes

1   *6-ounce can frozen orange juice*
3   *ounces whole milk*
6   *ounces light rum*
½   *teaspoon vanilla*
3   *ounces water*
½   *teaspoon sugar*
     ice

1. Put all ingredients in a blender. Fill with ice on top. Blend on medium high speed until slushy.
2. Serve in chilled glasses.

Add orange slice and cherry on a toothpick for pretty garnish. If you would wish a sweeter drink, add another ¼ teaspoon vanilla and ½ teaspoon sugar.

KAHLUA

*Yields: **1½ quarts***
Preparation Time: 10 minutes

1   *cup light brown sugar*
1½   *cups dark brown sugar*
2   *cups water*
½   *cup instant Nescafe coffee*
3   *cups 80 proof vodka*
2   *teaspoons vanilla or one vanilla bean*

1. Boil sugar and water for 5 minutes.
2. Add coffee and cool.
3. Add vodka and vanilla.
4. Pour in bottles. It will keep for 3 weeks.

QUIET AS A WHISPER
Must Make Ahead Of Time

Yields: **4 servings**
Preparation Time: 10 minutes
plus 2 hours set time

1   pint vanilla ice cream
1   ounce brandy
1   ounce white Creme de Cacao
2   ounces black coffee

1. Place all ingredients in a blender and blend on high speed until smooth. Refrigerate for at least 2 hours before serving.
2. Blend quickly on high just before serving.

PERCOLATOR PUNCH

Yields: **25 servings**
Preparation Time: 10 minutes

1   pint orange juice
1   pint apple cider
1   quart cranberry juice
1   teaspoon whole allspice
1   teaspoon whole cloves
3   sticks cinnamon
¼-½ cup sugar
½   fluid ounce almond extract

1. Combine liquid in electric coffee pot.
2. Combine sugar and spices in the coffee pot basket. Allow to heat through one cycle. Serve hot.

SCOTCH SOURS
"Even those who do not like scotch, love these"

Yields: **6 servings**
Preparation Time: 10-15 minutes

1   6-ounce can frozen lemonade
1   lemonade can of scotch
1   lemonade can of orange juice
     (orange juice that is already made)
2   lemonade cans of Seven-Up
10   ice cubes
     cherries and orange slices

1. In a blender, blend all liquid ingredients and ice on high speed until thoroughly mixed.
2. Pour over cracked ice in short high-ball glasses. Garnish with a cherry and orange slice.

FLOATING ISLAND PUNCH
Must Be Made Ahead Of Time

Yields: **30 servings**
Preparation Time: 20 minutes

1	46-ounce can orange juice
1	46-ounce can apple juice
1	46-ounce can pineapple juice
1	46-ounce can Hawaiian Punch
1	lemon (juice of)
1	quart gingerale
½	gallon of raspberry sherbet

1. Mix all juices together in punch bowl. Cover and refrigerate for several hours.
2. Just before serving, add gingerale and scoops of raspberry sherbet.

PICTURE PERFECT GRASSHOPPERS
"Deliciously Rich"

Yields: **8 servings**
Preparation Time: 10-15 minutes

Using a 1-ounce shot glass
6	shots of green Creme de Menthe
6	shots of white Creme de Cacao
8	shots of milk
1	quart of vanilla ice cream
10	ice cubes
	heavy cream, whipped (if desired)
	maraschino cherries (optional)

1. Combine first five ingredients in a blender. Blend thoroughly on high speed for 45 seconds - until thick and creamy.
2. Pour into champagne glasses. Top with a dollop of whip cream and cherry if desired.

CAROLYN'S IRISH COFFEE

Yields: **1 serving**
Preparation Time: 10 minutes

1	tablespoon dark brown sugar
½	ounce Irish Whiskey
½	ounce Kahlua
1	cup brewed coffee
	heavy cream, whipped

1. In each cup or Irish Coffee glass, put brown sugar, Irish Whiskey, and Kahlua. Stir well.
2. Pour in coffee. Stir again.
3. Top with a dollop of whipped cream.

KAHLUA VELVET FROSTY

Yields: **6 cups**
Preparation Time: 5 minutes

1   cup Kahlua
1   pint vanilla ice cream
1   cup light cream
1/8 teaspoon almond extract
1½   cups crushed ice

1. Combine first four ingredients in electric blender.
2. Add crushed ice. Blend on high speed until frothy.
3. Pour into chilled Champagne glasses.

A great throw together for a quick dessert.

SALLY'S WINE COOLER

"A Great Refresher"

Yields: **60 servings**
Preparation Time: 10 minutes

4   10-ounce boxes frozen sliced strawberries, thawed
4   6-ounce cans frozen lemonade, thawed
1   gallon rosé wine
2   bottles club soda

1. Combine all ingredients. Mix thoroughly. Serve chilled.

ORANGE JULIUS

Yields: **4 servings**
Preparation Time: 5 minutes

1   6-ounce can frozen orange juice
1   cup milk
1   cup water
1/3 cup sugar
1   teaspoon vanilla
     crushed ice

1. Put all ingredients in a blender. Blend on high speed to mix thoroughly.
2. Add crushed ice to desired consistency.

FISHING INDUSTRY

The more than 100 species of fish caught in Galveston area waters are significant to both the sports fishermen and to members of the commercial seafood industry. The Galveston Bay area attracts a greater number of sports fishermen than any other location on the Texas Coast. Commercially, the prolific waters of Galveston lure hundreds of small fishing boats and shrimp boats each year. Processing of most of the catches takes place in Galveston's industrial fish plants. It is estimated that the commercial fishing business contributes $7-$8 million to Galveston's economy annually.

Soups, Salads & Breads

FRESH STRAWBERRY SOUP

Yields: **4 servings**
Preparation Time: 30 minutes

1½   cups water
¾   cup Taylor Lake Country red wine
¼   cup sugar
2   tablespoons fresh lemon juice
1   quart strawberries, hulled and puréed
1   3-inch cinnamon stick
½   cup heavy cream, whipped
¼   cup sugar
1   lime, thinly sliced (optional)

1. In a large saucepan, bring water, wine, ¼ cup sugar, lemon juice, and cinnamon stick to a boil.
2. Boil gently for 15 minutes, stirring often. Add strawberry purée and simmer for 10 minutes. Discard cinnamon stick and chill soup for a minimum of 4 hours.
3. When ready to serve, whip cream and ¼ cup sugar until stiff.
4. Fold whipped cream into soup mixture and serve in individual bowls or cups.
5. Garnish with a slice of lime, if desired.

CORN CHOWDER

Yields: **4 servings**
Preparation Time: 30 minutes

2   slices bacon, finely chopped
½   medium onion, finely chopped
2   cups frozen corn
2   tablespoons butter
2   tablespoons flour
2   cups milk
1   teaspoon salt
½   teaspoon pepper
2   cups light cream

1. Fry bacon until crisp. Add onion and sauté in drippings until soft.
2. Defrost corn and put through a food chopper. Add to onion and bacon and cook until it begins to brown.
3. Add butter, then flour. Cook slowly for 3 minutes.
4. Add milk, salt and pepper. Cook until thickened. Reduce heat to low.
5. Add cream. Heat until smooth.

OMA'S GUMBO

Yields: **8 servings**
Preparation Time: 30 minutes

1	pound bacon, chopped fine
2	large onions, chopped
½	large green pepper, chopped
3	cloves garlic, minced
2	ribs celery, chopped
3-4	tablespoons parsley
2	13-ounce cans Italian tomatoes, puréed
2	tomato cans of water
3	dashes Worcestershire sauce
2	tablespoons ketchup
2	tablespoons salt
4	tablespoons flour
4	tablespoons water (more if needed)
2	tablespoons chili powder
1	small package frozen chopped okra
5	pounds shrimp, cleaned and deveined
4-5	cups cooked rice

Can be frozen.

1. Sauté bacon until crisp. Add onions, green pepper, garlic, and celery. Sauté until vegetables just begin to brown.
2. Add parsley, tomatoes, water, Worcestershire, ketchup, and salt. Bring to a boil.
3. Combine flour with enough water to blend well. Pour into vegetable mixture to thicken. Add chili powder. Add okra. Simmer for 30 minutes. Add shrimp and cook 10 minutes more.
4. Serve liberally over rice.

SUNDAY NIGHT CRAB BISQUE

Yields: **6 servings**
Preparation Time: 30 minutes

2	tablespoons butter or margarine
1	cup celery, minced
2	1-ounce packages white sauce mix
1	pint light cream
1	13¾-ounce can chicken broth
10	ounces fresh crabmeat
	salt and pepper to taste
	pats of butter
	celery leaves

1. In medium saucepan, melt butter. Sauté celery 5 minutes or until soft. Stir in sauce mix.
2. Gradually add cream and chicken broth. Stir over low heat until soup bubbles and thickens slightly. Stir in crabmeat.
3. Simmer 1 to 2 minutes. Add salt and pepper to taste.
4. Pour into serving bowls. Top with butter and celery leaves. Good with hot rolls or French bread and a salad.

FRENCH ONION SOUP

"Simply Superb"

*Yields: **6-8 servings***
Preparation Time: 1½-2 hours

5	cups yellow onions, sliced thin
3	tablespoons butter (do not substitute)
1	tablespoon vegetable oil
1	teaspoon salt
¼	teaspoon sugar
3	tablespoons flour
2	quarts beef stock or beef bouillon
½	cup dry white wine
3	tablespoons Cognac
8	slices day old French bread
1-2	cups Swiss cheese, grated salt and pepper to taste

1. In a 4-6 quart covered saucepan, slowly sauté onions in butter and oil for 15 minutes on low heat.
2. Uncover and stir in salt and sugar and cook 30-40 minutes over medium heat, stirring frequently, until onions are a deep golden brown.
3. Sprinkle with flour. Cook and stir 3 minutes. Remove from heat.
4. In a separate saucepan, bring stock or bouillon to a rolling boil. Stir boiling stock into onions.
5. Blend in wine. Season to taste. Simmer partially covered for 40 minutes. Skim the top occasionally.
6. Carefully adjust your seasonings and set aside, uncovered until serving time.
7. When ready to serve, reheat to simmer and add Cognac.
8. Put a round of French bread into individual soup crocks and add soup. Sprinkle with cheese and broil until it melts.
9. Serve with a salad and hot French bread on the side.

BEER CHEESE SOUP

*Yields: **4 servings***
Preparation Time: 30 minutes

¼	cup butter
½	cup onion, chopped
½	cup carrots, shredded
¼	cup flour
	salt and pepper
2½	cups milk
1	16-ounce jar Cheese Whiz
½	cup beer

1. Melt butter in saucepan. Add carrots and onions. Cook until tender.
2. Blend in flour, salt, and pepper to taste.
3. Add milk, stirring constantly until thickened. Add Cheese Whiz, then beer. Heat thoroughly.

SPLIT PEA SOUP

*Yields: **4-6 servings***
Preparation Time: 30 minutes

1	pound dried split peas
8	cups water
1	pound ham hocks
1½	cups onion, finely chopped
1	cup celery, chopped (tops included)
½	cup carrots, finely chopped
1	small potato, diced
2	cloves
2	bay leaves
1	clove garlic, minced
4	peppercorns
1	teaspoon salt
2	tablespoons white vinegar
1	teaspoon sugar

1. In a large dutch oven bring peas and water to a boil. Simmer 2 minutes. Remove from heat, cover, and let sit for 1 hour.
2. Add ham hocks, onion, celery, carrots, potato, cloves, bay leaves, garlic, and peppercorns. Simmer covered for 2½ - 3 hours. Remove from heat.
3. Remove ham hocks and pick meat. Set aside.
4. Put soup through sieve. Add meat. Refrigerate. When chilled, skim fat.
5. When ready to serve, heat through. Add sugar, salt, and vinegar. If desired, add more salt and pepper.

SKYWEEJUN

*Yields: **4 servings***
Preparation Time: 1 hour

2	links Polish sausage, cut into 1" pieces
4	turnips, diced
4	large carrots, chopped
½	pound green beans, cut (optional)
1	green pepper, diced
1	large onion, diced
½	teaspoon salt
½	teaspoon pepper
1	cup canned tomatoes
1	head cabbage, cut in 8 wedges
1	cup water

1. Place cabbage in bottom of a dutch oven. Add the rest of the ingredients.
2. Simmer over medium heat until cabbage is cooked (approximately 1 hour).

CREAM OF EGGPLANT SOUP

*Yields: **12-16 servings***
Preparation Time: 1½ hours

6	tablespoons butter
3	cups celery, diced
3	cups onion, diced
2	large eggplants, unpeeled and diced
3	cups potatoes, diced
1	teaspoon curry powder
½	teaspoon thyme
½	teaspoon sweet basil
	salt and pepper to taste
8	cups chicken stock
2	cups heavy cream
2	cups milk

1. Melt butter in 6 quart saucepan. Sauté celery, onions, eggplant, and potatoes.
2. Add seasonings, including salt and pepper to taste. Cook over medium heat, uncovered, stirring frequently, until potatoes are tender (15-20 minutes).
3. Stir in chicken stock, and cook uncovered until mixture starts to thicken (about 45 minutes).
4. Remove from heat. Purée 2 cups at a time in blender or food processor until finely chopped.
5. Add cream and milk and heat slowly so that soup doesn't boil or curdle.

AVGOLEMONO

*Yields: **4-6 servings***
Preparation Time: 25 minutes

6	cups chicken broth
½	cup rice
4	eggs
⅓	cup lemon juice

1. Bring broth to a boil. Add rice and cook uncovered until done.
2. Beat eggs until light and frothy. Slowly pour in lemon juice while beating.
3. Using a ladle, add a little of the hot broth into the egg mixture, blending well.
4. Slowly add egg mixture to broth and rice, stirring constantly. Heat through, but do not boil.

Cubed chicken may be added to soup.

HUNGARIAN CREAM OF GREEN BEAN SOUP

Yields: **2 servings**
Preparation Time: 45 minutes

1   10-ounce package frozen
     green beans, thawed or ½
     pound fresh green beans
3   cups chicken stock
½   onion, cut into quarters
1   medium potato, cut into
     pieces
2   cloves garlic, minced
2   tablespoons fresh dill weed
     or 2 teaspoons dry dill weed
½   teaspoon garlic salt
¼   teaspoon pepper
     salt to taste
3   tablespoons sour cream
1   tablespoon juice of lemon

1. Combine all ingredients in saucepan, except sour cream and lemon juice.
2. Bring to a boil and reduce to simmer until vegetables are tender, about 30 minutes. Adjust seasonings to taste.
3. Place in blender (several batches) and purée until smooth.
4. Return to saucepan and add sour cream and lemon juice. Heat thoroughly on low heat.

HOT TEXAS CHILI
"Oh Wow!"

Yields: **10 servings**
Preparation Time: 30 minutes

3   pounds ground chili meat or
     ground chuck
¼   cup olive oil
1   quart water
6   tablespoons chili powder
1   tablespoon salt
10   garlic cloves
1   teaspoon cumin
1   teaspoon marjoram
1   teaspoon crushed red pepper
½   teaspoon cayenne pepper
3   tablespoons cornstarch
6   tablespoons cornmeal

1. Brown chili meat in large skillet until it turns gray. Drain off fat.
2. Add olive oil and water. Simmer for three hours.
3. Add chili powder, salt, garlic, cloves, cumin, marjoram, crushed red pepper and cayenne. Cook over medium low heat for 30 minutes, stirring occasionally.
4. Remove one cup of juice from chili. Add cornstarch and cornmeal to juice. Stir well. Add this to chili. Cook about 5 minutes or until thickened. Add more cornstarch if not thick enough.
5. Serve with crackers.

CHILLED SUMMER GARDEN SOUP

Must Make Ahead Of Time

Yields: 1½ quarts
Preparation Time: 20 minutes

¼ cup olive oil
1 small onion, coarsely chopped
1 large clove garlic, minced
1 large sweet red pepper, coarsely chopped
2 small zucchini, coarsely chopped
2 small yellow squash, coarsely chopped
1 8-ounce can plum tomatoes, undrained
1½ teaspoons salt
1 teaspoon fennel seed
⅛ teaspoon dried thyme
⅛ teaspoon cayenne pepper
¾ teaspoon black pepper
½ pound cherry tomatoes
4 large fresh basil leaves or
1 teaspoon dried basil
4½ teaspoons red wine vinegar
1½ cup tomato juice
   lemon slices

1. In a 3-quart saucepan, heat olive oil until very hot, but not smoking. Add onion, garlic, red pepper, zucchini, squash, canned tomatoes, salt, fennel seed, thyme, cayenne, and black pepper. Stir and cook over medium high heat for 6 minutes.

2. Add cherry tomatoes and basil. Continue cooking for 10 more minutes. Add the vinegar and tomato juice. Reduce heat and cool a little.

3. Purée soup in batches in a blender or food processor. Chill well and serve ice cold. Garnish with very thin lemon slices.

OYSTER STEW

Yields: 4 servings
Preparation Time: 25-30 minutes

1   pint oysters
1   tablespoon onion, grated
½   cup celery, finely chopped
½   cup milk
3   tablespoons butter (do not
    substitute)
¼   teaspoon salt
⅛   teaspoon pepper
½   cup heavy cream
⅛   teaspoon paprika

1. In a small saucepan, combine oysters, oyster liquid, and onions. Bring to a boil until oyster edges begin to curl. Set aside.
2. In a separate pan, place celery and milk. Simmer 3 minutes. Add butter, then cream.
3. Bring to a boiling point. Add salt, pepper, and paprika.
4. Turn off heat and slowly add oysters and liquid to milk mixture. Heat through, but do not boil.

CHILLED AVOCADO-CUCUMBER SOUP

Yields: 6 servings
Preparation Time: 10 minutes plus 2 hours set time

Make 2 Hours Ahead Of Time

2   cucumbers, peeled, seeded
    and cubed
1   large avocado, peeled and
    cubed
½   bunch green onions, tops and
    bottoms, chopped
2   cups chicken broth
2   cups sour cream
4   tablespoons lime juice
    salt to taste
    Tabasco to taste

1. Combine all ingredients in a food processor or blender, processing until smooth.
2. Chill at least 2 hours.
3. Garnish with additional chopped cucumbers if desired.

Combine all ingredients in a large bowl. Add carefully to blender by batches.

HYANNIS CLAM CHOWER

Yields: 8 servings
Preparation Time: 1 hour

3	small onions, diced
1	green pepper, diced
2	potatoes, diced
1	slice of ham, diced
24	ounces clams, drained and diced (use chowder or cherrystones and weigh)
½	cup butter or margarine, divided
2	teaspoons salt
½	teaspoon white pepper
½	teaspoon celery salt
	Tabasco to taste (2-3 drops)
5	tablespoons flour
5	cups milk

1. Combine onions, pepper, potatoes, ham, clams, 4 tablespoons butter, salt, pepper, celery salt, and Tabasco. Cook for 20 minutes over medium heat.
2. Melt 4 tablespoons butter. Add flour and stir until flour is well cooked. Add flour mixture to clam mixture.
3. Add milk slowly, stirring occasionally until chowder is hot and potatoes are tender—approximately 15-20 minutes.
4. Serve piping hot with a small dot of butter (not margarine) on top.

Serve with crackers and a salad.

CREAM OF CARROT AND RICE SOUP

Yields: 6 servings
Preparation Time: 20 minutes

3	tablespoons butter
2	large carrots, thinly sliced
1	medium onion, thinly sliced
4	cups chicken stock or broth
¼	cup long-grain white rice
1	teaspoon salt
½	teaspoon white pepper
1	cup heavy cream
1	tablespoon fresh parsley, minced

1. Melt butter in heavy 3-quart saucepan over low heat, add carrots and onion. Cover and cook about 15 minutes, stirring occasionally. Stir in stock, rice, salt, and pepper.
2. Cover and simmer 30-40 minutes, until vegetables are tender. Transfer to blender or food processor in batches and purée.
3. Return to saucepan. Stir in cream. Place over low heat and bring to a simmer. Taste and adjust seasonings. Garnish with minced parsley.

GARLIC BROCCOLI SOUP

Yields: **6-8 servings**
Preparation Time: 30 minutes

1   *pound fresh broccoli*
1   *cup celery, chopped*
3   *cups chicken stock*
¼   *cup parsley, minced*
3   *garlic cloves, crushed*
1   *teaspoon cornstarch*
½   *teaspoon salt*
⅓   *cup heavy cream*

1. Cut and reserve flowerets from broccoli. Trim stalks and chop finely to measure 2 cups.
2. In large saucepan, combine broccoli stalks, celery, 2 cups chicken stock, parsley, garlic, and reserved flowerets.
3. Bring to boil, simmer covered for 10-15 minutes, or until broccoli is tender (not overcooked). Drain vegetables and reserve broth.
4. Put vegetables in a good processor and process for 10 seconds. Transfer to a saucepan. The mixture will be lumpy.
5. Add remaining cup of broth ¼ cup at a time, cornstarch and salt, stirring constantly. Bring soup to a boil and simmer.
6. Add heavy cream and simmer until soup is heated through.

CHEESY CARROT SOUP

Yields: **5 cups**
Preparation Time: 1 hour

3   *carrots, peeled and shredded*
1   *small onion, finely chopped*
½   *cup celery, finely chopped*
2   *cups chicken broth*
2   *cups milk*
¼   *cup all-purpose flour*
¼   *teaspoon salt*
1   *teaspoon black pepper*
1½   *cups medium Cheddar cheese, shredded*
   parsley, chopped (optional)

1. In a medium saucepan, combine first 4 ingredients. Bring to a boil. Reduce heat. Simmer for 15 minutes.
2. Combine next 4 ingredients in an electric blender. Blend until frothy.
3. Spoon ⅓ of the vegetable-broth mixture into blender. Blend 20 seconds. Repeat until all broth mixture has been blended. Pour mixture back into saucepan.
4. Stir cheese into saucepan. Cook over medium heat, stirring constantly until cheese is melted. Garnish with parsley, if desired.

53

AVOCADO AND TOMATO SOUP

Yields: 4-6 servings
Preparation Time: 30 minutes
(2 hours set time)

¼ *cup green onions, chopped*
2 *avocados*
2 *cups tomatoes, finely chopped*
¾ *cup sour cream*
1 *cup beef broth*
1 *teaspoon salt*
1 *tablespoon lemon juice*
   Tabasco to taste

1. Blend chopped green onions (reserving some for garnish), avocados and sour cream in food processor or blender. Add tomatoes and blend again.
2. Add remaining ingredients.
3. Chill at least 2 hours. Garnish with green onions.

VICHYSSOISE
Make 8-24 Hours Ahead Of Time

Yields: 2 quarts (serves 8-10)
Preparation Time: 30 minutes

2 *leeks, cut up*
1 *small onion, quartered*
¼ *cup butter*
3 *large potatoes, peeled and cut into 1-inch pieces*
6 *cups chicken stock*
2 *teaspoons salt*
½ *teaspoon white pepper*
2 *cups heavy cream*
   chopped chives for garnish

1. In food processor, fitted with metal blade, add leeks and onion. Process, turning on and off quickly, until evenly chopped.
2. Sauté leeks and onion in butter until tender. Transfer to soup kettle.
3. Add potatoes, chicken stock, salt, and pepper. Bring to a boil. Reduce heat and simmer, covered, until potatoes are tender. Strain vegetables, reserving liquid.
4. In food processor, fitted with metal blade, add ½ the cooked and drained vegetables and process until smooth. Continue processing and pour in ½ the cream. Transfer to storage container with reserved liquid from vegetables.
5. Repeat with remaining vegetables and cream. Cover and chill several hours or overnight. Garnish with chopped chives.

CAPITOL HILL BEAN SOUP

Make 24 Hours Ahead Of Time

Yields: 6 servings
Preparation Time: 1 hour

1	*pound dried navy beans*
1	*pound ham bones*
½	*cup mashed potatoes*
3	*cups celery, chopped*
3	*cups onion, chopped*
¼	*cup fresh parsley, chopped*
1	*clove garlic, pressed*
2	*teaspoons salt*
	pepper to taste

1. Place beans in large dutch oven. Cover with water and soak overnight. Drain beans.
2. Add ham bones and cover with water. Cover dutch oven and bring to a boil. Reduce heat and simmer 1 hour.
3. Add remaining ingredients and simmer another hour or until beans are tender. Remove ham and dice. Return ham to soup.
4. Serve soup by itself or with a garden fresh salad.

OKRA GUMBO

Yields: 4 servings
Preparation Time: 40 minutes

2	*large fresh tomatoes*
1	*8-ounce can tomato sauce*
1	*teaspoon salt*
½	*teaspoon pepper*
1	*tablespoon sweet basil*
1	*large onion, finely chopped*
¼	*cup bacon drippings*
2	*cloves of garlic, pressed*
1	*pound fresh okra*

1. Wash and peel tomatoes. Cut into small chunks.
2. In medium saucepan, combine tomatoes, tomato sauce, salt, pepper, and sweet basil. Heat over medium heat for 10 minutes.
3. Sauté onions in bacon drippings. Add garlic. Sauté 5 more minutes.
4. Wash and dry okra and cut into ¾-inch pieces. Add okra to tomato mixture and stir lightly in the middle. Simmer 15-20 minutes.

Variation: To make a main course, add ½ teaspoon garlic powder and one pound of peeled raw shrimp. Simmer for 12 minutes and serve over rice.

SHRIMP BISQUE

Yields: **4 servings**
Preparation Time: 1 hour, 15 minutes

2   cups butter or margarine,
    divided
1   large carrot, sliced
1   medium onion, chopped
1   stalk celery, chopped
1   dash of thyme
1   bay leaf
6   sprigs fresh parsley
1   dash of brandy (optional)
½   cup dry white wine
2   cups chicken stock, divided
1   cup light cream
6   tablespoons flour
½   teaspoon salt
2   pounds shrimp, uncooked,
    peeled, and deveined
    white pepper to taste
    sherry to taste (optional)

1. Sauté vegetables with thyme, bay leaf, and parsley in 4 tablespoons of butter until onions are transparent. Add white wine and 1 cup chicken broth; cook until vegetables are soft.
2. Remove bay leaf and blend mixture in blender or food processor until smooth.
3. Prepare white sauce by melting 6 tablespoons of butter in a saucepan over medium heat, then adding salt and flour, stirring vigorously with a wire whip until well blended. Add light cream and 1 cup chicken stock, continuously stirring until thickened.
4. Sauté shrimp in 6 tablespoons butter until pink (about 3 minutes). Blenderize ½ of the shrimp or chop very fine.
5. Combine all ingredients (except sherry) and heat thoroughly. Correct seasonings. Add a little sherry to each bowl, if desired, before serving.

May be served hot or cold. A full meal when served with French bread and green salad.

CRABMEAT SALAD WITH AVOCADO SLICES

Yields: **3 servings**
Preparation Time: 15 minutes

1   pound fresh crabmeat
1   cup good quality
    mayonnaise
2   tablespoons ketchup
1   teaspoon horseradish
½   tablespoon Dijon mustard
1   tablespoon lemon juice
1   teaspoon fresh parsley,
    minced
¼   teaspoon salt
1   cup cucumber, peeled and
    finely chopped
½   cup celery, finely chopped
1   avocado, sliced
1   head Boston lettuce
    capers (optional)

1. Drain crabmeat. Remove all shells and cartilage from crabmeat. Set aside.
2. Combine next 7 ingredients. Mix well.
3. Combine crabmeat, cucumbers, celery, and sauce. Toss thoroughly.
4. Serve on a bed of Boston lettuce and garnish with avocado slices. Sprinkle with capers, if desired.

RAW BROCCOLI SALAD

Must Make Ahead Of Time

Yields: **6 servings**
Preparation Time: 15 minutes

2   broccoli heads, finely
        chopped (2½ cups)
⅔   cup onion, finely chopped
1 or 2 stalks celery, chopped
½   cup Spanish olives, chopped
        but not drained
1   teaspoon garlic salt
¼   teaspoon pepper
4   hard boiled eggs
⅓   cup good quality
        mayonnaise
⅓   cup sour cream

1. Mix all ingredients and refrigerate overnight.

SPINACH SALAD FLAMBÉ

Yields: 4 servings
Preparation Time: 30 minutes

6   slices bacon, cut into ½-inch
     pieces
2   tablespoons honey
2   tablespoons red wine vinegar
1½   teaspoons Worcestershire
     sauce
½   teaspoon salt
1   pound spinach, torn into bite
     size pieces
½   pound fresh mushrooms,
     sliced
1   lemon, cut in half
¼   cup brandy

1. Fry bacon until crisp; drain, reserving 2 tablespoons of drippings.
2. Heat reserved fat and add next 4 ingredients. Heat to boiling.
3. Pour mixture on spinach and mushrooms and toss. Squeeze lemon over salad.
4. Heat bacon pieces and brandy in small skillet, just until warm. Ignite and pour on salad. Toss gently.

LENTIL AND SAUSAGE SALAD

Yields: 6 servings
Preparation Time: 45 minutes

Must Make Ahead Of Time

1½   cups water
1   cup lentils, picked over and
     rinsed
2   cups smoked sausage, sliced
⅓   cup green onions, minced
⅔   cup olive oil
⅓   cup lemon juice
1   teaspoon Dijon mustard
2   garlic cloves, pressed
     tarragon to taste
1   large beet, cooked and sliced
1   hard boiled egg, sliced
     parsley

1. Combine water and lentils in large saucepan and bring to a boil. Reduce heat and simmer 30 minutes, or until tender. Drain and transfer to bowl.
2. Add sausage and green onions. Combine oil, lemon juice, mustard, cloves of garlic, and tarragon. Pour over lentils and sausage and toss well. Chill.
3. Garnish with egg and beet slices and parsley.

GERMAN POTATO SALAD

*Yields: **8-10 servings***
Preparation Time: 45 minutes

½	pound bacon, fried crisp (reserve drippings)
⅓	cup bacon drippings
1	tablespoon flour
1	tablespoon sugar
1½	teaspoons salt
½	teaspoon ground black pepper
1	teaspoon celery seed
½	cup chicken broth
½	cup red wine vinegar
6	cups hot potatoes, sliced
½	cup green onion, thinly sliced
2	tablespoons parsley, minced

1. Combine all ingredients in a large bowl. Mix thoroughly.
2. Serve hot. Adjust seasonings if needed.

SPINACH-MUSHROOM SALAD

*Yields: **6 servings***
Preparation Time: 15 minutes

½	bunch leaf or butter lettuce
½	bunch romain lettuce
1½	pounds fresh spinach
½	pound fresh mushrooms
½-1	pound bacon, cooked and crumbled
1	avocado, cut in chunks
¼	red onion, separated into rings

Dressing:

1	teaspoon sugar
½	cup vegetable oil
3	tablespoons white wine vinegar
1	tablespoon onion, grated
2	teaspoons Dijon mustard
1	teaspoon salt
	freshly ground pepper

1. Remove stems from spinach. Wash thoroughly and pat leaves dry. Tear into bite size pieces.
2. Quickly rinse mushrooms in cold water. Drain well and cut into thin slices.
3. Combine salad ingredients in large bowl. Add dressing and toss until well coated. Sprinkle with bacon.

Dressing:

1. Combine all ingredients and shake well to blend.

VEGETABLE SALAD

Yields: **8 servings**
Preparation Time: 20 minutes

1   10-ounce package frozen lima
     beans, cooked and drained
2   cups raw beets, shredded
     (about 4 medium-size)
2   tablespoons Italian dressing
6   cups salad greens, torn into
     pieces
1   green onion, cut into 1/4-
     inch pieces, tops and bottoms
1   8-ounce package Swiss cheese,
     sliced into strips

Cucumber Dressing:

1   medium cucumber, finely
     chopped
1   cup sour cream
1   tablespoon vinegar
1   teaspoon grated onion
½   teaspoon salt

1. Season beans and beets with 1 tablespoon Italian dressing in separate bowls. Chill.
2. Before serving, fill salad bowl with mixed greens.
3. Arrange circle of beets, green onion rings and lima beans on top.
4. Fill center with cheese strips. Serve with cucumber dressing.

Cucumber Dressing:

1. Pare and quarter cucumber; remove seeds. Fold in sour cream and season with remaining ingredients.

SWEET AND SOUR ASPARAGUS

Yields: **6-8 servings**
Preparation Time: 5 minutes

Make 24 Hours Ahead Of Time

¾   cup white vinegar
½   cup sugar
½   cup water
3   cinnamon sticks
½   teaspoon salt
1   teaspoon whole cloves
1   teaspoon celery seed
2   14½-ounce cans asparagus
     spears, drained

1. Combine all ingredients (except asparagus) in medium saucepan. Boil 3 minutes. Pour over asparagus in shallow dish.
2. Cover and chill overnight. Drain and serve.

Can substitute 1½ pounds of fresh asparagus for canned.

GREEN BEANS WITH SOUR CREAM
Must Make Ahead Of Time

Yields: **6 servings**
Preparation Time: 15 minutes

2   packages French-cut green beans, frozen
1   slice bacon
1   onion, thinly sliced
1   cup sour cream, seasoned to taste with lemon juice, salt and Tabasco

Salad Dressing:

¾   cup oil
4   tablespoons vinegar
     salt
     pepper

1. Add bacon to water and cook beans, using ½ cup less water than required on the package. Drain and cool. Add sliced onions.
2. To serve, place in bowl and serve with seasoned sour cream.

Salad Dressing:

1. Combine ingredients and pour over green beans and onions. Marinate overnight.

NITA'S RICE SALAD
Must Make Ahead Of Time

Yields: **10 servings**
Preparation Time: 20 minutes

2   cups Minute Rice
1   cup Italian dressing
1   bunch green onions, chopped
1   4-ounce can chopped mushrooms
1   can sliced water chestnuts
1   cucumber, chopped
1   jar stuffed green olives, sliced
1   10-ounce package frozen green peas
     mayonnaise, optional

1. Cook rice in 1 cup water and 1 cup dressing. Cool. Add onions, mushrooms, water chestnuts, cucumber, and olives. Set aside.
2. Cook peas 3 minutes; drain. Add peas to rice mixture.
3. You may add 1 teaspoon of mayonnaise, if desired.
4. Add salt and pepper to taste. Mix and let sit overnight in refrigerator.

CURRIED CHICKEN SALAD

Yields: **8 servings**
Preparation Time: 1½ hours

Must Make Ahead Of Time

2	*cups cooked chicken, cut into bite size pieces*
4	*green onions, chopped*
4	*ribs celery, chopped*
1	*apple, unpeeled and chopped*
1	*15-ounce can pineapple chunks, drained*
1	*cup seedless white grapes*
1	*cup water chestnuts, sliced*
½	*cup good quality mayonnaise*
½	*cup sour cream*
1	*teaspoon lemon juice*
¼	*teaspoon chicken bouillon granules*
1	*teaspoon curry powder*
	salt and pepper to taste

1. Combine chicken, onion, celery, apple, pineapple, grapes, and water chestnuts. Set aside.
2. Combine rest of ingredients. Mix well. Add to chicken mixture and toss lightly.
3. Season with salt and pepper. Chill before serving.

1 chopped banana may be added if desired.

CAULIFLOWER SALAD

Yields: **6 servings**
Preparation Time: 20 minutes

Make 24 Hours Ahead Of Time

1	*large head cauliflower*
1	*head lettuce*
1	*small onion, finely diced*
1	*pound bacon*

Dressing:

2	*cups good quality mayonnaise*
¼	*cup sugar*
⅓	*cup Parmesan cheese, grated*
1	*teaspoon salt*
¼	*teaspoon pepper*

1. Break cauliflower and lettuce into small pieces.
2. Cook and drain bacon. Crumble.
3. Place layer of: lettuce, cauliflower, bacon, lettuce, cauliflower, onion, bacon, onion.

Dressing:

1. Mix all ingredients and pour over salad.
2. Cover with plastic wrap and let set overnight.

ELLEN'S CRAZY PARTY SALAD

*Yields: **15-20 servings***
Preparation Time: 1 hour

Make 24 Hours Ahead Of Time

Dressing:

¼	*cup sugar*
1	*teaspoon salt*
1	*cup vegetable oil*
½	*cup vinegar*
¼	*cup ketchup*
1	*teaspoon onion or garlic powder*

Salad:

1	*15-ounce can green beans, drained*
1	*15-ounce can wax beans, drained*
1	*15-ounce can red beans, drained*
1	*15-ounce can lima beans, drained*
1	*bunch green onions, chopped*
1	*5-ounce jar stuffed olives*
2	*cups shrimp, cooked*
2	*cups chicken, diced*
2	*cups ham, diced*
2	*cups roast, diced*
2	*cups good quality mayonnaise*
	pecans or almonds

1. Mix dressing ingredients. Drain all vegetables, then mix with green onions, olives, and dressing in a large mixing bowl. Cover and marinate at least overnight.
2. Before serving, drain off marinade, then mix in meats and mayonnaise.
3. Top with one cup toasted pecans or almonds.

You may use any combination of meat (such as shrimp with ham and chicken), but you must use 8 cups. Do not freeze. Serve on a bed of lettuce accompanied by a hot vegetable, bread, and a fruit salad.

STRAWBERRY CRANBERRY SALAD

Yields: **10 servings**
Preparation Time: 30 minutes

Must Make Ahead Of Time

1   6-ounce package strawberry jello
2   cups boiling water
1   12-ounce package cranberries
½   cup sugar
1   10-ounce box frozen strawberries
1   8¼-ounce can crushed pineapple, drained

1. Dissolve jello in boiling water. Cool until slightly thickened.
2. Grind the cranberries. Add the sugar and stir until the sugar is dissolved.
3. Combine all the ingredients and mix thoroughly. Chill for several hours before serving.

RICE AND ARTICHOKE SALAD

Yields: **5 servings**
Preparation Time: 30 minutes

1   cup uncooked rice
2   cups chicken broth
¼   cup green onion, chopped
¼   cup green pepper, chopped
1   6-ounce jar marinated artichoke hearts, drained and chopped
¼   cup sliced pimiento-stuffed olives
½   cup good quality mayonnaise
¼   teaspoon dried dill weed
½   teaspoon salt
⅛   teaspoon pepper

1. Boil broth and stir in rice.
2. Cook 20 minutes or until done, covered. Cool. Stir in remaining ingredients. Chill.

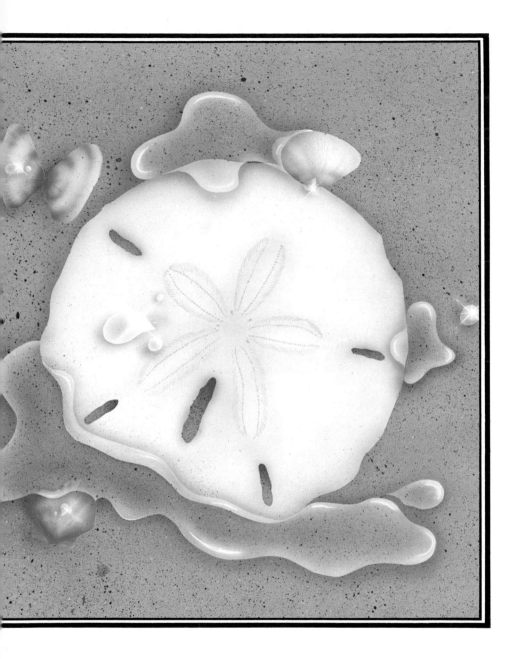

SAND DOLLARS

A beachcombing excursion along the Galveston beaches is sure to turn up a collection of a sand dollar—flat circular shells with five slits along the outer edge. You'll notice that the entire shell is penetrated by many small brown spines giving the shell a velvety appearance and enabling the animal to move about.

According to the legend the five slits along the edge represent the five wounds of the body of Christ. In the center of the top of the sand dollar is an Easter lily design which has a five-pointed star of Bethlehem in its center. On the back is the outline of a Christmas poinsettia. If the shell is broken, five small cells reveal replicas of the doves of good will and peace.

PASTA AND VEGGIE SALAD

Yields: **12 servings**
Preparation Time: 30 minutes

Must Make Ahead Of Time

1   *cup medium-sized shell macaroni, cooked and drained*
²/₃   *cup Italian salad dressing*
½   *cup zucchini, sliced*
½   *cup fresh mushrooms, halved or whole*
½   *cup broccoli flowerets, broken into bite size pieces*
½   *cup marinated artichoke hearts, cut in quarters*
1   *large tomato, cut into thin wedges*
½   *avocado, peeled and cubed*

1. Combine all ingredients except tomato and avocado in large bowl.
2. Cover and refrigerate at least 3 hours.
3. Stir in tomato and avocado before serving.

RASPBERRY-CRANBERRY SALAD

Yields: **6 servings**
Preparation Time: 30 minutes

1   *6-ounce package raspberry jello*
1   *16-ounce can whole cranberry sauce*
1   *8-ounce can crushed pineapple and juice*
½   *cup burgundy wine*
½   *cup nuts*
    fresh orange and grapefruit slices

1. Dissolve jello in 2 cups hot water. Stir in next 3 ingredients. Pour into 6-cup ring mold.
2. When partially set, add ½ cup nuts. Chill until firm.
3. Add fresh fruit slices to center of mold.

RAINBOW COMPOTE
Make 24 Hours Ahead Of Time

Yields: **10 servings**
Preparation Time: 30 minutes

½ cup honey
2 tablespoons lemon juice
1 tablespoon candied ginger, finely snipped (optional)
1 teaspoon orange peel, finely shredded
4 oranges, peeled and sliced crosswise
1½ cups blueberries
2 cups honeydew melon, cubed
1½ cups halved strawberries

1. Combine first 4 ingredients.
2. Pour over orange slices in bowl. Cover and refrigerate overnight.
3. Chill remaining fruit.
4. Drain oranges, reserving dressing.
5. Arrange orange slices in bottom of compote. Top with a layer of blueberries, melon cubes, and strawberries. Pour dressing over fruit.
6. Garnish with whole strawberries.

GREEK SALAD

Yields: **6-8 servings**
Preparation Time: 20 minutes

1 medium head of lettuce
1 medium cucumber, thinly sliced
2 large tomatoes, cut in wedges
1 5½-ounce jar pitted olives, chopped
½ teaspoon salt
⅛ teaspoon pepper
2 green onions, chopped
¼ pound feta cheese, grated
½ cup olive oil
3 tablespoons red wine vinegar
1 teaspoon oregano

1. Into large chilled salad bowl, tear lettuce into bite-size pieces.
2. Peel lengthwise strips of skin from cucumbers to give stripped effect.
3. Add cucumbers and tomatoes to lettuce mixture with olives, green onions and feta cheese. Set aside.
4. In cup, combine olive oil, red wine, and oregano.
5. Pour over salad. Toss to mix well.

COLD CHICKEN VEGETABLE PLATTER

*Yields: **10-12 servings***
Preparation Time: 2 hours

1	*whole chicken, cut up or enough to make 4-5 cups cooked chicken*
1	*stalk celery*
1	*onion*
1	*1-pound bag carrots, julienned*
6	*red potatoes, peeled and sliced*
1	*10-ounce package frozen whole green beans*
1	*10-ounce package frozen peas*
8	*radishes, sliced*
½	*pound fresh mushrooms, sliced*
1	*6-ounce can artichoke bottoms, sliced*
1	*2¼-ounce can pitted black olives, chopped*
1	*bunch green onions, chopped*
½-1	*package cherry tomatoes*

Dressing:

1	*10-ounce jar Durkee's Famous Sauce*
1	*pint sour cream*
5	*tablespoons good quality mayonnaise juice of 1 lemon*
1½	*teaspoons dill weed To taste: Worcestershire sauce, onion powder, Tabasco, and garlic powder.*

1. Boil chicken in water with one carrot, one onion, and one stalk of celery.
2. Cook for 1 hour, cool chicken, and debone. Reserve 4 cups of stock.
3. Boil potatoes in 4 cups chicken stock until barely cooked. Drain potatoes and reserve stock again.
4. Bring stock to a boil, add frozen peas and green beans, and cook according to package directions (except undercook by 1-2 minutes). DO NOT OVERCOOK. Drain vegetables and cool; reserve stock.
5. Cook carrots in stock until tender—do not overcook. Drain and cool.
6. Slice radishes and mushrooms; drain artichoke bottoms and slice; drain olives.
7. On large platter, place vegetables in layers, starting with potatoes, carrots, green beans, peas, mushrooms, radishes, artichokes, and green onions.
8. On top, place strips of cold chicken and garnish with olives and tomatoes. Cover all with dressing and garnish with dill weed.

Dressing:

1. Blend all ingredients well.

Very pretty when a few tomatoes, olives, and green onions are reserved to garnish the top of dressing. A bed of lettuce may be used as a first layer if desired. Dressing is even better if made 24 hours ahead.

THE GREAT SALAD
"Enough Said"

Yields: **8 servings**
Preparation Time: 30 minutes

1	large bunch fresh spinach
1	head iceberg lettuce
1	head red tip lettuce
½	head romaine lettuce
2	tablespoons fresh chives, finely chopped
2	tablespoons parsley, chopped
1-2	teaspoons fresh tarragon
1	teaspoon prepared mustard
1	teaspoon salt
1	egg
1	lemon (juice of)
½	cup oil
1	cup sour cream
2-3	drops Tabasco
2	cups small shrimp, cooked, deveined, and cut in half seasoned croutons freshly cracked pepper

1. Wash and dry greens thoroughly and refrigerate. (May be done a day ahead).
2. Just prior to serving, in a large salad bowl, combine chives, parsley, tarragon, mustard and salt. Add egg, lemon juice, and mix thoroughly with whisk.
3. Slowly add oil, beating briskly until thickened. Blend in sour cream and Tabasco. Fold in shrimp. Add greens and toss gently. Sprinkle with fresh ground pepper and croutons. Serve immediately.

ROCCHI'S PERUVIAN SALAD

Yields: **6 servings**
Preparation Time: 30 minutes plus 2 hours set time

5	ears fresh yellow corn, cooked, cooled and removed from ears
1	rib celery, thinly sliced
¾	pound fresh Parmesan cheese, cut into small chunks
1	can hearts of palm, sliced
2	large lemons (juice of)
½	cup olive oil salt and pepper to taste

1. Mix all ingredients in order and cover.
2. Let chill for at least 2 hours, preferably more.

CHICKEN ARTICHOKE SALAD

Yields: 8-10 servings
Preparation Time: 1 hour

Must Make Ahead Of Time

1	*chicken, boiled and deboned*
1	*package chicken Rice-A-Roni*
1/2	*bell pepper, chopped*
1/2	*cup pimento-stuffed olives, sliced*
2	*jars marinated artichoke hearts, reserving liquid*
1/4	*teaspoon curry*
1/3	*cup good quality mayonnaise*
1/2	*cup green onion, chopped*

1. Cook Rice-a-Roni as directed, omitting butter.
2. Cool to room temperature.
3. Add green onions, pepper, olives, and artichokes.
4. Add chicken.
5. Mix curry, mayonnaise, and artichoke liquid from 1 jar.
6. Pour over salad and chill 24 hours.

MARINATED TOMATOES

Yields: 4-6 servings
Preparation Time: 20 minutes

Must Make Ahead Of Time

4	*large tomatoes, peeled*
1/3	*cup parsley, chopped*
1	*clove garlic, crushed*
1/3	*cup olive oil*
2	*tablespoons cider vinegar*
1	*teaspoon salt*
1/2	*teaspoon leaf basil*
1/4	*teaspoon Tabasco*

1. Cut tomatoes into 1/2-inch slices. Place in shallow dish. Set aside.
2. Combine other ingredients. Pour over tomatoes.
3. Chill 4 hours or overnight. Serve over lettuce.

CREAMY VEGETABLE SALAD

Yields: 6-8 servings
Preparation Time: overnight

1   10-ounce package frozen
     broccoli spears
1   10-ounce package frozen
     french style green beans
1   10-ounce package frozen cut
     asparagus
2   10-ounce packages artichokes
1   green pepper, sliced
1   cucumber, thinly sliced

Dressing:

½   cup light cream
3   tablespoons lemon juice
2   tablespoons garlic vinegar
1   cup good quality mayonnaise
¼   cup onion, finely chopped
3   teaspoons anchovy paste
     salt and pepper to taste

1. Cook vegetables half the pre-scribed time on the package.
2. Drain and chill.
3. Add cucumber and green peppers.
4. Pour dressing over salad and refrigerate overnight.

Dressing:

1. Combine all ingredients and shake well to blend.

MEXICAN SALAD BOWL

Yields: 6 servings
Preparation Time: 10 minutes

½   cup good quality mayonnaise
¼   cup green onions, minced
2-3 tablespoons chili sauce
2   tablespoons cider vinegar
1   teaspoon onion salt
½   teaspoon chili powder
4   drops hot pepper sauce
1   13-ounce can whole kernel
     corn
1   15-ounce can red kidney
     beans
1   7-ounce can pitted ripe olives
2   cups lettuce, shredded

1. Combine mayonnaise, onions, chili sauce, vinegar, salt, chili powder, and hot pepper sauce. Cover and chill.
2. Drain and combine next three ingredients. Spoon into lettuce-lined bowl. Serve with dressing.

Crushed corn chips make a great addition.

VERMICELLI SALAD
Make 24 Hours Ahead Of Time

*Yields: **4-6 servings***
Preparation Time: 30 minutes

1	10-ounce package Vermicelli
½	cup vegetable oil
¼	cup lemon juice
1	medium-size bunch green onions, finely chopped
1	4¼-ounce jar chopped pimiento
1	3½-ounce can chopped black olives
½	cup good quality mayonnaise
1	cup celery, finely chopped
1	cup green pepper, finely chopped
	salt and pepper to taste

1. While still in package, crush Vermicelli into small pieces. Drop Vermicelli into boiling water and cook for 8 minutes. Drain Vermicelli.
2. In a medium-size bowl, combine oil and lemon juice with pasta and place in freezer for 10 minutes.
3. Combine remaining ingredients. Add to pasta. Mix thoroughly. Set in refrigerator overnight. Adjust seasonings with salt and pepper.

Great summer salad!

SUPER SEAFOOD SALAD
Make 4 Hours Ahead Of Time

*Yields: **6-8 servings***
Preparation Time: 45 minutes plus 1 hour set time

1½	cups fresh white crabmeat
1½	cups medium shrimp, cooked, shelled, and deveined
1¼	cups 1" fresh pineapple, chunks
2	tablespoons chutney
1	cup celery, sliced
1¼	cups green onions, sliced (including some tops)
1	cup sliced water chestnuts
½	cup toasted almonds, slivered
1¼	cups good quality mayonnaise (not salad dressing)
½	cup sour cream plus 2 tablespoons
1¼	teaspoons curry powder

1. Using a large bowl, combine crabmeat, shrimp, pineapple, chutney, celery, green onions, water chestnuts, and almonds. Toss together lightly. Cover and refrigerate.
2. In a small bowl, combine mayonnaise, sour cream, and curry. Mix well. Cover and refrigerate for at least 2 hours.
3. An hour before serving, pour dressing over seafood and mix lightly, making sure all ingredients are covered thoroughly. Let set in refrigerator for an hour for flavors to set.
4. Serve in tomato halves, avocado halves, or on a bed of lettuce.

ORIENTAL TOSSED SALAD

Yields: **6 servings**
Preparation Time: 15 minutes

1   *head lettuce, torn*
4   *green onions, sliced*
3   *ounces almonds, sliced*
4   *teaspoons sesame seeds*
6-8 *slices bacon, crisp and crumbled*
½   *cup Chinese noodles*

Dressing:

2-4 *tablespoons sugar*
2   *teaspoons salt*
2   *teaspoons Accent*
¼   *teaspoon black pepper*
½   *cup vegetable oil*
6   *tablespoons white vinegar*

1. Combine lettuce and onions.
2. Toss with dressing and add remaining ingredients.

Dressing:

1. Combine all ingredients and shake well to blend.

SHRIMP SALAD

Make 24 Hours Ahead Of Time

Yields: **6-8 servings**
Preparation Time: 20 minutes

1   *cup large elbow macaroni, uncooked*
1   *cup celery, diced*
1   *medium onion, chopped*
¼   *cup green pepper, chopped*
¼   *cup pimiento, chopped*
1⅓   *cups shrimp, cooked, shelled, and deveined*
2   *hard boiled eggs, peeled and chopped*
½   *teaspoon salt*
¼   *teaspoon paprika*
1   *cup good quality mayonnaise*
¾   *cup French dressing*

1. Cook macaroni according to package directions. Drain and rinse.
2. In large bowl, combine macaroni, celery, onion, green pepper, pimiento, shrimp, and eggs. Set aside.
3. In a small bowl, combine salt, paprika, mayonnaise, and French dressing. Pour over ingredients in the large bowl. Mix well.
4. Chill overnight in refrigerator. Serve on a bed of lettuce.

SHRIMP REMOULADE

Yields: **2 cups**
Preparation Time: 1 hour

Shrimp:

1   *quart water*
1   *tablespoon caraway seeds*
1   *slice lemon*
3   *peppercorns*
½   *teaspoon salt*
2   *pounds raw shrimp, uncleaned*

Sauce:

2   *tablespoons vegetable oil*
2   *yolks of hard boiled eggs*
1   *raw egg*
1   *teaspoon dry mustard*
1   *tablespoon parsley*
1   *tablespoon chives*
½   *green pepper, chopped*
¼   *cup capers*
¼   *onion, chopped*
½   *cup vinegar*
⅛   *clove garlic, minced*
2   *teaspoons salt*
½   *teaspoon pepper*

Shrimp:

1. Boil water with seasoning for 5 minutes and add shrimp.
2. Boil for 5 minutes.
3. Drain, clean, devein, and refrigerate.

Sauce:

1. Combine all ingredients in a covered jar and shake. ·
2. This is a very thin sauce.
3. Pour sauce over shrimp. Serve with crackers.

COWBOY SLAW

Yields: **8-10 servings**
Preparation Time: 30 minutes

1½   *quarts cabbage, shredded*
1   *small green pepper, chopped, optional*
1   *medium onion, finely chopped*
1   *cup white or cider vinegar*
¾   *cup sugar*
⅔   *cup vegetable oil*
1   *teaspoon dry mustard*
1   *teaspoon celery seed*
1   *teaspoon salt*

1. Combine cabbage, green pepper, and onion. Set aside.
2. In a medium sauce pan, bring to a boil the vinegar, sugar, oil, dry mustard, celery seed and salt. Pour hot liquid immediately over the cabbage mixture. Serve warm or chilled.

COBB SALAD

Yields: **8-10 servings**
Preparation Time: 12 hours

Salad:

1	head romaine lettuce, finely chopped
8	slices of bacon, crisp and crumbled
1/4	pound Roquefort cheese, broken into pieces
3	tomatoes, peeled, seeded, and finely chopped
2	avocados, peeled, seeded, and finely diced
2	hard boiled eggs, finely chopped

Dressing:

1/4	cup pear or cider vinegar
1/2	cup salad oil
1	teaspoon lemon juice
1	clove garlic, crushed
1	teaspoon salt
1/8	teaspoon fresh ground pepper

1. Chop all ingredients for salad (except avocado) into very small pieces, (about lima bean size). This may be done early in the day and refrigerated.
2. Just before serving, dice avocado and mix with other ingredients.
3. Pour dressing over top and toss.

Dressing:

1. Combine all ingredients and shake well to blend.

CRAB-SHRIMP SALAD

Yields: **6 servings**
Preparation Time: 2 hours

1	cup good quality mayonnaise
1	teaspoon dry mustard
1	tablespoon onion, minced
2	tablespoons celery, finely chopped
1	tablespoon sweet pickle relish
1/2	teaspoon tarragon
1/2	teaspoon salt
1/2	teaspoon Tabasco
1 1/2	cups fresh crabmeat
1/2	pound shrimp, cooked and cleaned

1. Blend first 8 ingredients.
2. Combine with flaked crabmeat and chopped shrimp.
3. Chill at least 2 hours.

74

STAINED GLASS FRUIT SALAD

Yields: *6-8 servings*
Preparation Time: 10 minutes

"Looks So Pretty"

2   *11-ounce cans mandarin oranges, drained*
1   *16-ounce can pineapple chunks, drained*
1   *10-ounce package frozen sliced strawberries (not drained)*
1   *20-ounce can peach pie filling*
3-4 *bananas, sliced*

1. Mix all together thoroughly in a large bowl.
2. Transfer to a large glass bowl and chill.

A trifle bowl is perfect for this.

HOT FRUIT COMPOTE

Yields: *6-8 servings*
Preparation Time: 45 minutes

1   *16-ounce can pears cut into large pieces*
1   *16-ounce can white Royal Anne cherries*
1   *16-ounce can pineapple chunks*
1   *16-ounce can sliced peaches*
¼   *cup golden raisins*
3   *oranges, unpeeled*
    Retain 1 cup drained fruit juice

Sauce:

½   *cup sugar*
2   *tablespoons flour*
1   *tablespoon butter*
1   *cup juices, reserved from canned fruit*
½   *cup dry sherry*

1. Slice unpeeled oranges into wedges.
2. Cover with water and cook until tender, about 10 minutes.
3. Drain and add to other fruits. Transfer to 9"× 9" casserole. Add sauce and bake in 300° oven for 30 minutes.

Sauce:

1. Cook first 4 ingredients until smooth. Cool and add sherry.
2. Cool before adding fruit.

Temperature: *300 °*
Time: *30 minutes*

Best if made the day before to allow flavors to blend.

OLEANDER BLOSSOM SALAD

Must Make Ahead Of Time

Yields: 12 servings
Preparation Time: 1½ hours

1   3-ounce package lemon gelatin
1½ cups boiling water
¼   cup lemon juice
1   8-ounce package cream cheese, softened
1   cup medium Cheddar cheese, shredded
1   cup pecans, chopped
1   15¼-ounce can pineapple chunks, packed in its own juice
2   3-ounce packages orange gelatin
2   cups Champagne or gingerale
2   11-ounce cans mandarin orange sections, drained
    lettuce for garnish
    orange sections for garnish
    frosted grape clusters for garnish

1. In a small saucepan, dissolve lemon gelatin in boiling water. Stir in lemon juice.

2. Place cream cheese in a medium size bowl. Gradually add lemon gelatin mixture to cream cheese, beating with electric mixer on medium speed until smooth. Refrigerate until partially set.

3. When partially set, fold in Cheddar cheese and pecans. Turn into a lightly oiled 10-cup ring mold. Refrigerate until almost firm.

4. Drain pineapple chunks, reserving juice. Cut each chunk in half. Set aside. Add water to pineapple juice to make 1½ cups. Bring pineapple juice to a boil. Add orange gelatin and stir until dissolved. Slowly stir in Champagne or gingerale. Refrigerate until partially set.

5. When partially set, fold in orange sections and pineapple chunks. Pour over cream mixture in mold. Refrigerate 8 hours or overnight until firm.

6. When ready to serve, arrange lettuce leaves on platter. Unmold salad on plate. Garnish with orange sections and frosted grapes.

To frost grapes, brush with beaten egg white and sprinkle with granulated sugar. Dry completely on rack.

FESTIVE STRAWBERRY SALAD

Must Make Ahead Of Time

Yields: **15-20 servings**
Preparation Time: *45 minutes*

2	*cups pretzels, crushed*
¾	*cup butter or margarine, melted*
3	*tablespoons brown sugar*
2	*3-ounce packages strawberry jello*
2	*cups hot water*
2	*10-ounce packages frozen strawberries*
1	*8-ounce package cream cheese, softened*
1	*9-ounce container whipped topping*
⅓	*cup sugar*

1. Mix crushed pretzels, butter, and brown sugar. Spread in a 9" × 13" pan and bake in 350° oven for 15 minutes.
2. Dissolve jello in hot water. Add frozen strawberries. Stir until slightly thickened. Pour over pretzel crust. Chill until set (about 2 hours set time).
3. Mix cream cheese, whipped topping, and sugar until creamy. Spread over chilled jello. Cut into squares.

Temperature: **350 °**
Time: *15 minutes*

MANHATTEN DELI SALAD

Yields: **6 servings**
Preparation Time: *15 minutes*

¼	*pound hard salami*
1	*package spiral pasta, cooked according to package directions*
¼	*cup pitted ripe olives, sliced*
1	*cup green pepper, sliced*
1	*small red onion, cut into rings*
¼-½	*cup grated Parmesan cheese*
¼	*cup parsley*
¾	*cup Italian dressing*

1. In a large bowl, combine salami in thin strips and all other ingredients.
2. Serve at room temperature or chilled.

PAPER CUP FROZEN SALAD

Must Make Ahead Of Time

*Yields: **12 servings***
Preparation Time: 15 minutes

2	*cups sour cream*
2	*tablespoons lemon juice*
½	*cup sugar*
⅛	*teaspoon salt*
1	*8-ounce can crushed pineapple, drained*
1	*banana, diced*
¼	*cup pecans, chopped*
4	*drops red food coloring*
1	*16-ounce can pitted bing cherries, drained*

1. Combine all ingredients. Spoon into paper cups in muffin pan. Cover with plastic wrap. Freeze.
2. Remove 15 minutes before serving and transfer to a bed of lettuce.

MOMMA'S CHIVE SALAD DRESSINGS

Make 12-24 Hours Ahead Of Time

*Yields: **8-10 servings***
Preparation Time: 10 minutes

1	*garlic clove, minced*
2	*teaspoons onion, grated*
2	*teaspoons capers*
1	*teaspoon parsley, chopped*
1	*teaspoon chives, chopped*
½	*teaspoon sugar*
½	*cup olive oil*
4	*tablespoons tarragon vinegar*
	salt and pepper to taste

1. Combine all ingredients.
2. Set aside for at least 12 hours.

Best if made with fresh herbs.

GAIDO'S ROMANO CHEESE DRESSING

Yields: 1½ cups
Preparation Time: 10 minutes

1	whole egg
1	clove garlic, minced
½	cup vegetable oil
½	cup Romano cheese, grated
⅓	teaspoon red pepper
½	teaspoon salt
5	teaspoons white vinegar

1. Combine all ingredients in blender and blend until smooth.
2. Refrigerate until ready to serve.

POPPY SEED DRESSING I

Yields: 3½ cups
Preparation Time: 10 minutes

¼	onion, finely chopped
1½	cups sugar
1	teaspoon dry mustard
2	teaspoons salt
⅔	cup vinegar
2	cups vegetable oil
3	tablespoons poppy seeds

1. Combine first 5 ingredients in food processor or blender. Mix well 4-5 seconds.
2. With blade in motion, slowly add oil until mixture thickens.
3. Add poppy seeds and process just to blend. Refrigerate.

POPPY SEED DRESSING II

Yields: 2 cups
Preparation Time: 10 minutes

2	teaspoons poppy seeds
1	teaspoon dry mustard
1	teaspoon paprika
¼	teaspoon salt
½	cup sugar
1	teaspoon dried onions, minced
⅓	teaspoon honey
6	tablespoons white vinegar
3	tablespoons lemon juice
1	cup vegetable oil

1. Soak poppy seeds 2 hours in water.
2. Drain thoroughly in cheesecloth. Mix next 8 ingredients.
3. *Slowly* add oil while beating with electric mixer or food processor.
4. Add drained poppy seeds.

BRASS RAIL DRESSING

Yields: **2 cups**
Preparation Time: 10 minutes

1¼ cups good quality
mayonnaise
½ cup oil
¼ cup honey
¼ cup prepared mustard
¼ teaspoon dry mustard
3 tablespoons lemon juice
2 green onions, minced
1 tablespoon parsley
1 teaspoon celery salt or celery
seed
¼ teaspoon curry powder

1. Mix all ingredients in a jar.
2. Shake until well blended.
3. Toss with shrimp or chicken and serve over lettuce.

BLEU CHEESE DRESSING AT ITS BEST

Yields: **2½ cups**
Preparation Time: 10 minutes

¾ cup sour cream
½ teaspoon dry mustard
½ teaspoon black pepper
½ teaspoon salt
⅓ teaspoon garlic powder, scant
1 teaspoon Worcestershire
sauce
1⅓ cups good quality
mayonnaise
1 4-ounce package Danish bleu
cheese

1. Using a blender, combine first 6 ingredients. Blend on low speed.
2. Add mayonnaise and blend ½ minute at low speed, then blend 2 minutes at medium speed. Crumble bleu cheese and add to mixture. Blend on low speed 3½-4 minutes. DO NOT BLEND ANY LONGER.
3. Pour into jar and cover tightly. Refrigerate until ready to use.

RUBY'S SALAD DRESSING

Yields: 1 cup
Preparation Time: 1 hour

1-½   *teaspoons salt*
3   *tablespoons sugar*
½   *large lemon, squeezed*
2   *small cloves garlic, pressed*
½   *teaspoon celery seed*
½   *teaspoon beau monde*
¼   *teaspoon sweet basil or 3*
         tablespoons sweet basil
         vinegar
4   *tablespoons red wine vinegar*
4   *tablespoons olive oil*
2   *tablespoons vegetable oil*

1. Mix all ingredients in a jar. Shake well.
2. Let stand at least 1 hour. Pour over salad greens.

WHITE FRENCH DRESSING

Yields: 2-½ cups
Preparation Time: 15 minutes

½   *cup sugar*
½   *cup vinegar*
¼   *cup water*
1   *cup oil*
1   *teaspoon salt*
½   *teaspoon white pepper*
1   *pod garlic*
4   *green onions and tops,*
         chopped

1. In a blender, mix first 3 ingredients.
2. Slowly add oil, then next 3 ingredients.
3. Add green onions and mix by hand. Chill until ready to serve.

SPINACH SALAD DRESSING

Yields: 8-10 servings
Preparation Time: 5 minutes

1   *cup vegetable oil*
½   *cup red wine vinegar*
½   *cup sugar*
⅓   *cup ketchup*
         salt and pepper to taste

1. Combine all ingredients in bowl. Mix well.
2. Pour into quart sized jar. Shake well.

Will keep several weeks in a tightly covered jar. Great also on regular tossed salad.

SWEET AND SOUR HERBED DRESSING

Yields: 1 cup
Preparation Time: 10 minutes

¾ *cup vegetable oil*
¼ *cup red wine vinegar*
1 *clove garlic, minced*
1-½ *tablespoons sugar*
1 *teaspoon salt*
1 *teaspoon paprika*
1 *teaspoon dry mustard*
½ *teaspoon tarragon*
½ *teaspoon thyme*
½ *teaspoon oregano*
¼ *teaspoon pepper*

1. Combine all ingredients in pint-sized jar. Shake well and chill until serving time.

CAESAR SALAD DRESSING

Yields: 6-8 servings
Preparation Time: 10 minutes

1 *clove garlic*
1 *egg*
¼ *teaspoon dry mustard*
¼ *teaspoon coarse ground pepper*
½ *teaspoon salt*
½ *cup Parmesan cheese, grated*
6 *tablespoons olive oil*
4 *tablespoons lemon juice*
2-3 *head Romaine lettuce croutons*

1. Grate the garlic clove into a wooden salad bowl. Beat in the egg. Add the rest of ingredients and mix with a wire whisk.
2. Clean and tear 2-3 heads Romaine lettuce. Coat with dressing and add croutons.

GOLDEN RAISIN CASEROLE BREAD

Yields: **2 loaves of bread**
Preparation Time: 2 hours, 45 minutes

*1	cup milk
½	cup sugar
*1	teaspoon salt
*¼	cup butter or margarine
½	cup warm water (105°-115°)
2	packages dry yeast
*1	egg
4½	cups unsifted flour
1	cup golden raisins
1	teaspoon cinnamon
¼	teaspoon allspice

1. Scald milk. Stir in sugar, salt, and butter. Cool to lukewarm. Set aside. Add warm water to a large warm bowl. Sprinkle in yeast; stir until dissolved.

2. Stir in lukewarm milk mixture, egg, and 3 cups flour. Beat by hand or with electric mixer until smooth. Add remaining flour and spices. Mix well.

3. Cover. Let rise in warm place for about 1 hour until double in bulk.

4. Punch batter down. Stir in raisins. Divide dough in half. Place each half in a 5" × 9" bread pan or 1-quart casserole dish. Bake in 350° oven for 40-45 minutes.

Temperature: **350 °**
Time: 40-45 minutes

Freezes well. Makes excellent toast. Great for Christmas gifts.

For A Heart Healthy Recipe Make These Substitutions:

*1	cup skim milk
*½	teaspoon salt
*¼	cup corn oleo
*¼	cup cholesterol free egg substitute

SPICED APPLE MUFFINS

Yields: **12 muffins**
Preparation Time: 15 minutes

2	cups flour
½	cup sugar
4	teaspoons baking powder
½	teaspoon salt
½	teaspoon cinnamon
1	egg
1	cup milk
¼	cup butter or margarine, melted
1	cup apples, chopped

Topping:

2	tablespoons sugar
½	teaspoon cinnamon

1. Sift together flour, sugar, baking powder, and salt into a large bowl. Add cinnamon.
2. Beat egg and combine with milk and butter. Add to dry ingredients. Beat thoroughly. Fold in chopped apples and mix well.
3. Drop by tablespoons into greased muffin tin. Sprinkle topping on dough.
4. Bake in a 425° oven for 15 minutes.

Temperature: **425 °**
Time: 15 minutes

CHEESE BREAD

Yields: **2 loaves**
Preparation Time: 2 hours

3½	cups flour, divided
1	tablespoon yeast
¼	cup sugar
1	teaspoon salt
½	cup milk
½	cup water
2	eggs
1-1½	cups sharp Cheddar cheese, grated
½	cup vegetable oil
½	teaspoon pepper

1. Combine 1-1½ cups flour and yeast.
2. Heat next 5 ingredients over low heat, stirring to blend. (Do not boil.)
3. Add liquid mixture to flour and yeast and beat until smooth. Blend in remaining ingredients and flour. Beat until smooth and elastic.
4. Spoon into 2 well greased 1-pound coffee cans. Cover with lids and let rise 1 hour.
5. Remove lids - batter should be ¼ to ½ inch below top rim. Bake in cans at 375° for 30-35 minutes.
6. Allow to cool before removing from can.

Temperature: **375 °**
Time: 30-35 minutes

APRICOT BUBBLES

Yields: **12-14 servings**
Preparation Time: 2½ hours

1   package yeast
¼   cup lukewarm water
½   cup milk
1   cup sugar, divided
⅓   cup shortening
1   teaspoon salt
3½   cups flour, divided
2   eggs
1   teaspoon cinnamon
¼   cup butter
⅔   cup apricot or pineapple
     preserves
1   cup walnuts, finely chopped

1. Dissolve yeast in water.
2. Scald milk. Add ⅓ cup sugar, shortening and salt to scalded milk. Add 1 cup flour. Add yeast and beaten eggs.
3. Mix in remaining flour to make a soft dough. Mix thoroughly.
4. Place dough in greased bowl, cover, and let rise in a warm place. When double in size, punch down and let rise 10 minutes.
5. Divide dough into 20 pieces and form into balls.
6. Mix remaining ⅔ cup sugar with cinnamon.
7. Melt butter. Roll each ball in butter and then in sugar mixture. Place a layer of 10 balls in a well-greased 10-inch tube pan.
8. Drop a spoonful of preserves between each ball, and sprinkle with half the nuts.
9. Follow the same procedure with second layer. Cover and let rise until double in size.
10. Bake in 350° oven for 35 minutes, or until done. Cool 10 minutes before removing from pan.

Temperature: **350 °**
Time: **35 minutes**

CINNAMON MONKEY BREAD

Yields: **8-10 servings**
Preparation Time: **30 minutes**

3	cans "Butter Me Not" biscuits
½	cup sugar
½	teaspoon cinnamon
½	cup butter
¾	cup sugar
¾	teaspoon cinnamon
½	cup pecans, chopped

1. Grease and flour a bundt pan.
2. Quarter the biscuits and roll each quarter in mixture of ½ cup sugar and cinnamon combined.
3. In a saucepan, melt butter. Add ¾ cup sugar and cinnamon. Heat until sugar melts. Pour over biscuits. Sprinkle chopped pecans over biscuits.
4. Bake in 350° oven for 30-35 minutes. Remove from oven. Let stand 10 minutes and invert on cake plate.

Temperature: **350 °**
Time: **30-35 minutes**

BRAN MUFFINS
"Great For Quick Breakfast"

Yields: **50 muffins**
Preparation Time: **30 minutes**

5	cups flour
3	cups sugar
5	teaspoons baking soda
2	teaspoons salt
1	15-ounce box raisin bran
1	quart buttermilk
1	cup vegetable oil

1. In a large mixing bowl combine all ingredients. Mix well.
2. Store mixture in jars until ready to use. This will keep 6 weeks in refrigerator.
3. When ready to bake, spoon mixture into cupcake liners in muffin tins. Bake in 400° oven for 15 minutes.

Temperature: **400 °**
Time: **15 minutes**

This is nice for winter mornings.

SOUR CREAM COFFEE CAKE

Yields: **12 servings**
Preparation Time: 20 minutes

½	cup butter, room temperature
1	cup sugar
2	eggs, room temperature
2	cups flour, sifted
½	teaspoon salt
1	teapsoon baking soda
1	teaspoon baking powder
1	cup sour cream, room temperature
1	teaspoon vanilla
⅓	cup brown sugar
1	teapsoon cinnamon
⅓	cup nuts, chopped

1. Cream butter and 1 cup sugar together. Add eggs, and flour (sifted together with salt, baking soda, and powder) alternately.
2. Fold in sour cream and vanilla. Put one-half the batter in a greased and floured tube pan. Sprinkle with half the brown sugar, cinnamon, and nuts. Cover with remaining batter.
3. Bake in 350° oven for 45 minutes. Do not open oven until cake has baked 45 minutes. Sprinkle top with remaining brown sugar, nuts, and cinnamon while cake is still hot.

Temperature: **350** °
Time: 45 minutes

ENGLISH MUFFINS

Yields: 8
Preparation Time: 2½-3 hours

1	cup milk
2	tablespoons sugar
1	teaspoon salt
3	tablespoons butter
1	package dry yeast
1	cup warm water
3	cups flour
	cornmeal

1. Scald milk, sugar, salt, and butter in double boiler. Cool slightly.
2. Add yeast that has been dissolved in one cup warm water.
3. Beat in 3 cups flour, and let rise one hour.
4. Punch down, roll out, and cut in 3 inch circles.
5. Dust with cornmeal, and place on ungreased cookie sheets. Let rise one hour.
6. Bake in 350° oven 10 minutes on each side. (Turn muffins after 10 minutes.)

"BEGINNER'S" ROLLS

Must Make Ahead Of Time

Yields: **4 dozen**

Preparation Time: 30 minutes
plus set time

2   *packages yeast, dry or*
compressed
1   *cup lukewarm water*
1   *cup shortening*
²/₃ *cup sugar*
1½ *teaspoons salt*
1   *cup boiling water*
2   *eggs, beaten*
6   *cups flour*
½   *cup butter or margarine,*
melted

1. Dissolve yeast in warm water. Set aside. Using a 3-quart mixing bowl, combine shortening, sugar, salt, and boiling water. Mix with electric mixer until thick. Stir in yeast and eggs. Slowly add in flour and mix well.
2. Refrigerate for 12 hours.
3. Roll out on a floured board and cut with round cookie cutter.
4. Lightly grease baking pan. Dip each roll in melted butter and fold over. Note: Rolls may be frozen at this point.
5. Let rise for 2 hours or more, then bake in 425° oven for 10 minutes.

*Temperature: **425** °*
Time: 10 minutes

BANANA NUT BREAD

Yields: **1 loaf**
Preparation Time: 20 minutes

1   *cup sugar*
½   *cup butter or margarine*
3   *large ripe bananas*
2   *eggs*
2   *cups flour*
1   *teaspoon salt*
1   *teapoon baking soda*
¼-½ *cup nuts, chopped*

1. Cream together sugar and butter. Add bananas and eggs. Mix thoroughly. Set aside.
2. Sift together flour, salt, and baking soda. Add to banana mixture. Fold in nuts.
3. Pour into a greased and floured bread pan. Bake in 350° oven for 1 hour.

*Temperature: **350** °*
Time: 1 hour

Freezes well.

OVERNIGHT REFRIGERATOR ROLLS

Yields: 40-50 rolls
Preparation Time: 1 hour

Must Make Ahead Of Time

1	*cup shortening*
⅔	*cup sugar*
1	*cup all-bran cereal*
1½	*teaspoons salt*
1	*cup boiling water*
2	*packages granular yeast*
1	*cup lukewarm water*
2	*eggs, beaten*
6½	*cups flour, sifted*

1. In a large mixing bowl, combine shortening, sugar, cereal, and salt. Add boiling water, stirring until shortening is melted. Let stand until lukewarm.

2. Soften yeast in lukewarm water. Add to bran mixture. Add eggs. Stir in half the flour and beat until smooth. Add remaining flour and beat thoroughly. Cover bowl and refrigerate overnight or until ready to use.

3. Shape into rolls and let rise until double in bulk (about 2 hours).

4. Bake in 425° oven about 15 minutes.

Temperature: 425 °
Time: 15 minutes

Alternate method: After refrigerating, make rolls and freeze individually. Take out as needed and let rise - then bake. This is also great for monkey bread.

QUICK BUTTERMILK ROLLS

Yields: *1½ dozen*
Preparation Time: *2 hours*

1	cup buttermilk, lukewarm and thick
½	teaspoon baking soda
1	teaspoon sugar
1	teaspoon salt
1	cake compressed yeast
3	tablespoons vegetable oil
2½	cups sifted all-purpose flour

1. In a large mixing bowl, mix together first 4 ingredients. Crumble yeast into mixture. Stir until dissolved.
2. Add oil and flour. Mix well and knead.
3. Shape into any desired shapes. Let rise until double in size (45-60 minutes). Grease pan and place dough in it.
4. Bake in 400° oven for 15 minutes or until golden brown.

Variation: For whole wheat rolls use 1¼ cups whole wheat flour and 1¼ cups white flour.

Temperature: **400** °
Time: *15 minutes*

Freezes well for up to 3 months. Use heavy freezing bags and seal tightly.

# PINEAPPLE FRITTERS

Yields: **4 servings**
Preparation Time: *30 minutes*

1	14-ounce can chunk pineapple
1⅓	cups flour
2	teaspoons baking powder
¼	teaspoon salt
⅔	cup milk
1	egg, beaten
3-4	tablespoons pineapple juice powdered sugar

1. Drain pineapple, reserving juice.
2. In large mixing bowl, combine next 6 ingredients. Mix well.
3. Dip pineapple in mixture and fry in deep, hot fat.
4. Drain, and sprinkle with powdered sugar. Great for a breakfast treat!

BROILED FRENCH TOAST

Yields: **4 servings**
Preparation Time: 20 minutes

¼   **cup butter or margarine, softened, divided**
4   **eggs**
1⅓ **cups evaporated milk**
½   **teaspoon salt**
8   **slices white bread**
¼   **cup butter or margarine, melted**
     powdered sugar

1. Spread 2 tablespoons of the soft butter over bottom of two 9" × 9" pans.
2. Beat eggs with evaporated milk and salt until well blended. Pour ½ egg mixture into each pan. Place 4 slices bread side by side in each pan. Turn slices over and let stand 5 minutes.
3. Place pans about 4 inches from heat in broiler. Broil until golden. Turn slices over and brown on other side. Remove to warm platter. Brush with melted butter and dust with powdered sugar. Serve with warm syrup.

Temperature: Broil
Time: 5 minutes

You can eliminate the syrup and use sugar and cinnamon.

SIMPLE SPOON BREAD

Yields: **4-6**
Preparation Time: 10 minutes

1   **heaping tablespoon butter**
1   **large egg, beaten at room temperature**
¾   **cup white corn meal**
1½ **cups buttermilk, room temperature**
½   **teaspoon soda**
½   **teaspoon salt**

1. Melt butter in a 400° oven using a quart casserole suitable for serving.
2. In a large mixing bowl, mix the beaten egg with other ingredients. Stir until smooth.
3. Pour into the HOT baking dish and bake about 20 minutes or until just set.
4. Serve immediately with butter, or the gravy from a roast or turkey.

Temperature: **400 °**
Time: 20 minutes

HEALTH BREAD

Yields: **3 loaves**
Preparation Time: **2 hours**

6½   cups flour
1   cup whole wheat flour
2   packages active dry yeast
1   cup quick cooking oats,
      uncooked
1   cup whole bran cereal
1   cup raisins, optional
2½   cups boiling water
1½   cups cottage cheese
2   tablespoons shortening
2   teaspoons salt
½   cup molasses

1. In large mixer bowl, stir 2 cups flour, whole wheat flour and yeast.
2. In separate bowl, combine oatmeal, cereal, raisins, water, cottage cheese, shortening, and salt. Stir until shortening melts and let mixture come to 115°-120°. Add molasses.
3. Add dry ingredients and heat ½ minute to combine ingredients. Then beat 3 minutes on high speed and stir in enough remaining flour to form a stiff dough.
4. On floured surface, knead dough until smooth, 5-7 minutes.
5. Place in greased bowl and let rise until double. Punch down and let rest 10 minutes. Shape into 3 loaves and let rise again until double in loaf pans. Bake in 375° oven for 35-40 minutes.

Temperature: **375 °**
Time: **35-40**

JALAPEÑO CORNBREAD

Yields: **12-16 servings**
Preparation Time: **30 minutes**

2   cups cream style corn
2   cups cornbread mix
1   cup vegetable oil
4   eggs, beaten
2   cups sour cream
1½   cups Cheddar cheese, grated
1   4-ounce can chopped
      jalapeños, or 4 medium
      jalapeño peppers, seeded and
      diced
1   cup onion, chopped

1. In large mixing bowl, combine all ingredients in the order given. Pour into a greased 9" × 13" glass pan.
2. Bake in 350° oven for 1 hour.

Temperature: **350 °**
Time: **1 hour**

STRAWBERRY BREAD

Yields: 2 loaves
Preparation Time: 15 minutes

3	*cups flour*
1	*teaspoon baking soda*
1	*teaspoon salt*
½	*teaspoon cinnamon*
2	*cups sugar*
4	*eggs, beaten*
1¼	*cups vegetable oil*
2	*cups fresh strawberries, sliced or 2 cups frozen, thawed strawberries (No sugar)*

1. In a large mixing bowl, combine flour, baking soda, salt, cinnamon, and sugar. Mix well. Add eggs, oil, and strawberries. Stir until moistened.
2. Grease loaf pans. Spoon mixture into loaf pans.
3. Bake at 350° for 1 hour and 10 minutes.

Temperature: 350 °
Time: 1 hour 10 minutes

Mix a little strawberry juice with cream cheese. Spread between two pieces of bread for party sandwiches.

CRANBERRY NUT BREAD

Yields: 1 loaf
Preparation Time: 15 minutes

2	*cups flour*
1	*cup sugar*
1½	*teaspoons baking powder*
1	*teaspoon baking soda*
½	*teaspoon salt*
¼	*cup shortening*
¾	*cup orange juice*
1	*tablespoon orange rind, grated*
1	*egg, beaten*
½	*cup nuts, chopped*
1	*cup fresh cranberries, chopped*

1. Sift together dry ingredients. Cut in shortening until mixture resembles coarse corn meal.
2. Combine juice, rind and egg. Add to dry mixture. Stir only until dampened. Add nuts and cranberries.
3. Pour into a greased and floured large loaf pan. Bake in 350° oven for 1 hour.

Temperature: 350 °
Time: 1 hour

ZUCCHINI BREAD

*Yields: **10 servings***
Preparation Time: 2 hours

3   eggs
2   cups sugar
2   cups zucchini, shredded
1   cup vegetable oil
2   teaspoons vanilla
3   cups flour
1   teaspoon salt
1   teaspoon soda
1   teaspoon baking powder
2   teaspoons cinnamon
½   teaspoon nutmeg
¼   teaspoon cloves
½   cup nuts, chopped

1. Beat eggs until foamy. Stir in sugar, zucchini, oil, and vanilla. Add remaining ingredients and mix well.
2. Pour into two 9" × 5" greased (bottoms only) pans and bake in 325° oven for 50-60 minutes.
3. Cool in pans 10 minutes and then turn onto cooling racks.

*Temperature: **325 °***
Time: 50-60 minutes

CLOUD BISCUITS
"Light As A Feather"

*Yields: **15 biscuits***
Preparation Time: 30 minutes

2   cups flour, sifted
1   teaspoon salt
4   teaspoons baking powder
6   heaping tablespoons of
     shortening
⅔   cup milk

1. Sift together dry ingredients. Add shortening and cut in. Slowly add milk to make dough soft (might not use the full amount).
2. Knead and roll out ½-1 inch thick. Cut with floured biscuit cutter and place on ungreased cookie sheet.
3. Bake in 425-450° oven for 10-12 minutes.

*Temperature: **425-450 °***
Time: 10-12 minutes

BLUEBERRY COFFEECAKE

*Yields: **10-12 servings***
Preparation Time: 45 minutes

½	cup butter or margarine
1	cup sugar
3	eggs, slightly beaten
1	teaspoon baking powder
1	teaspoon baking soda
¼	teaspoon salt
2	cups flour, unsifted
1	cup sour cream
2	cups fresh or frozen blueberries

Topping:

1	cup brown sugar
¼	cup butter
¼	cup flour

1. Cream butter and sugar. Add next four ingredients.
2. Alternately add flour and sour cream to the egg mixture with a spoon. Fold in blueberries.
3. Pour mixture into greased 9" × 13" greased baking dish.

Topping:

1. Cream brown sugar and butter. Add flour to get a semi-dry mixture. Spread on top of batter.
2. Bake in 350° oven for 30 minutes.

*Temperature: **350** °*
Time: 30 minutes

CORNMEAL DINNER ROLLS

*Yields: **3 dozen***
Preparation Time: 4½ hours

2	cups milk, scalded
1	package yeast
¼	cup water
¼	cup butter
¼	cup shortening
½	cup sugar
1	tablespoon salt
7½	cups sifted flour, divided
2	eggs, beaten
1½	cups cornmeal

1. Scald milk slowly in double boiler; do not boil.
2. Dissolve yeast in lukewarm water. Add butter, shortening, sugar, and salt to scalded milk. Add 3 cups flour, eggs, and yeast. Mix thoroughly.
3. Mix in remaining flour and cornmeal. Knead until smooth. Let rise 1¾ hours.
4. Knead and make into rolls (pinch into balls and cook on cookie sheet, or make cloverleaf rolls using a muffin tin).
5. Let rise 2 hours. Bake in 375° oven for 15 minutes.

*Temperature: **375** °*
Time: 15 minutes

ORANGE JUICE MUFFINS WITH HONEY SPREAD

Yields: **1 dozen**
Preparation Time: 20 minutes

*2   cups biscuit mix
2   tablespoons sugar
*1   egg
1   teaspoon orange rind, grated
⅔   cup orange juice
2   tablespoons sugar
⅛   teaspoon ground nutmeg
¼   teaspoon ground cinnamon

Honey Spread:

*¼   cup butter or margarine, softened
¼   cup honey

1. In a large mixing bowl, combine first 5 ingredients. Stir until all ingredients are moistened.
2. Spoon mixture into greased muffin tins, filling ⅔ full.
3. In a medium mixing bowl, combine sugar, nutmeg, and cinnamon. Sprinkle over muffin batter.
4. Bake in 400° oven for 15 minutes or until golden brown. Serve hot with honey spread.

Honey spread:

1. Combine butter and honey. Mix well.

Temperature: **400 °**
Time: 15 minutes

For A Heart Healthy Recipe Make These Substitutions:

*2   cups no cholesterol Bisquick mix
*¼   cup cholesterol free egg substitute
*¼   cup corn oleo, softened

HIBISCUS

The reason you see so many hibiscus blossoms in the yards of Galvestonians is that the bushes are so well suited to the local climate. Only a severe freeze will kill the plants and since they seem to thrive with nothing more than the moisture from the normal yearly rainfall, additional watering is rarely necessary.

Interestingly, color hues and the dimensions of the blooms are dictated by the weather; the darker shaded flowers indicate that the weather has turned cool.

Cheese, Eggs & Pasta

SPANISH POTATO OMELETTE

Yields: **4 servings**
Preparation Time: 45 minutes

6	slices bacon, cut into 1-inch pieces
1	medium potato, cut into ½-inch cubes
1	medium onion, chopped
6	eggs
¾	teaspoon salt
⅛	teaspoon pepper
½	cup medium cheddar cheese, grated
	parsley for garnish

1. Fry bacon in a 10-inch skillet over medium heat, until crisp. Remove bacon and drain, reserving 4 tablespoons bacon fat in skillet.
2. Add potato and onion to reserved bacon fat, cooking and stirring until potato is golden brown, about 10 minutes. Stir bacon into potato mixture.
3. Beat eggs with salt and pepper. Add eggs to potato mixture. Mix and top with cheese.
4. Cover and cook over low heat until eggs are set and light brown on bottom, about 10 minutes.
5. Cut into wedges to serve; garnish with parsley.

Serve with buttered toast and fresh juice as a brunch.

CREAMY PIMIENTO SPREAD

Yields: **1½ cups**
Preparation Time: 20 minutes

1	cup mild cheddar cheese, grated (4 ounces)
1	cup Monterey Jack cheese, grated (4 ounces)
⅓	cup salad dressing
¼	cup pimiento, chopped
2	tablespoons milk
1½	tablespoons green onion (including tops), chopped

1. Combine all ingredients and stir until well blended. (This can be mixed with a hand mixer for creamy consistency.)

STRAND STREET GASLIGHTS

An important facet of the historic Strand, the famed commercial avenue of the 19th century, were the charming gaslights. Today, facsimiles of those original fixtures illuminate the now-revived street. The luminare was specially cast to resemble the earlier Victorian model.

STRAW AND HAY

Yields: **3-4 servings**
Preparation Time: 20 minutes

4	ounces white linguini
4	ounces green linquini
½	cup butter or margarine
1½	cups cooked ham, cut in thin strips
¾	cup peas, cooked
1	2½-ounce jar sliced mushrooms, drained
2	egg yolks, well beaten
1	cup heavy cream
1	cup fresh Parmesan cheese, grated

1. In a 6-quart heavy sauce pan or dutch oven, cook linguini according to package directions until just tender. Drain well. Return linguini to pot.
2. Add butter, ham, peas, and mushrooms. Set aside.
3. In a small bowl, beat egg yolks and cream with a fork or wisk until foamy. Slowly add cream mixture to linguini. Mix well. Stir in ½ cup Parmesan cheese. Stir gently over medium high heat, until mixture is thickened. Sprinkle with remaining Parmesan cheese.
4. Serve hot or cold.

Could substitute thin noodles for the linguini.

CHILI CHEESE BITS

Yields: **35-40 squares**
Preparation Time: 30 minutes

2	4-ounce cans green chili peppers (green chilies)
1	pound sharp Cheddar cheese, shredded
1	pound pork sausage, cooked and drained
8	eggs
½	cup milk
	salt and pepper

1. Grease a 13" × 9" pan. Take seeds out of chili peppers and cover bottom of pan. Cover chili peppers with cheese and sausage.
2. In a mixing bowl, beat eggs with milk, salt, and pepper. Pour over sausage mixture.
3. Bake at 325° for 30 minutes or until light brown. Cut into squares and serve.

Temperature: **325 °**
Time: 30 minutes

Excellent for a brunch menu. The chili peppers are the secret.

GREEN VERMICELLI

Yields: **4-6 servings**
Preparation Time: 30 minutes

½   cup butter or margarine, divided
1   tablespoon fresh parsley
1   teaspoon basil leaves
1   8-ounce package cream cheese
⅛   teaspoon white pepper
⅔   cup boiling water
1   8-ounce package Vermicelli or thin spaghetti
2   cloves garlic
¾   cup Romano cheese, grated

1. In a medium saucepan or on top of a double boiler, combine ¼ cup of butter, parsley, and basil. Blend in cream cheese and pepper.
2. Stir in boiling water. Blend thoroughly and keep warm over a pan of hot water.
3. Cook Vermicelli according to package directions until it is just soft. Set aside (keep warm).
4. Sauté garlic in ¼ cup of butter for 2 minutes. Pour over Vermicelli. Toss Vermicelli with half of the grated cheese.
5. Transfer Vermicelli to serving platter and spoon sauce on top. Sprinkle with remaining cheese over all. Serve warm.

BRUNCH CASSEROLE

Must Make Ahead Of Time

Yields: **8-10 servings**
Preparation Time: 30 minutes

6   slices bread, buttered and decrusted
1   1-pound package breakfast sausage, browned
5-6 ounces medium-sharp Cheddar cheese, grated
5   eggs
1   teaspoon dry mustard
1   teaspoon salt
1   pint light cream

1. Place bread in bottom of 9" × 13" greased glass pan.
2. Place browned sausage on bread. Sprinkle cheese on top of sausage.
3. Beat eggs, salt, cream, and mustard. Pour mixture over cheese. Refrigerate overnight.
4. Bake in 350° oven for 40 minutes.

Temperature: **350 °**
Time: 40 minutes

If desired, you may use an additional pound of sausage.

HANGTOWN FRY

Yields: *4*
Preparation Time: *20 minutes*

½	pound bacon, cut into large pieces
2	tablespoons butter
12	medium oysters flour for breading
1	egg, slightly beaten for dipping oysters
1	cup plain bread crumbs
6	eggs, lightly beaten salt and freshly ground pepper to taste

1. Fry bacon in a large skillet until crisp. Remove and drain. Remove bacon grease and clean pan.
2. Melt butter in skillet. Dip each oyster in flour, egg, then bread crumbs (in that order) and fry in skillet over medium heat until golden brown.
3. Add eggs and cook until set, stirring gently. Top with bacon, heat, and serve immediately. Season with salt and pepper.

A good Sunday night supper with a salad and garlic bread.

MAMA II'S MACARONI AND CHEESE

Yields: **6-8 servings**
Preparation Time: *20 minutes*

3	cups elbow macaroni, uncooked
4	tablespoons butter or margarine salt and pepper to taste
1½	pounds Velveeta cheese, sliced
½	pound Colby cheese
½	cup milk

1. Cook macaroni according to package directions. Drain thoroughly. Pour into a 3 quart long flat glass casserole.
2. Dot macaroni with butter and sprinkle with salt and pepper. Lay Velveeta slices over in order to completely cover macaroni. Dot with Colby cheese cut in chunks. Cover all with milk.
3. Bake in 350° oven for 30 minutes.

Temperature: **350 °**
Time: *30 minutes*

May be frozen before milk is added. Seal with foil, and before baking, add ½ cup milk.

MUSHROOM SPINACH LASAGNA

Yields: **8 servings**
Preparation Time: **45 minutes**

1	pound fresh spinach, coarsely chopped
½	cup water
4	tablespoons vegetable oil
1	pound fresh mushrooms
1	cup onion, chopped
1	cup green pepper, chopped
2	large cloves garlic, chopped
1	12-ounce can tomato paste
1	32-ounce can stewed tomatoes
1¼	teaspoons salt
1¼	teaspoons oregano
1	16-ounce package lasagna noodles
1	cup sharp Cheddar cheese, shredded
24	slices Mozzarella cheese
3	tablespoons Parmesan cheese, grated and divided

1. Cook spinach in water until tender. Drain well. Set aside.
2. Heat oil in a large skillet. Add mushrooms, onion, pepper, and garlic. Cook rapidly, stirring often until almost tender (about 5 minutes).
3. Add tomato paste, tomatoes, salt, and oregano. Bring to a boil. Reduce heat and simmer covered for 15 minutes. Add spinach. Mix thoroughly.
4. While sauce is simmering, cook lasagna noodles according to package directions. Drain well.
5. In a 9" × 13" pan, ladle ¼ of the sauce. Layer ⅓ of lasagna noodles, ¼ of sauce, ⅓ Cheddar cheese, 8 slices of Mozzarella, and 1 tablespoon of Parmesan cheese. Repeat layers two more times.
6. Cover with foil. Bake in 375° oven for 20 minutes. Uncover and bake 5 minutes more.

Temperature: **375 °**
Time: *20 minutes*
Time: *5 minutes*

May be made ahead and frozen. Thaw before baking.

FETTUCINE VERDE

Yields: **4 servings**
Preparation Time: **20 minutes**

12	ounces fresh fettucine or 1 8-ounce package
6	tablespoons butter
1	cup green onions, sliced
2	cloves garlic, minced
½	pint whipping cream
1½	cups Parmesan cheese
	salt and pepper to taste

1. Cook fettucine according to package directions. Drain well.
2. Melt butter in skillet and add onions and garlic, stir-frying for 2 minutes.
3. Add cream and boil rapidly until slightly thickened with large shiny bubbles forming, about 2 minutes.
4. Add hot noodles to pan and toss gently. Add ½ cup of Parmesan cheese and toss until noodles are evenly coated.
5. Add remaining cheese. Salt and pepper to taste. Toss again.

If you are using fresh fettucine, cook 4-6 minutes in boiling water.

BRUNCH PIE
Make 24 Hours Ahead Of Time

Yields: **6 servings**
Preparation Time: **30 minutes**

8	slices bacon, fried crisp
1	tablespoon reserved bacon drippings
½	cup corn flake crumbs
5	eggs
2½	cups frozen hashed brown potatoes
1½	cups Swiss cheese, grated
⅓	cup milk
1	green onion, thinly sliced
1	teaspoon salt
⅛	teaspoon pepper
4	drops Tabasco

1. Crumble bacon; set aside.
2. Mix corn flake crumbs with reserved bacon drippings; set aside.
3. In medium-sized bowl, beat eggs until foamy. Stir in remaining ingredients.
4. Pour into greased 9-inch pie pan. Sprinkle with crumb mixture and bacon. Cover and refrigerate overnight.
5. Cover and bake in 325° oven for 50 minutes, or until knife inserted near center comes out clean.

Temperature: **325 °**
Time: **50 minutes**

CONFETTI SANDWICH

Yields: **6-8 servings**
Preparation Time: 40 minutes

9   hard boiled eggs, chopped
¼   cup sour cream
⅓   cup fresh spinach, chopped
½   cup carrots, shredded
½   cup stuffed olives, chopped
6   English muffins
     butter
6   slices bacon, fried crisp and crumbled
1   cup sharp Cheddar cheese, grated

1. In a large bowl, combine eggs, sour cream, spinach, carrots, and olives. Mix thoroughly.
2. Split English muffins. Toast muffins and spread lightly with butter.
3. Spread egg mixture over each muffin half. Sprinkle with cheese and bacon.
4. Broil 6 inches from heat until cheese melts (3-5 minutes). Serve open-faced.

Temperature: Broil
Time: 3-5 minutes

GREEN ENCHILADAS

Yields: **4-6 servings**
Preparation Time: 30 minutes

1   dozen corn tortillas
     vegetable oil
2   cups Monterey Jack cheese, grated
1   cup onion, chopped
¼   cup butter
¼   cup flour
2   cups chicken broth
1   cup sour cream
1   4-ounce can jalapeño peppers, seeded and chopped

1. Fry tortillas one at a time in hot oil for 15 seconds on each side.
2. Put two tablespoons cheese and one tablespoon onion on each tortilla. Roll up and place seam side down in 2-quart flat baking dish.
3. In a saucepan, melt butter and blend in flour. Add chicken broth and cook, stirring constantly until thick. Stir in sour cream and peppers. Cook until heated through. DO NOT BOIL.
4. Pour sauce over enchiladas in baking dish, covering completely.
5. Bake in 425° oven for 20 minutes. Sprinkle remaining cheese on top. Return to oven for 5 minutes. Serve hot.

Temperature: **425 °**
Time: 20 minutes
Time: 5 minutes

SOUTH OF THE BORDER EGG CASSEROLE

*Yields: **8-10 servings***
Preparation Time: 15 minutes

10 eggs
1   4-ounce can chopped green chilies, drained
1   pound Monterey Jack cheese, grated
1   24-ounce container large curd cottage cheese
½   cup flour
1   teaspoon baking powder
½   cup butter or margarine, melted

1. Beat eggs with a wire whisk. Blend in the chopped chilies.
2. Add all other ingredients. Mix thoroughly.
3. Grease a 9″ × 13″ glass baking dish. Pour in mixture and spread evenly.
4. Bake in 400° oven for 15 minutes. Reduce heat to 350° and bake 30 minutes more until golden and bubbly.
5. Serve with picante sauce on the side.

*Temperature: **400** °*
Time: 15 minutes
*Temperature: **350** °*
Time: 30 minutes

CORN FRITTERS

*Yields: **4-6 servings***
Preparation Time: 10 minutes

2   17-ounce cans whole kernel corn
     milk (if necessary)
4   tablespoons butter or margarine melted
1   cup flour
1½   teaspoons baking powder
1   teaspoon salt
⅛   teaspoon black pepper
4   eggs, beaten
     shortening for frying
     warm maple syrup

1. Drain corn in strainer, pressing slightly so that all the liquid is removed and reserved.
2. Measure corn liquid and add milk if necessary to make ⅔ cup.
3. Mix all ingredients except syrup with the liquid; mix thoroughly.
4. Melt shortening or oil in large skillet. Pour batter into hot skillet forming small pancakes. Fry until golden brown on both sides. Serve with warm maple syrup.

CREPES BENEDICT
"Great Brunch"

*Yields: **12 servings***
Preparation Time: 2 hours

3   *eggs*
1   *cup flour*
1¼   *cups milk*
⅛   *teaspoon salt*
1   *tablespoon fresh parsley,*
       finely chopped
       vegetable oil
12   *poached eggs*
12   *thin slices of ham*
2   *egg yolks at room*
       temperature
2   *tablespoons lemon juice at*
       room temperature
½   *cup butter, melted*
       dash of cayenne

1. Combine first 5 ingredients and mix by hand until batter is smooth. DO NOT BEAT. REFRIGERATE BATTER FOR AT LEAST ONE HOUR.
2. Place 1 tablespoon of vegetable oil in skillet. When skillet is hot, pour in 2 tablespoons of batter. Tilt pan quickly so that batter covers entire pan. Cook one minute on the first side, turn and cook 30 seconds on second side.
3. Use wax paper to stack crepes.
4. Pan must be hot and well-oiled before making each additional crepe.

EGGS

Poach the 12 eggs.

HOLLANDAISE SAUCE

1. Blend egg yolks and lemon juice in a blender at high speed until thick. Add melted butter very slowly.
2. Blend until all the butter is absorbed. Add salt and cayenne to taste. Set aside.

ASSEMBLING

1. Place a slice of ham and a poached egg on each warm crepe. Fold crepe and place in a buttered shallow baking dish.
2. Top with Hollandaise sauce and broil (as far as possible from heat source) until bubbly. Serve immediately.

Temperature: Broil
Time: 3-5 minutes—watch carefully

Use a 6" or 8" skillet (not larger than an 8" skillet).

MIGAS

Yields: **10-12 large servings**
Preparation Time: 45 minutes

1	package corn tortillas
1/3	cup oil
2	cloves garlic, minced
1	medium onion, chopped
4	tomatoes, diced
1/4	cup butter
2	dozen eggs
10	ounces medium sharp Cheddar cheese, grated
10	ounces Monterey Jack cheese, grated
	salt, pepper, and garlic powder to taste
	Chorizo sausage (hot Mexican sausage)
	flour tortillas
	salsa

1. Fry corn tortillas in oil until crisp.
2. Sauté garlic, onions, and tomatoes in butter until tender.
3. Beat eggs with salt, pepper, and garlic powder to taste. Add egg mixture to tomato mixture.
4. Cook over medium-low heat until soft.
5. Crumble the fried tortilla chips. Add chips and both grated cheeses to egg mixture. Stir until cheeses melt and the chips softened.
6. Serve with Chorizo sausage, flour tortillas, and fresh salsa.

CARBONARA

Yields: **4-6 servings**
Preparation Time: 40 minutes

1/2	pound thick sliced bacon, cut in 2-inch pieces
4	cloves garlic, sliced thin
2	tablespoons olive oil
1	tablespoon butter or margarine
1/4	cup dry white wine
5	tablespoons Romano cheese, freshly grated
3/4	cup Parmesan cheese, freshly grated
1/8	teaspoon black pepper, freshly ground
2	tablespoons Italian parsley
3	eggs, beaten
1	pound linguini

1. Fry bacon and reserve 1/4 cup of the bacon drippings. Set aside.
2. Sauté garlic in olive oil and butter. Add reserved bacon drippings.
3. Add the wine and cook over medium heat until wine boils away. Set aside.
4. In large bowl, combine cheeses, pepper, parsley, and eggs. Mix thoroughly. Set aside.
5. Cook linguini according to package directions. Drain well.
6. Combine linguini with egg and cheese mixture.
7. Reheat bacon mixture. When piping hot, pour over linguini and serve.

Great with tossed salad and garlic bread!

SHRIMP QUICHE
"A Nice Touch"

Yields: **6 servings**
Preparation Time: 30 minutes

¾	pound medium headless shrimp, cooked, peeled, and deveined
1	cup fresh mushrooms, sliced
¼	cup green onions, chopped
¼	cup butter, melted
4	eggs, beaten
1½	cups light cream
1	teaspoon salt
⅛	teaspoon dry mustard
⅛	teaspoon nutmeg
1	cup Mozzarella cheese, grated
1	9-inch pie shell, unbaked

1. Chop shrimp. Set aside.
2. In saucepan, cook mushrooms and green onions in butter until tender.
3. In large bowl, combine eggs, light cream, salt, dry mustard, nutmeg, and cheese. Fold in shrimp and mushroom mixture.
4. Pour mixture into 9-inch pie shell.
5. Bake at 400° for 15 minutes. Reduce heat to 300° and bake for 30 minutes, or until knife inserted in center of quiche comes out clean.
6. Let stand 10-15 minutes before cutting into pie shape wedges.

Temperature: **400** °
Time: 15 minutes
Temperature: **300** °
Time: 30 minutes

ITALIAN SAUSAGE QUICHE

Yields: **6-8 servings**
Preparation Time: 25 minutes

1	pound mild Italian bulk sausage
½	cup onion, chopped
2	tablespoons flour
1	10-inch pie shell, pre-baked 7-8 minutes
1	13-ounce can evaporated milk
4	eggs
2	cups sharp Cheddar cheese, shredded
2	tablespoons fresh parsley, chopped

1. Crumble sausage and cook over medium heat. Drain fat. Sauté onion with sausage.
2. Add flour. Mix thoroughly. Transfer mixture to pre-baked pie shell. Set aside.
3. In a separate bowl, combine milk, eggs, and cheese. Pour over sausage mixture.
4. Top with parsley. If desired, sprinkle more cheese on top. Bake in 400° oven for 25 minutes.
5. Let set 15 minutes before cutting.

Temperature: **400** °
Time: 25 minutes

TIROPETA

Yields: **8 servings**
Preparation Time: *30 minutes*

1	*pound Feta cheese, crumbled*
1	*pound small curd cottage cheese*
1	*cup fresh Romano cheese, grated*
4	*large eggs, beaten with fork*
½	*teaspoon white pepper*
1	*pound fillo*
	clarified butter

1. In a large mixing bowl, combine cheeses, eggs, and pepper. Set aside.
2. Butter bottom and sides of a 15" × 10" pan. Place 10-12 layers of fillo on bottom, buttering each sheet with clarified butter.
3. Spread cheese mixture over fillo. Cover top with remaining fillo, again buttering each sheet with clarified butter.
4. Bake in 375° oven for 30 minutes. Reduce heat to 350° and bake for 1 hour more.

Temperature: **375** °
Time: *30 minutes*
Temperature: **350** °
Time: *1 hour*

THREE CHEESE MANICOTTI

Yields: **4 servings**
Preparation Time: *20 minutes*

2	*cups Mozzarella cheese, shredded and divided*
1	*cup Ricotta or small curd cottage cheese*
½	*cup Parmesan cheese, grated*
2	*eggs, beaten*
½	*teaspoon salt*
⅛	*teaspoon pepper*
1	*teaspoon fresh parsley*
8	*manicotti shells, cooked*
2	*cups spaghetti sauce (homemade or jar)*

1. In large bowl, combine 1 cup Mozzarella cheese, Ricotta, Parmesan, eggs, salt, pepper, and parsley. Stir gently.
2. Stuff manicotti shells with cheese mixture.
3. Pour ½ cup of sauce in the bottom of a 2-quart casserole. Arrange shells on top. Pour rest of sauce on top. Sprinkle with remaining cheese.
4. Bake uncovered in 350° oven for 25-30 minutes or until bubbly.

Temperature: **350** °
Time: *25-30 minutes*

MEXICAN QUESADILLAS

*Yields: **6 servings***
Preparation Time: 15 minutes

1   package of 12 flour tortillas
*½   cup butter
*1   12-ounce package of
      medium Cheddar cheese or
      Monterey Jack cheese, cut in
      strips lengthwise

1. Spread butter on both sides of tortillas. Place strip of cheese on flat tortilla and roll up and place seam down.
2. Bake in a 400° oven on an ungreased cookie sheet for 10 minutes or until bubbly.

*Temperature: **400 °***
Time: 10 minutes

For a zesty flavor, use Monterey Jack cheese with jalapeños, or make some with all three types of cheese. These are a great crowd pleaser! These also make a great appetizer.

For A Heart Healthy Recipe Make These Substitutions:

*½   cup corn oleo
*1   12-ounce package Weight
      Watchers Monterey Jack or
      Cheddar cheese, cut in strips
      lengthwise

DAVISON HOME

For several years members of the Junior League of Galveston County, Inc. have acted as docents at the Davison Home in Texas City. This building has played a significant role in the city for almost a century. Frank Davison who built the mansion in 1897 was active in the community and the house, a Gothic Revival design, became a cultural center. Today the Victorian house is open to the public as a community center and a respository for historical data and valuable local artifacts.

Meats

OVEN-SMOKED BRISKET

Make 24 Hours Ahead Of Time

Yields: 6-8 servings
Preparation Time: 20 minutes

*1	4-6 pound beef brisket
1	3-ounce bottle liquid smoke
*	garlic salt
*	celery salt
*	salt
2	onions, coarsely chopped
½-1	cup Worcestershire sauce
¾	cup barbecue sauce

1. The day before serving, place brisket in a large roasting pan. Pour liquid smoke over meat and season liberally with salts. Sprinkle chopped onions over meat.

2. Cover pan with foil and refrigerate overnight.

3. Next day, pour off liquid smoke and douse meat well with Worcestershire sauce.

4. Recover with foil and bake at 275° for 5 hours. Uncover and pour barbecue sauce over meat.

5. Continue cooking uncovered for one hour more. Remove from oven and let meat set for 15 minutes before slicing.

Temperature: 275 °
Time: 6 hours

For A Heart Healthy Recipe Make These Substitutions:

* trim fat before cooking
* garlic powder
* celery powder
* omit salt

STEAK DIANNE

4	*8-12 ounce each sirloin strip steaks or top sirloins with fat trimmed and reserved coarse black pepper*
2½	*tablespoons butter*
1	*clove garlic, pressed*
2	*tablespoons shallot bulbs, chopped*
4	*mushroom caps, sliced*
¼	*cup A-1 sauce*
¼	*cup Worcestershire sauce*
2	*tablespoons red wine*
⅛	*teaspoon dry mustard*
1	*tablespoon parsley*
2	*tablespoons shallot tops, chopped*
½-¾	*cup domestic brandy*

1. Season steaks with pepper. Brown in a frying pan with reserved fat, over a high heat for approximately 1½ minutes per side. Cover and set aside.
2. Melt butter in chafing dish over moderate heat. Add garlic and shallot bulbs and cook for 3 minutes.
3. Add sliced mushrooms and cook for two more minutes. Add A-1, wine, Worcestershire sauce, and mustard.
4. Add beef, parsley, and shallot tops. Cook 2 minutes, turning frequently. With fluid bubbling, add brandy and ignite immediately. Turn beef while brandy flames.
5. Remove beef to plates when flame subsides. Pour sauce over meat.

STEAK AU POIVRE

4	*top sirloin steaks*
1½	*tablespoons coarse cracked pepper*
¼	*cup brandy*
1	*cup beef broth*
½	*cup heavy cream*
¼	*cup butter*

1. Press pepper into both sides of steak. Slightly flatten steaks with meat pounder.
2. Over moderately high heat, rub skillet with piece of fat trimmed from the steaks.
3. Sear the steaks for 1½ minutes on each side. Reduce heat to moderate and cook steaks 1-2 minutes more on each side for rare meat. Transfer to heated platter.
4. Pour off fat, add brandy and ignite. Shake pan until flame goes out and add broth and cream.
5. Reduce liquid over high heat by half and swirl in butter sliced and pour sauce over steaks.

MIKE'S PRIME RIB

Yields: **2 servings per pound**
Preparation Time: 15 minutes

1   *rib roast*
     seasoned salt
     seasoned pepper

1. Have butcher cut prime rib to desired size.
2. Preheat oven to 500°. Using an open roasting pan, place prime rib in pan. Sprinkle with seasonings.
3. When oven has been completely preheated, cook roast 5 minutes per pound. When meat has cooked the allotted time, turn off the oven. Leave the meat in the oven to rest for at least 1 hour. It can wait up to two hours. DO NOT OPEN THE OVEN DOORS FROM THE TIME YOU HAVE PUT THE MEAT IN THE OVEN UNTIL YOU ARE READY TO SERVE.
4. When ready to serve, remove from oven and slice. Meat will be rare and juicy.

Temperature: **500 °**
Time: 5 minutes per pound

For medium-rare, add 5 minutes to total cooking time. For medium, add 10 minutes total cooking time before turning off the oven.

YORKSHIRE PUDDING

Yields: **4-6 servings**
Preparation Time: 15-20 minutes

6   *teaspoons hot beef drippings*
     (add shortening to make 6
     teaspoons)
1   *cup flour*
1   *teaspoon salt*
1   *cup milk*
2   *eggs*

1. Put meat drippings in a 2-quart casserole with high sides. Set aside.
2. Sift flour and salt. Add remaining ingredients. Beat with rotary beater or hand mixer until blended. Refrigerate for 1 hour.
3. Add to meat drippings. Bake *uncovered* for 30 minutes in 425° oven. Serve immediately or pudding will fall.

Temperature: **425 °**
Time: 30 minutes

PEPPER STEAK

*1-1½ pounds sirloin steak, 1" thick
*¼ cup vegetable oil
1 clove garlic, crushed
*1 teaspoon salt
½ teaspoon black pepper
1 teaspoon ground ginger
3 large green peppers, cut into strips
2 large yellow onions, thinly sliced
½ cup celery, diced
*¼ cup soy sauce
½ cup sugar
*½ cup beef bouillon
1 8-ounce can sliced water chestnuts
1 tablespoon cornstarch
¼-½ cup cold water
4 green onions, cut in 1" pieces
cooked rice

1. Cut steak in ⅛-inch slices. Heat oil in large skillet. Add garlic, salt, pepper, and ginger. Sauté until garlic is golden.
2. Add steak slices and brown lightly for two minutes. Remove meat.
3. Add green pepper, onions, and celery.
4. Return meat to pan. Mix soy sauce, sugar, bouillon, and water chestnuts. Add to meat mixture.
5. Dissolve cornstarch in cold water and add to mixture. Add green onions. Simmer 10-15 minutes or until sauce thickens. Serve over hot rice.

The use of an electric skillet is a great help in preparing this.

 For A Heart Healthy Recipe Make These Substitutions:

* trim fat before cooking
*¼ cup safflower oil
* omit salt
*¼ cup low salt soy sauce
*½ cup low salt beef bouillon

MOUSSAKA

Yields: *12 servings*
Preparation Time: 1 hour

Meat Sauce:

1½	pounds ground chuck or ground lamb
1	cup onion, finely chopped
1	clove garlic, crushed
3	tablespoons butter or margarine
½	teaspoon dried oregano leaves
1	teaspoon dried basil leaves
½	teaspoon cinnamon
1	teaspoon salt
⅛	teaspoon black pepper
2	8-ounce cans tomato sauce
2	eggplants, washed and dried
2	tablespoons butter or margarine, melted

Cream Sauce:

2	tablespoons butter or margarine
2	tablespoons flour
½	teaspoon salt
⅛	teaspoon black pepper
2	cups milk
2	eggs
½	cup Parmesan cheese, grated
½	cup medium Cheddar cheese, grated
2	tablespoons dry bread crumbs

1. Sauté meat, onion, and garlic in butter in a 3½ quart dutch oven until brown. Add herbs, spices, and tomato sauce. Bring to a boil, stirring constantly. Reduce heat. Simmer uncovered ½ hour.
2. Halve *unpared* eggplant lengthwise. Slice crosswise ½-inch thick. Place in bottom of broiler pan. Sprinkle lightly with salt. Brush lightly with melted butter. Broil 4-inches from heat, 4 minutes per side.
3. Make cream sauce. In medium saucepan, melt butter. Remove from heat. Stir in flour, salt, and pepper. Return to heat. Add milk gradually. Bring to a boil, stirring constantly until mixture thickens. Remove from heat.
4. In small bowl, beat eggs with wire whisk. Beat in some hot cream sauce mixture. Return egg mixture to hot sauce mixture in saucepan. Mix well and set aside.
5. In bottom of a shallow 2 quart dish layer half of eggplant slices, overlapping slightly. Sprinkle each layer with 2 tablespoons of each cheese. Stir bread crumbs into meat sauce. Spoon evenly over eggplant. Then sprinkle again with 2 tablespoons of each cheese. Repeat with rest of eggplant slices.
6. Pour cream sauce over all. Top with remaining cheese. Bake in 350° oven for 35-40 minutes.
7. Cool slightly and cut into squares.

Temperature: Broil
Time: 8 minutes
Temperature: 350 °
Time: 35-40 minutes

Can be baked ahead of time, frozen and reheated.

DELUXE CHERRY BRISKET
Make 2 Days Ahead Of Time

Yields: **6-8 servings**
Preparation Time: 2 days

1	5-pound brisket
	Soy sauce to taste
	Worcestershire sauce to taste
1	package Lipton onion soup mix
	caraway seeds
	celery seeds
	rosemary
1	20-ounce can cherry pie filling

1. Season brisket with first 2 ingredients. Sprinkle soup mix on brisket. Add rosemary, caraway seeds, and celery seeds. Marinate 2 days.
2. Wrap brisket and seasonings in 2 layers of aluminum foil and bake in 325° oven for 4 hours. Let cool before unwrapping.
3. Pour gravy into one container and place meat in another; refrigerate.
4. Scrape off all seasonings and slice cold meat.
5. Put gravy in bottom of pan and put slices on top of gravy. Pour cherry pie filling over meat and bake in 350° oven for 30-45 minutes.

Temperature: **325** °
Time: 4 hours
Temperature: **350** °
Time: 30-45 minutes

STEAK MARCHAND DE VIN

Yields: **4 servings**
Preparation Time: 25 minutes

½	cup green onions, minced
1-2	tablespoons garlic, minced
6	tablespoons butter
1	cup fresh mushrooms, minced
2	tablespoons flour
½	cup ham, minced
½	cup dry red wine
1	cup beef broth
	salt and pepper to taste
4	fillet steaks

1. In a skillet, sauté onions and garlic in butter until onions are softened. Stir in mushrooms and cook for 5 minutes.
2. Stir in flour and cook over moderate heat, stirring for 3 minutes. Add ham and wine, then cook over medium heat for 5 minutes.
3. Add beef broth. Salt and pepper to taste.
4. Reduce the heat to low and simmer for 10 minutes.
5. Cook fillets to desired doneness. Serve sauce over fillets.

BEEF BRACIOLA

Yields: 6-8 servings
Preparation Time: 2 hours

12	slices top round or sirloin, about ¼″ thick
¼	pound Italian salami, minced
¼	pound veal, ground
½	cup Parmesan, grated
2	tablespoons butter, softened
1	cup soft white bread crumbs
½	cup milk
2	tablespoons parsley, minced
1	egg, beaten
	salt and pepper to taste
12	slices of Prosciutto, very thinly sliced
2	tablespoons olive oil
2	tablespoons butter
1	large clove garlic
1	large onion, chopped
2	carrots
1	bay leaf
1	cup dry white wine
1	2 pound can plum tomatoes, sieved

1. Flatten slices of beef as thinly as possible.

2. Soak bread crumbs in milk and squeeze dry. Mix ground meats, cheese, butter, bread crumbs, parsley, and egg. Season with salt and pepper.

3. Place slice of prosciutto on each piece of beef, spread with stuffing. Roll slices tightly and tie with a string.

4. Heat oil and butter together in large skillet. Add garlic, onion, carrots, and bay leaf; sauté.

5. Add beef rolls and brown well on all sides. Stir in wine and cook over moderate heat until most of liquid has evaporated.

6. Add tomatoes and bring to boil. Reduce heat to low and simmer 1 hour or until beef is tender. Remove beef to warm platter.

7. Strain pan liquid and return to skillet and cook for a few minutes until thickened. Pour over beef rolls and serve hot.

BOEUF EN DAUBE

Yields: **6 servings**
Preparation Time: 4-5 hours

*4	pounds beef pot roast
*	salt and pepper to taste
1	clove garlic, pressed
2	large onions, sliced
2	carrots, sliced
¼	cup parsley, chopped
*2	teaspoons salt
8	whole peppercorns
½	cup French red wine vinegar
1	cup French dry red wine
*1	10½-ounce can condensed beef broth
*¼	cup butter
½	cup tomato purée
1	tablespoon cornstarch

1. Sprinkle roast with salt and pepper, and rub with garlic.
2. Place in large glass or earthenware bowl and add onions, celery, carrots, parsley, salt, peppercorns, vinegar, wine, and broth. Cover and let stand 2 hours. Drain meat, reserving marinade.
3. Heat butter in dutch oven and brown meat on all sides. Add marinade and bring to boil. Lower heat and simmer 2-2½ hours or until meat is tender.
4. Remove roast to platter. Skim excess fat from pan juices. Mix last 2 ingredients and stir into pan juices. Cook, stirring over low heat until bubbly.
5. Slice beef and top with gravy.

For A Heart Healthy Recipe Make These Substitutions:

*	trim fat before cooking
*	omit salt
*1	10½-ounce can low salt beef broth
*¼	cup corn oleo

 BEEF WELLINGTON
Start 3 Days Ahead Of Time

Yields: **8 servings**
Preparation Time: **6½ hours**

Beef:

1	*12-inch long beef tenderloin*
1	*long strip of beef suet, split lengthwise (available at your butcher's)*

Marinade:

1½	*cups dry red wine*
1	*tablespoon Worcestershire sauce*
1	*lemon (juice of)*
¼	*teaspoon fresh ground black pepper (several grinds from the pepper mill)*

Duxelles:

2	*tablespoons butter*
1-1½	*pounds fresh mushrooms, finely diced*
5	*green onions, finely minced*
1	*clove garlic, pressed*
¼	*cup parsley, finely chopped*
½	*cup Madeira wine salt and pepper*
1	*4 or 5-ounce can paté de foie gras (goose liver paté) (may use less if desired)*

Madeira Sauce:

	pan juices
½	*cup beef consommé*
½	*cup Madeira wine salt and pepper to taste*
2-3	*tablespoons reserved marinade*
2	*teaspoons arrowroot or cornstarch dissolved in a few tablespoons cold water*
½	*pound truffles (available at gourmet shops)*

2 DAYS BEFORE SERVING

1. Mix marinade ingredients and pour over beef in a shallow pan. Cover and refrigerate for 24 hours.

Day Before

1. Drain marinade from meat and reserve. Fold tail under meat and tie securely to form a 12" length piece of meat with uniform thickness.
2. Place one strip of suet on bottom and one strip of suet on top of meat. Insert meat thermometer.
3. Bake in 425° oven for 30 minutes, turning once. Replace suet. Thermometer will indicate very rare. (If your final measure of doneness is well-done, cook slightly longer at this point).
4. Remove meat from pan. Cool and refrigerate. Reserve pan juices.
5. Skim fat from pan juices and discard. In a medium saucepan, combine all ingredients for Madeira Sauce (except arrowroot). Cook down for about 5 minutes. Adjust seasonings. Add dissolved arrowroot, stirring constantly over low heat until thickened. Add truffles. Cover and refrigerate until ready to reheat.
6. Make Duxelles in a large skillet by sautéing mushrooms, green onions, and garlic for 8-10 minutes until mixture is quite dry. Drain if necessary. Add parsley, then wine and boil down until wine has almost evaporated. Season with salt and pepper. Blend in paté. Do not add too much paté. Cover and refrigerate.
7. In medium sized mixing bowl,

Pastry:

3   *cups Wondra all-purpose flour*

2   *teaspoons salt*

14   *tablespoons butter, chilled*

4   *tablespoons shortening, chilled*

¾   *cup cold bouillon mixed with ice water (to total no more than ¾ cup)*

1   *egg, beaten with 1 tablespoon of water*

mix flour and salt. Using a pastry blender, cut in butter and shortening until coarse granules form for pastry. Sprinkle bouillon, small amounts at a time, tossing constantly, until dough holds together. Wrap in waxed paper and refrigerate.

3-4 Hours Before Serving

1. Remove Duxelles and meat from refrigerator. Remove string. Allow meat to come to room temperature.
2. When meat has come to room temperature, remove pastry from refrigerator. When soft enough to roll, roll pastry out in a 9″ × 14″ rectangle, ¼″ thick (large enough to envelop meat).
3. Stir Duxelles to soften and spread evenly over pastry leaving 1-inch border all around. Place meat in center and fold pastry over meat, sealing seams well by moistening edges. Place seam side down on greased cookie sheet.
4. Decorate top with pastry cut outs from left over dough and brush top with egg and water. Prick on all sides with tines of fork.
5. Bake in 400-425° oven for 15 minutes. Reduce heat to 350°-375° for 30 minutes more or until golden brown.
6. Allow to stand 20 minutes before cutting. Gently reheat sauce.
7. Slice meat in 1¼-inch portions and serve with Madeira Sauce.

Temperature: **425** °
Time: 30 minutes
Temperature: **400-425** °
Time: 15 minutes
Temperature: **350-375** °
Time: 30 minutes

Great served with fresh asparagus and crisp green salad.

GRILLED BEEF TENDERLOIN
Must Make Ahead Of Time

Yields: 6 servings
Preparation Time: 20 minutes

¼   *cup Soy sauce*
¼   *cup Worcestershire sauce*
1½ *cups brown sugar*
2   *large cloves garlic, pressed*
1   *3½-4 pound beef tenderloin*

1. In a small bowl, combine Soy sauce, Worcestershire sauce, sugar, and garlic. Set aside.
2. Prepare tenderloin by peeling membrane and excess fat with a very sharp knife. If you want the same degree of doneness throughout the tenderloin, cut the tenderloin into two pieces where the diameter becomes noticeably smaller.
3. Rub mixture liberally on the meat at least two hours before cooking.
4. Cook on a covered charcoal grill with indirect heat (coals not under meat) for 18-20 minutes to make meat medium rare. Cook slightly less for smaller cut.
5. Finish cooking tenderloin directly over coals—approximately 2 minutes per side.

MULLER'S HOT ENCHILADAS

Must Make Ahead Of Time

Yields: *8 servings*
Preparation Time: *30-40 minutes*

*2	pounds ground chuck
1	large onion, chopped
2	tablespoons chili powder
2-3	teaspoons ground cumin
*1	teaspoon salt
1	15-ounce can Ranch-Style beans
6	flour tortillas
*1½	cups Swiss cheese, grated
*1	10-ounce can tomatoes, drained (save juice)
1	10-ounce can green chilies
1	10¾-ounce can cream of mushroom soup, undiluted

1. In a large skillet, cook meat and onion until done. Drain well. Add chili powder, cumin, and salt. Stir well. Cook meat mixture over low heat for 10 minutes.
2. Spoon meat mixture into a 13" × 9" baking dish. Layer beans, tortillas, and cheese over meat mixture. Pour tomato liquid over cheese.
3. Chop the tomatoes. Combine with green chilies and spread over cheese. Spread soup over all.
4. Cover baking pan and refrigerate over night.
5. Bake uncovered in 350° oven for one hour.

Temperature: *350 °*
Time: *1 hour*

For A Heart Healthy Recipe Make These Substitutions:

*2	pounds extra lean ground beef
*	omit salt
*1½	cups Weight Watchers Swiss cheese, grated
*1	10-ounce can low salt tomatoes, drained (save juice)

DELUXE PIZZA
"A Meal In Itself"

Yields: 10 servings
Preparation Time: 2 hours

1	recipe for 12" pizza crust
1	bunch green onions, sliced (plus tops)
¼-½	pound fresh mushrooms, sliced
1	large bell pepper, thinly sliced
2	tablespoons butter or margarine
1	pound ground chuck
1	teaspoon salt
½	teaspoon black pepper
1	8-ounce can tomato sauce
¼	teaspoon garlic powder
¼	teaspoon basil leaves
¼	teaspoon oregano leaves
1	4½-ounce can ripe pitted olives, sliced
2	medium zucchini, sliced
2	medium squash, sliced
8	ounces Mozzarella cheese, shredded
8	ounces Provolone cheese, shredded

1. Follow directions for your favorite pizza crust and press into a greased 9" × 13" pan.
2. Sauté onions, mushrooms, and bell pepper in butter until soft. Set aside.
3. Brown meat with salt and pepper, breaking it up with a fork as it cooks until crumbly. Drain well. Set aside.
4. In a small bowl, combine tomato sauce, garlic, basil, and oregano.
5. Layer ingredients on top of prepared crust in following order until filled topping with cheese: tomato sauce, meat, olives, cooked vegetables, zucchini, yellow squash, and cheeses. (layering can vary according to your preference, only layer it twice).
6. Bake in 375° oven for 45 minutes.

Temperature: 375 °
Time: 45 minutes

Warms well the next day and freezes well.

BRAISED LAMB SHANKS

Yields: ***4-6 servings***
Preparation Time: 20 minutes

6   *lamb shanks*
1½   *teaspoons salt*
¼   *teaspoon black pepper*
3   *tablespoons butter or*
      vegetable oil

Sauce:

¼   *cup white vinegar*
½   *cup water*
2   *tablespoons sugar*
1   *tablespoon prepared mustard*
½   *teaspoon black pepper*
¼   *teaspoon cayenne pepper*
1   *thick slice of lemon*
1   *cup onions, thinly sliced*
½   *cup ketchup*
2   *tablespoons Worcestershire*
      sauce

1. Have butcher cut shanks into 2-inch pieces.
2. Season shanks with salt and pepper.
3. Melt butter (oil will not burn) in large frying pan. Add shanks; simmer and brown evenly. If using a skillet, transfer to a 3-quart casserole.
4. In a medium saucepan, combine all ingredients for basting sauce. Mix thoroughly and bring to a boil. Reduce heat and simmer for 10 minutes.
5. Pour basting sauce over shanks and bake for 2-2½ hours in 300° oven or until tender. Stir several times while baking.
6. Remove from oven.
7. Allow shanks to sit at room temperature until fat rises to the top. Skim off fat and discard. Use juice to serve over meat.

Temperature: ***300** °*
Time: 2-2½ hours

CELEBRATION LAMB CHOPS

"So Simple"

Yields: ***4 servings***
Preparation Time: 20 minutes

6   *1½-inch loin lamb chops*
      lemon juice
      minced garlic
      oregano
      black pepper

1. Coat one side of each lamb chop with the following ingredients in the following order: lemon juice, garlic, oregano, and pepper.
2. Place chops on broiling pan or grill with seasoned side to heat. Season other side the same way.
3. Cook 8 minutes per side for medium rare. Turn once.

STUFFED BREAST OF VEAL

Yields: *6 servings*
Preparation Time: *1 hour*

3	slices bacon
1	medium onion, chopped
½	pound ground pork
1	cup soft bread crumbs
1	6-ounce can sliced mushrooms
2	tablespoons fresh parsley, chopped
1	teaspoon dill weed
½	teaspoon basil
½	teaspoon tarragon
½	teaspoon salt
⅓	cup sour cream
1	egg, beaten
1	4-pound veal breast, boned or
1	4-5 pound veal round, roast, boned, rolled, and tied
3	tablespoons flour
1½	cups chicken broth
2	tablespoons sour cream

1. Cook bacon until crisp; crumble and set aside. In same skillet, sauté onions and ground pork, until brown.

2. In bowl, mix ground pork, onions, bread crumbs, bacon, mushrooms, and all seasonings. Add ⅓ cup sour cream and egg.

3. Make deep split if using breast and fill with stuffing. If using rolled veal, untie meat, fill, re-roll, and tie with strings.

4. Brown roast in butter, then place in roasting pan. Cover and roast at 350° for 2½ hours. (Cook 1 hour longer for rolled roast.)

5. Remove veal from pan and keep warm. Mix flour into pan drippings, add chicken broth, and stir until thickened.

6. Add 2 tablespoons sour cream and mix well. Serve sauce with meat.

*Temperature: **350** °*
Time: 2½ or 3½ hours

VEAL BROCCOLI AND SAUCE

Yields: **5-6 servings**
Preparation Time: **40 minutes**

*1   egg
¼   cup water
*1   teaspoon salt
1   teaspoon black pepper
2   pounds veal cutlets
1   cup bread crumbs
*½   cup oil
2   10-ounce packages frozen broccoli spears
1   10-ounce can cream of asparagus soup
*½   soup can of milk
¼   cup dry sherry
½   teaspoon garlic powder
½   teaspoon cayenne pepper
½   cup Velveeta cheese, cubed
*¼   cup sharp Cheddar cheese, grated

1. Beat egg with water, salt, and pepper. Dip cutlets in egg mixture and then coat thoroughly with bread crumbs.
2. Fry cutlets in hot cooking oil—about 8-10 minutes. Drain on paper towel and set aside.
3. Cook broccoli according to package directions. Drain thoroughly.
4. Heat soup, milk, sherry, spices, and Velveeta, stirring constantly until cheese melts and mixed thoroughly.
5. Place cutlets in bottom of 9″ × 13″ glass baking dish. Place broccoli on top of cutlets. Cover entire dish with soup mixture. Sprinkle Cheddar cheese on top.
6. Bake uncovered in 350° oven for 30 minutes.

Temperature: **350 °**
Time: *30 minutes*

For A Heart Healthy Recipe Make These Substitutions:

*2   egg whites
*   omit salt
*½   cup safflower oil
*½   soup can skim evaporated milk
*¼   cup Weight Watchers Cheddar cheese, grated

VEAL WITH MUSHROOMS AND CAPERS

*Yields: **4 servings***
Preparation Time: 25 minutes

1-1½ pounds milk-fed baby veal,
　　 cut in narrow strips
　　 flour, seasoned with salt and
　　 pepper
2　 tablespoons vegetable oil
6　 green onions, sliced
1　 clove garlic, minced
½　 pound fresh mushrooms,
　　 sliced
2　 tablespoons capers
1　 10½-ounce can beef
　　 consommé
½　 cup sour cream
2-3　 cups cooked rice

1. Dredge veal slices in seasoned flour. Sauté lightly in oil.
2. Add green onions and garlic. Sauté 3 minutes. Add mushrooms and capers. Sauté another 5 minutes.
3. Add consommé and simmer 20 minutes. Stir in sour cream. heat thoroughly, but do not allow to boil.
4. Serve over rice.

VEAL CUTLETS SUPREME

*Yields: **4-6 servings***
Preparation Time: 35-45 minutes

6　 (¼-inch thick) veal cutlets
3　 eggs
1½　 teaspoons salt
¾　 teaspoon coarsely ground
　　 black pepper
1　 cup flour
1½　 cups plain dry bread crumbs
¾　 cup butter or margarine
6　 ounces Gruyere cheese, thinly
　　 sliced
3　 tablespoons parsley flakes
　　 lemon slices for garnish

1. Using wax paper and a meat mallet, pound the cutlets until ⅛ inch thick. Set aside.
2. Combine eggs, salt, and pepper in a shallow dish. Beat well.
3. Dredge cutlets in flour, dip in egg mixture and then coat with bread crumbs. Set aside for 10-15 minutes for coating to set.
4. In an electric skillet or other large skillet, melt butter over medium heat. Sauté cutlets in butter 4-5 minutes on one side. Turn and cook 2 minutes on other side.
5. Top with cheese slices. Cover and cook 3-4 minutes. Sprinkle with parsley flakes. Remove to platter and garnish with lemon slices.

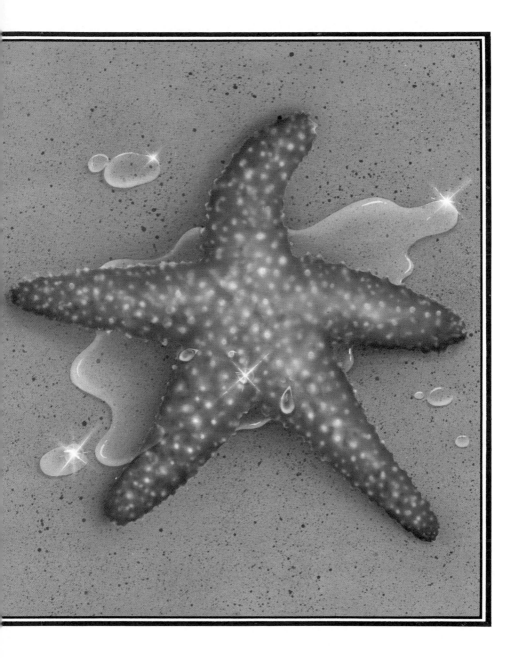

STAR FISH

Star fish or sea stars are spiny, five-rayed creatures that dwell in the sea—never in fresh water. Sea water flows through tubes in the body, and the animal moves via a process of pumping water into its many small tube feet. Just like sea urchins and sand dollars, the star fish has a mouth in the center of its body. The star fish possesses miraculous regenerative powers: if the creature drops a single one of its rays, it has the ability to grow a new one, and the abandoned ray has the power to grow a whole new body.

VEAL MARSALA

Yields: **4 servings**
Preparation Time: 20 minutes

1	pound veal scallops, sliced thin
½	teaspoon salt
⅛	teaspoon black pepper
1	cup flour
3	tablespoons unsalted butter
½	cup dry Marsala wine
½	pound fresh mushrooms, sliced thin
2	tablespoons butter or margarine
¼	teaspoon Kitchen Bouquet
¼	cup beef bouillon

1. Season scallops with salt and pepper. Sprinkle flour on pastry board and pound scallops into the flour. Turn and repeat on the other side.
2. Heat unsalted butter in skillet and sauté scallops 2-3 minutes per side. Remove to warm oven.
3. Add Marsala to skillet and deglaze pan. Cook 3 minutes. While Marsala is heating, sauté mushrooms in remaining butter in another skillet for 3 minutes.
4. Add mushrooms to Marsala. Pour in bouillon and add Kitchen Bouquet. Cook 3 minutes more. Pour over veal scallops and serve immediately.

VEAL PARMESAN

Yields: **4 servings**
Preparation Time: 20 minutes

4-5	veal steaks
2	tablespoons butter or margarine
2	green peppers, chopped
1	14½-ounce can tomatoes
1	6-ounce can tomato paste
1	package Italian seasoning mix
	garlic powder to taste
	pepper to taste
4-5	slices Mozzarella cheese

1. Brown steaks in butter on both sides.
2. Arrange veal in a 9″ × 9″ baking dish.
3. Combine peppers, tomatoes, tomato paste, and seasonings to taste. Top with cheese slices.
4. Bake uncovered in 350° oven for 30-40 minutes.
5. Place under broiler to brown cheese.

Temperature: **350 °**
Time: 30-40 minutes

Temperature: Broil
Time: 3-5 minutes

EASY STIR FRIED PORK AND SHRIMP ORIENTAL

Yields: 6 servings
Preparation Time: 1½-2 hours

1	*pound boneless pork, cut into 1" pieces*
2	*tablespoons flour*
1¼	*teaspoons ginger*
3	*tablespoons vegetable oil, divided*
1½	*teaspoons instant chicken bouillon*
1½	*cups boiling water*
1	*pound large shrimp, shelled and deveined*
1	*pound fresh mushrooms, sliced*
6	*ribs celery, cut diagonally*
8	*green onions with tops, cut in 1-inch pieces*
2	*tablespoons sugar*
2	*tablespoons soy sauce*
3	*cups cooked rice (prepared according to package directions)*

1. Coat pork with mixture of flour and ginger. In a large skillet, brown pork in 2 tablespoons of oil.

2. Add bouillon and water. Heat to boiling. Reduce heat. Cover and simmer until pork is tender (about 1 hour).

3. Stir fry shrimp in one tablespoon oil in wok or skillet (2 minutes). Remove shrimp from wok.

4. Stir fry celery in same skillet for 2 minutes. Stir in mushrooms, onions, pork mixture, sugar, and soy sauce. Stir fry until vegetables are tender (about 3 minutes).

5. Add shrimp and stir fry about 1 minute.

6. Serve over rice.

The use of a wok makes this a real snap.

PORK MEDALLIONS WITH MUSTARD CREAM SAUCE

Yields: **4-6 servings**
Preparation Time: 20 minutes

12	pork medallions
	salt and pepper to taste
	flour
5	tablespoons butter or
	margarine
1/3	cup white vinegar
8	peppercorns, crushed
2	cups heavy cream
1/3	cup Dijon mustard

1. Between 2 sheets of wax paper, flatten 12 pork medallions until they are ½-inch thick. Sprinkle with salt, pepper, and dust with flour.
2. In a large skillet, melt 3 tablespoons butter. Sauté medallions for 2 minutes per side. Keep warm.
3. Add vinegar and crushed peppercorns to the skillet. Boil mixture until it is reduced by ⅔. Add heavy cream. Simmer 5 minutes or until mixture thickens.
4. Remove skillet from heat and swirl in Dijon mustard and 2 tablespoons butter cut into pieces.
5. Season with ½ teaspoon salt, if desired. Pour sauce over warm medallions and serve.

OVEN BARBECUED PORK CHOPS

Yields: **3-4 servings**
Preparation Time: 15 minutes

6	pork chops
1/2	cup ketchup
1	teaspoon celery seed
1	bay leaf
2	tablespoons brown sugar
4	tablespoons white vinegar
1	cup water
1	teaspoon prepared mustard

1. Brown pork chops. Arrange in bottom of a shallow baking pan so they do not overlap.
2. While chops are browning, mix all other ingredients in small saucepan and heat. Pour over chops and bake uncovered at 375° for 1 hour. Check after 45 minutes to see that sauce is not getting too thick. If so, cover for remaining 15 minutes.

Temperature: **375 °**
Time: 1 hour

HAM LOAF
"Eat One-Freeze One"

Yields: **2 loaves - each 6-8 servings**
Preparation Time: 20 minutes

Loaf:

2	*pounds ground ham*
2	*pounds ground pork*
1½	*cups fresh cracker crumbs*
⅓	*cup onion, chopped*
4	*eggs, well beaten*
1¼	*teaspoons salt*
2	*cups milk*
2	*tablespoons parsley*

Glaze:

½	*pound brown sugar*
¼	*cup cider*
1½	*tablespoons dry mustard (or less if desired)*

Sauce:

½	*cup good quality mayonnaise*
½	*cup sour cream*
¼	*cup prepared mustard*
1	*tablespoon minced chives*
1-1½	*teaspoons lemon juice*
2	*tablespoons horseradish*

1. Mix ham, pork, and cracker crumbs. Add onion, eggs, salt, milk, and parsley. Work together until thoroughly blended.
2. Shape into two loaves and place into two loaf pans. Bake at 350° for 30 minutes. After 30 minutes, remove from oven and set pans in a jelly roll pan.
3. Prepare glaze by combining all ingredients for glaze and bring to boil for one minute.
4. Baste all of glaze onto the two loaves. Bake at 350° for one hour more.
5. If ready to serve, remove from oven and slice.
6. If not serving immediately, cool and wrap in foil. Freeze until ready to use. When ready to serve, remove from freezer. Do not thaw. Bake frozen at 325° for 1½ hours.
7. Combine ingredients for sauce and heat over medium heat. Do not boil.
8. Serve ham loaf with sauce over it.

*Temperature: **350** °*
Time: 30 minutes, 1 hour

BOLIVAR LIGHTHOUSE

To the east of Galveston across Galveston Bay is the Bolivar Peninsula. Not far from the ferry landing on Bolivar Peninsula is a lighthouse which has been preserved even though it's not been used for many years. Built in 1872 to replace an earlier version that had been in place since before the Civil War, this lighthouse is a captivating feature of the history of Galveston and its environs.

Poultry & Game

CHICKEN DUMPLET CASSEROLE

Yields: **10 servings**
Preparation Time: 30 minutes

4	teaspoons flour
4	teaspoons butter
1	cup evaporated milk
2	cups chicken stock
2	8-ounce packages cream cheese
1	teaspoon pepper
1	teaspoon salt
1	4¼-ounce can chopped or sliced ripe olives, drained
1	2½-ounce can sliced mushrooms, drained
4	cups cooked chicken, diced
4	cups rippled egg noodles, cooked and drained
	buttered bread crumbs or sliced almonds

1. In a saucepan, combine flour, butter, milk, and chicken stock to make the cream sauce.
2. Cube the cream cheese, add to white sauce and stir until melted. Blend in salt, pepper, drained olives, and drained mushrooms. Fold in chicken and noodles.
3. Place mixture in a 9" × 13" baking dish. Top with buttered crumbs and/ or sliced almonds. Bake in 350° oven for 30 minutes.

Temperature: **350 °**
Time: 30 minutes

Can be frozen, defrosted and reheated at 350° for 30 minutes.

HAWAIIAN CHICKEN

Yields: **4-6 servings**
Preparation Time: 45 minutes

⅓	cup cornstarch
1½	teaspoons salt
2	teaspoons paprika
1	whole fryer or 6-8 pieces of chicken
¼	cup vegetable oil
1	16-ounce can pineapple chunks
1	cup celery, sliced
1	green pepper, sliced
1	tablespoon cornstarch
2	tablespoons brown sugar
2	tablespoons soy sauce
3	cups cooked rice
¼	cup raisins

1. Shake together in a bag, cornstarch, salt, paprika and chicken.
2. In a large skillet, brown chicken parts lightly in oil. Reduce heat and cook 20 minutes.
3. Drain pineapple (reserve juice). Add pineapple chunks, celery, and pepper slices to chicken. Cook 5 minutes.
4. In a small mixing bowl, combine cornstarch, brown sugar, Soy sauce, and reserved pineapple juice. Pour over chicken and cook for 10 minutes.
5. Serve over rice sprinkled with raisins.

I LOVE THESE CHICKEN LIVERS

*Yields: **4-6 servings***
Preparation Time: 30 minutes

1	pound chicken livers
½	cup clarified butter
¼	cup flour
½	teaspoon salt
⅛	teaspoon black pepper
1½	large yellow onions, sliced into ½" rings
1	teaspoon garlic, minced
2	cups large mushrooms, sliced
2	cups Rhine wine
1	teaspoon crushed thyme
1	cup parsley, minced
4	slices white bread, crust removed

1. Rinse chicken livers in cold water. Drain on paper towels and dry well. Heat ½ of the clarified butter in dutch oven. Put flour, salt, and pepper in plastic bag and shake well. Add livers and shake to coat.
2. Add onions and garlic to hot butter and stir until onions are soft. Sauté livers in remaining butter in another pan. When brown (about 2 minutes) add to onions along with mushrooms.
3. Deglace liver pan with wine and add to livers. Add thyme and parsley. Bring to a boil. Reduce heat and cook until sauce thickens.
4. Fry bread in about 1-inch of clarified butter in 2-quart saucepan. When brown, drain on paper towel. Serve livers over bread. Sprinkle extra parsley on top if desired.

May be cooked hours or days ahead. Flavor improves. Reheat on low heat. Bread does not keep long.

CHICKEN-HAM ARTICHOKE CASSEROLE

*Yields: **4-5 servings***
Preparation Time: 20 minutes

2	cups cooked chicken, diced
1	cup ham, cut in large chunks
1	small can unmarinated artichokes, quartered
1	10¾-ounce can cream of chicken soup
½	cup good quality mayonnaise
½	teaspoon lemon juice
¼	teaspoon curry powder
2	slices bread, toasted, buttered, and cubed
1	cup Cheddar cheese, grated

1. Layer chicken and ham in the bottom of a 1½-2 quart shallow casserole. Place artichokes on top.
2. Combine soup, mayonnaise, lemon juice, curry powder, and pour over meat. Add cheese to top.
3. Sprinkle bread crumbs on top. Bake uncovered in 350° oven for 30 minutes.

*Temperature: **350 °***
Time: 30 minutes

135

ARROZ CON POLLO
(Chicken with rice)

*Yields: **4 servings***
Preparation Time: 1 hour

2	pounds chicken, cut in serving pieces
2	tablespoons vegetable oil
1	10½-ounce can condensed chicken broth
1	1-pound can tomatoes
⅓	cup water
½	cup onion, chopped
2	medium cloves garlic, minced
1	teaspoon salt
½	teaspoon saffron or turmeric dash of pepper
1	bay leaf
1	10-ounce package frozen peas
1	cup rice, uncooked
½	cup olives, sliced (stuffed or ripe)

1. In skillet, brown chicken in oil. Pour off fat.
2. Add broth, tomatoes, water, onion, and seasonings. Cover and cook on low for 15 minutes.
3. Add remaining ingredients. Cover and cook for 30 minutes.

CHICKEN BREASTS IN CREAM

*Yields: **4-6 servings***
Preparation Time: 25 minutes

6	boneless chicken breasts salt pepper
1	egg, beaten
1½	cups dry bread crumbs
¼	cup butter
¼	cup vegetable oil
2	cups heavy cream
1	clove garlic, crushed
½	teaspoon paprika

1. Season chicken breasts with salt and pepper. Dip chicken into egg and roll in bread crumbs.
2. Melt butter in large skillet. Add oil. Sauté chicken until golden brown. Remove from pan and place in a large baking dish.
3. Combine cream, salt, and garlic and pour over chicken. Sprinkle top with paprika.
4. Bake in 350° oven 45 minutes to an hour, basting occasionally.

*Temperature: **350 °***
Time: 45 minutes-1 hour

FRIED CHICKEN AND POTATOES WITH SOUR CREAM SAUCE

Yields: 4-6 servings
Preparation Time: 45 minutes

⅓	cup flour
1	teaspoon salt
2	teaspoons paprika
¼	teaspoon black pepper
1	pound chicken breasts
1	pound chicken thighs
⅓	cup butter or margarine
1	10¾-ounce can cream of mushroom soup
8	small potatoes
1	cup onion, sliced
1	cup sour cream
2	teaspoons parsley, minced

1. Mix flour, salt, paprika, and pepper in a large bag. Shake 2-3 pieces of chicken at a time.
2. Melt butter in a large skillet. Add chicken and brown on all sides. Add potatoes, onion, and soup. Cover and cook until tender.
3. Remove chicken. Keep warm. Add sour cream and bring to a boiling point.
4. Pour sauce over chicken and garnish with minced parsley and remaining paprika.

CHICKEN ENCHILADAS SWISS

Yields: 8 servings
Preparation Time: 2 hours

2	packages corn tortillas
2	cups cream of chicken soup
2	fryers (boiled and cubed)
2	cups Rotel tomatoes
1½	cups Swiss cheese, grated
1½	cups Cheddar cheese, grated
2½	cups Monterey Jack cheese, grated
2	cups sour cream
	salt and pepper to taste

1. Dip tortillas in heated soup.
2. Mix chicken, Swiss and Cheddar cheese, 1 cup tomatoes, and salt and pepper.
3. Place a generous amount of cheese-mixture in each tortilla. Roll and place seam-side down in a baking dish.
4. Mix soup with 1 cup tomatoes (mashed), Monterey Jack cheese, and sour cream. Pour over tortillas.
5. Bake in 350° oven until bubbly (about 20 minutes).

Temperature: 350 °
Time: 20 minutes

GEORGE GOURLEY'S STUFFED CHICKEN BREASTS

Yields: 8-10 servings
Preparation Time: 45 minutes
to 1 hour

2   tablespoons butter
1   cup fresh mushrooms, sliced
      thin
2   tablespoons flour
½   cup light cream
¼   teaspoon salt
⅛   teaspoon cayenne pepper
1¼   cups sharp Cheddar cheese,
      grated
12   boneless chicken breasts
1½   cups flour
1   teaspoon salt
½   teaspoon black pepper
¾   cup dry bread crumbs
2   eggs, beaten
      oil for frying

1. Melt butter and sauté mushrooms for five minutes. Blend in two tablespoons flour.
2. Stir in cream, salt, and cayenne pepper. Cook over medium heat, stirring constantly until thick.
3. Add cheese and blend thoroughly until cheese is melted. Remove from heat and chill for one hour.
4. Pound chicken breasts until very thin. Place a heaping teaspoon of the cheese mixture in center of the chicken breast. Fold in sides and roll up breasts.
5. Combine 1½ cups flour, 1 teaspoon salt, and ½ teaspoon black pepper.
6. Dip chicken breast rolls in seasoned flour, then egg, then bread crumbs.
7. Deep fry chicken breasts about 10-15 minutes until golden brown. Drain on paper towels.
8. Serve with creamy mushroom gravy (below).

Temperature: 325 °
Time: 30-45 minutes

These may be wrapped individually and frozen. To reheat, bake at 325° for 30-45 minutes. This makes it great to prepare ahead of time for a dinner party.

CREAMY MUSHROOM GRAVY

2   tablespoons butter
½   cup fresh mushrooms, sliced
      thin
2   tablespoons flour
¾   cup light cream
      salt and pepper to taste

1. Melt butter and sauté mushrooms for three minutes. Blend in flour.
2. Slowly pour in cream and cook until slightly thickened.
3. Add salt and pepper to taste.

CREAMY CHICKEN AND WILD RICE

Yields: *8 servings*
Preparation Time: *30 minutes*

½   cup uncooked wild rice
1   teaspoon salt, divided
½   cup uncooked long-grain rice
½   cup onion, chopped
½   cup butter or margarine
¼   cup flour
1   6-ounce can broiled sliced
     mushrooms
     chicken broth
1½   cups light cream
3   cups cooked chicken, diced
¼   cup pimiento, chopped,
     (optional)
¼   cup parsley, snipped
¼   cup slivered almonds, toasted
⅛   teaspoon black pepper

1. Rinse wild rice in cold water. Combine 2 cups water and ½ teaspoon salt. Bring to a boil. Add wild rice. Cook 20 minutes. Add long-grain rice, 1 cup boiling water and rest of salt. Cook 20 minutes longer.
2. In a separate skillet, sauté onion in butter until tender. Remove from heat and stir in flour.
3. Drain mushrooms, reserving liquid. Add enough chicken broth to liquid to measure 1½ cups. Stir into flour mixture. Add cream. Cook, stirring constantly until mixture thickens.
4. Add cooked rice, mushrooms, chicken and rest of ingredients except almonds and pepper. Turn into two-quart casserole. Top with nuts and sprinkle with black pepper.
5. Bake in 350° oven for 25-30 minutes.

Temperature: *350 °*
Time: *25-30 minutes*

SWEET AND SOUR CHICKEN

Yields: *5-6 servings*
Preparation Time: *10 minutes*

1   8-ounce bottle Russian salad
     dressing
1   envelope dry onion soup mix
1   8-ounce jar of apricot or
     peach preserves
6-8 chicken pieces (your choice)
3   cups rice, cooked according
     to directions on package

1. Combine first 3 ingredients. Mix well. Set aside.
2. Lightly grease 9" × 13" baking dish. Lay chicken pieces in a single layer. Pour sauce over all.
3. Bake uncovered in a 350° oven for 60 minutes. Serve over rice.

Temperature: *350 °*
Time: *1 hour*

SUSANNE'S SHERRIED CHICKEN

"An Elegant Company Dish"

Yields: **8 servings**
Preparation Time: 2 hours

8-10 chicken breasts
¼   teaspoon seasoned salt
½   teaspoon salt
¼   teaspoon black pepper
¼   cup butter
¾   cup dry sherry, divided
6   cups cooked rice
2   cans cream of chicken soup
1   cup sour cream
½   cup good quality mayonnaise
1   tablespoon parsley flakes
1   teaspoon paprika

1. Sprinkle chicken breasts with seasoned salt, salt, and pepper. Set aside.
2. In a 9" × 13" pan, melt butter in oven. Remove from oven. Roll each chicken piece in butter and leave in pan with breasts skin side up.
3. Pour ¼ cup sherry over chicken pieces.
4. Bake in 350° oven for 1 hour or until done.
5. When chicken is cool enough to handle, debone breasts without breaking skin. Set aside.
6. Place cooked rice in 4-5 quart casserole.
7. To drippings in pan, add soups, sour cream, mayonnaise, parsley, paprika, and ½ cup sherry. Mix thoroughly.
8. Pour half the sauce over rice. Arrange chicken breasts on top. Pour remaining sauce over all.
9. Bake in 350° oven for 40 minutes or less — until bubbly.
10. Serve with chicken resting on a bed of rice smothered in this delicious sauce.

Temperature: **350 °**
Time: 40 minutes

CHICKEN PAILLARDS WITH SESAME SEEDS
"Best Done On A Grill"

Yields: **4-6 servings**
Preparation Time: *20 minutes
plus 2 hours set time
or overnight*

2	tablespoons Soy sauce
2	tablespoons white-wine vinegar
2	tablespoons medium dry sherry
1	tablespoon sugar
8	boneless chicken breasts, skin removed
2	tablespoons sesame seeds vegetable oil

1. In a small bowl, combine Soy sauce, vinegar, sherry, and sugar. Stir until sugar is dissolved.
2. Flatten the chicken breasts until they are ¼-inch thick. Combine chicken breasts and sauce in a plastic bag or shallow bowl. Refrigerate for at least 2 hours or overnight.
3. In a small skillet, toast the sesame seeds over moderate heat, stirring constantly for 1-2 minutes until golden brown and fragrant.
4. Heat grill until hot. Brush with oil and arrange chicken breasts. Sear breasts 30 seconds. Shift them a quarter turn for 30 seconds more to achieve a diamond pattern. Shift again for 20 seconds and then again for 20 seconds more.
5. Turn over and repeat on other side. Transfer breasts to warm plate and sprinkle with toasted sesame seeds.

If preparing in a skillet, sear 1 minute on one side turn breasts and sear for 40-60 seconds on the other side.

141

DUCK AND DRESSING CASSEROLE

Must Make Ahead Of Time

Yields: **6 servings**
Preparation Time: 2 hours

6	sprig, widgeon or other large ducks, not teal
1	onion sliced
1	potato, peeled and sliced
1	bay leaf
1	teaspoon salt
½	teaspoon pepper

Dressing:

2	cups duck broth
½	cup butter or margarine
1	package Pepperidge Farm Herb Season Stuffing Mix
½	cup celery, chopped
1½	cups onion, chopped
2	eggs, beaten
1	10¾-ounce can cream of mushroom soup
¾	cup whole milk

1. In a three or four quart pan, cover ducks with water. Add onion, potato, bay leaf, salt, and pepper. Cook until tender. Remove from pot. Strain and reserve two cups broth.

2. Cool ducks and remove meat from bone. Cut meat into fairly large pieces.

3. Bring two cups broth and butter to a boil. Pour over stuffing mix in a bowl. Add celery and onion. Mix thoroughly.

4. Add eggs and duck meat. Mix thoroughly again. Put mixture in a greased 11" × 9" baking dish.

5. Combine soup and milk. Pour over duck mixture. Let stand several hours or overnight.

6. Bake uncovered in 400° oven for 1-1½ hours — or until lightly browned. Cover with foil if it browns too quickly.

Temperature: **400** °
Time: 1½ hours

SHERRIED CHICKEN VELVET

Yields: 8 servings
Preparation Time: 1½ hours

2 *whole fryers*
1 *cup celery, coarsely chopped*
1 *cup green pepper, coarsely chopped*
1 *cup onion, coarsely chopped*
4 *tablespoons butter or margarine*
1 *8-ounce package cream cheese*
¾-1 *pound Velveeta Cheese*
1 *cup light cream*
¾ *cup long grain rice*
2 *tablespoons jalapeño juice*
½ *cup dry sherry*

1. Cook fryers in boiling water until tender. Debone chicken and set aside. Cut chicken into bite-size pieces. Reserve broth to cook rice.
2. Sauté celery, green peppers, and onions in butter for five minutes. Set aside.
3. In a large saucepan, or dutch oven, combine cream cheese, Velveeta, and cream. Heat over medium-low heat until cheese is melted, stirring constantly to keep cheese from sticking to bottom of pan.
4. Cook rice according to package directions using chicken broth in place of the water. Add cooked rice to cheese mixture.
5. Add chicken and vegetable mixture to cheese and rice. Mix thoroughly. Add jalapeño juice and sherry; then stir well.
6. Pour into three or four quart baking dish. Bake in 350° oven for 30 minutes or until hot and bubbly.

Temperature: 350 °
Time: 30 minutes

SOUR CREAM CHICKEN ENCHILADAS

*Yields: **12 servings***
Preparation Time: 2 hours

1	*whole chicken fryer*
1	*carrot, sliced*
1	*onion, sliced*
3	*sprigs parsley, chopped*
	salt
	pepper
	poultry seasonings
	garlic powder
1	*tablespoon bacon grease*
1	*package taco seasoning mix*
½	*cup water*
1	*large onion, diced*
1	*tablespoon Picante sauce*
1	*16-ounce container sour cream*
1	*8-ounce package Monterey Jack cheese, grated*
1	*8-ounce package mild Cheddar cheese, grated*
12	*corn tortillas*
2	*avocados*
	green chili sauce
	Picante sauce

1. In a large pan, cover chicken with water. Add carrot, onion, and parsley. Season water with salt, pepper, poultry seasoning, and garlic powder. When cooked chicken has cooled, debone and cut into bite-size pieces. Set aside.

2. In frying pan put 1 tablespoon of bacon grease and the cooked chicken pieces, taco seasoning mix, ½ cup water, and onion. Cook mixture until onion is tender.

3. Add 1 tablespoon of Picante sauce to sour cream (or to taste). Mix well.

4. Tortillas may be softened by frying in a little hot oil for a few seconds.

5. To assemble enchiladas, place chicken mixture, sour cream, and cheeses on counter. Dip tortillas in water (or prepare as described in Step #3). Place on tortilla, one tablespoon chicken mixture and 2 dollops of sour cream; sprinkle both kinds of cheese over top. Roll up and place in large oiled casserole. Cover enchiladas with remaining sour cream. Cover with the rest of cheese. Add 1 tablespoon of water to bottom and cover with aluminum foil.

6. Bake in 350° oven for 20 minutes or until cheese is melted.

7. Add sliced avocados to top of enchiladas when serving. Serve with green chili sauce and Picante sauce.

*Temperature: **350 °***
*Time: **20 minutes***

CHICKEN BARBARA

Yields: *6 servings*
Preparation Time: 1 hour

3	whole chicken breasts, split
1	teaspoon salt
1/4	teaspoon pepper
1	teaspoon rosemary
1	rib celery, top and leaves
1	large onion, sliced
1	cup water
1	clove garlic, halved

Batter:

1	cup sifted flour
1½	teaspoons baking powder
1/4	teaspoon salt
1	egg yolk, beaten
1/4	cup vegetable oil
2/3	cup milk
1/4	cup salad oil

Cream Sauce:

3/4	cup reserved chicken stock
3	tablespoons flour
1/2	teaspoon salt
	dash pepper
1/4	cup light cream
1	tablespoon lemon juice
2	drops yellow food coloring

1. Place chicken breasts in a two-quart casserole. Sprinkle with salt, pepper, and rosemary. Add celery, onion, and water. Cover and bake at 375° for about one hour (until chicken is tender). Reserve stock. Cool chicken.

2. Remove skin and bones from chicken breasts. Rub each breast well with cut clove of garlic. Set aside while preparing batter and cream sauce.

3. To make batter, sift together flour, baking powder and salt. Combine egg yolk, milk, and oil. Stir into flour mixture. Fold in stiffly beaten egg white, leaving a few fluffs. DO NOT OVERMIX.

4. Dip chicken breast in batter. Fry in deep hot fat until nicely browned (about three minutes). Serve hot with cream sauce.

5. In a medium saucepan, make cream sauce. Heat reserved stock over low heat.

6. Blend in flour, salt, and pepper. Add cream. Stir and cook quickly until mixture thickens slightly and bubbles.

7. Stir in lemon juice and food coloring. Serve over chicken breasts.

*Temperature: **350** °*
Time: 1 hour

AUNT KATES CHESAPEAKE CHICKEN

Yields: **6 servings**
Preparation Time: 45 minutes

1	*8-ounce box long grain and wild rice*
6	*boneless chicken breasts, skin removed*
8	*ounces smoked ham, thinly sliced*
1	*pint oysters*
	liquid from oysters
3	*slices bacon, uncooked and halved*
1	*10¾-ounce can cream of chicken soup*
½	*cup sour cream*
½	*cup light cream*
¼	*cup dry sherry*
2	*teaspoons fresh parsley, chopped*
1	*generous pinch of tarragon*
	salt to taste
	pepper to taste
¼	*cup fresh Parmesan cheese, grated*
	paprika

1. Cook long grain and wild rice according to package instructions. Lay rice mixture in the bottom of a shallow 7"× 12" or 9"× 13" baking dish.
2. Cover rice with a layer of smoked ham slices. Place oysters on ham and cover with chicken breasts. Top each chicken breast with a slice of bacon.
3. Combine soup, liquid from oysters, sour cream, light cream, sherry, parsley, and tarragon. Mix thoroughly. Add salt and pepper to taste.
4. Pour sauce over the chicken. Sprinkle top with Parmesan cheese and paprika.
5. Bake in 300° oven for 1-1½ hours or until hot and bubbly.

Temperature: **300 °**
Time: 1-1½ *hours*

You can make this early in the day or the night before and then bake when you are ready to have dinner.

ROAST ROCK CORNISH GAME HENS

Yields: **6 servings**
Preparation Time: **20 minutes**

6	cornish hens
1½	teaspoons salt
¼	teaspoon black pepper
1	teaspoon tarragon
½	cup butter, softened
6	slices bacon
¾	pound green grapes

Sauce:

1	10½-ounce can beef broth
⅓	cup water
⅓	cup Madeira wine
1	tablespoon brandy
1	tablespoon butter
1	tablespoon flour

1. Wash hens and pat dry. Sprinkle cavity of each hen with salt, pepper, and tarragon.
2. Put one teaspoon butter inside each cavity. Truss birds and rub skin with remaining butter.
3. Blanch bacon slices by simmering bacon in water for 10 minutes. Lay blanched bacon over hens.
4. Place birds in roasting pan and put on middle rack in oven.
5. Roast in 400° oven until brown and tender — about one hour, basting often with dripping. During final ten minutes of cooking, place grapes, cut in six clusters, around hens and baste.
6. When hens are done, remove bacon. Spoon Madeira sauce over hens and serve.

Sauce:

1. Make sauce in roasting pan. Pour off fat. Add broth, water, Madeira, and brandy to pan. Bring to a boil, stirring occasionally.
2. Cook until sauce has been reduced to about one cup.
3. Work the softened 1 tablespoon of butter and flour together with your fingers. Add to sauce. Cook, stirring occasionally, for 2-3 minutes until slightly thickened. Pour over hens.

Temperature: **400 °**
Time: **1 hour**

BRANDIED CHICKEN BREASTS

*Yields: **6-8 servings***
Preparation Time: 30 minutes plus
1 hour set time

12	*boneless chicken breasts*
1	*tablespoon dried marjoram*
½	*cup brandy*
6	*tablespoons butter*
¼	*cup dry sherry*
2	*cups heavy cream*
3	*egg yolks*
	salt
	white pepper
1	*pound fresh mushrooms, halved*
¼	*cup butter*
¼	*cup dry bread crumbs*
½	*cup Parmesan cheese, grated*
2	*tablespoons fresh parsley, chopped*

1. Rub chicken breasts with majoram and pour brandy over all. Place breasts in glass 9" × 13" baking dish and refrigerate one hour.

2. In large skillet, heat six tablespoons butter over moderate heat. Remove chicken from marinade (reserve marinade) and sauté 2-3 minutes on each side until golden. Remove to large baking dish.

3. Return pan to high heat, add sherry, ignite, and allow to burn off and reduce by one-half its volume.

4. Add cream to pan and bring to a boil until it forms a thick sauce so that it coats a spoon well.

5. Add reserved marinade. Remove pan from heat for two minutes. Add egg yolks one at a time, stirring well after each addition. Season with salt and white pepper.

6. Sauté half of the mushrooms in two tablespoons butter. Remove. Add remaining butter and sauté remaining mushrooms. Add all the mushrooms to the sauce. Stir well and pour over chicken in baking dish.

7. Sprinkle bread crumbs and Parmesan cheese over chicken and sauce.

8. Bake in 350° oven for 15 minutes. Place under broiler 2-3 minutes to lightly glaze the surface.

9. Sprinkle top with chopped parsley and serve at once.

HOT AND SPICY CHICKEN

Yields: 6-8 servings
Preparation Time: 1 hour

4-6	tablespoons butter or margarine
3	large onions, cut in thin strips
1	large green pepper, cut in thin strips
12	pieces of chicken (your choice)
1	14½-ounce can stewed tomatoes
1	15-ounce can tomato sauce
1	can Rotel tomatoes
½	cup green stuffed olives sliced
⅛	teaspoon garlic salt
1	teaspoon oregano
1	14½-ounce can artichokes
4	small zucchini, cut round cooked rice

1. In an electric skillet or a large frying pan, melt butter. Sauté onions and peppers. Add chicken and sauté until light brown.
2. Reduce heat to 250° (medium-low). Add stewed tomatoes, tomato sauce, Rotel tomatoes, olives, and seasonings. Cover and cook one hour.
3. Add artichokes and zucchini the last 10 minutes. Serve over rice.

CHAMPAGNE CHICKEN

Yields: 4-6 servings
Preparation Time: 1 hour

1	broiler/fryer, cut up in serving pieces
¼	cup flour
¼	teaspoon ginger
¼	cup butter or margarine
1	onion, quartered
1	carrot, sliced into 4 pieces
1	bay leaf
1	cup champagne or dry white wine
1	5-ounce package long grain and wild rice
1	cup heavy cream, whipped
1	8-ounce can white seedless grapes
	salt and pepper to taste

1. Shake chicken pieces in flour which has been seasoned with salt, pepper, and ginger.
2. In a skillet, brown chicken slowly in melted butter. Add onion, carrot, bay leaf, and champagne. Cover pan and simmer 25-30 minutes or until chicken is tender.
3. Prepare rice according to package directions. Arrange rice on heated serving platter. Place chicken over rice. Discard onion, carrot, and bay leaf. Add cream and grapes to sauce and heat without bringing to a boil. Spoon sauce over chicken and rice.

149

STIR FRY CHICKEN PRIMAVERA

Yields: **6 servings**
Preparation Time: 25 minutes

6	*tablespoons olive oil, divided*
3	*whole chicken breasts, boned and skin removed, cut in 1-inch pieces*
4	*large cloves garlic, crushed*
2	*medium carrots, peeled and julienned into ¼" × 1" strips*
1	*medium green pepper, seeded and sliced into thin strips*
1	*bunch broccoli, including flowerets*
1½	*pounds linguini, cooked al dente*
1	*pimiento, cut into tiny squares*
½	*pound mushrooms, quartered*
12	*pitted black olives, quartered lengthwise*
½	*cup fresh Parmesan cheese, grated*
2	*tablespoons parsley, minced salt and pepper to taste*

1. Heat 3 tablespoons of the olive oil over moderately high heat and sauté chicken pieces until lightly browned. Set chicken aside.

2. Add rest of oil and sauté garlic until light brown. Add carrots, pepper, and broccoli. Stir until tender. DO NOT overcook.

3. Add chicken, linguini, pimiento, mushrooms, and olives. Stir fry until heated thoroughly. Adjust seasoning. Add Parmesan cheese and toss. Sprinkle lightly with parsley and serve.

STUFFED CORNISH GAME HENS

Yields: **6 servings**
Preparation Time: 45 minutes

1 cup onion, finely chopped
½ cup green pepper, finely chopped
6-8 slices of bacon, cooked and crumbled (reserve bacon drippings)
3 cups small dry bread cubes
1 cup pecans, finely chopped
3 teaspoons salt, divided
½ teaspoon dried thyme
1 teaspoon sage, divided
3 cornish game hens
½ cup butter, melted
½ cup dry white wine
1 clove garlic, crushed

Sauce:

3 tablespoons flour
1 cup red wine
1 cup currant jelly
1 tablespoon dry mustard
1 teaspoon salt

1. Sauté onion and green pepper in bacon drippings for about eight minutes or until they are tender. Remove from heat.
2. In a large bowl, mix the bacon, onion, green pepper, bread cubes, pecans, 1½ teaspoons of salt, one and one-half teaspoon sage. Toss lightly until well mixed.
3. Stuff the cavities of the hens loosely and close openings securely. Arrange the hens breast side up in a small roasting pan. Set aside and preheat oven to 400°.
4. In a small saucepan, combine butter, wine, garlic, remaining sage, and 1½ teaspoons salt. Cook over low heat for 2-3 minutes.
5. Bake hens for one hour in 400° oven, basting every fifteen minutes.
6. When hens are cooked, remove from oven to a warming platter and keep in oven on warm while preparing sauce.
7. Remove drippings from roasting pan, reserving ⅔ cup. Add flour to reserved drippings in roasting pan and cook over low heat, stirring constantly until mixture is smooth.
8. Add the wine, jelly, mustard, and salt. Bring mixture to a boil using a heavy spoon to remove the bits from the bottom of the pan. Reduce heat and simmer 10 minutes or until the sauce is thickened.
9. Remove hens from oven and split in half. Drizzle a small amount of sauce over the hens and serve remaining sauce on the side.

Temperature: **400** °
Time: 1 hour

CHICKEN VERONIQUE

Yields: 6-8 servings
Preparation Time: 1 hour

2   cups dry white wine, divided
2   teaspoons garlic salt
    juice of ½ fresh lemon
1   medium onion, sliced
3   tablespoons vegetable oil,
    divided
10 boneless chicken breasts
4   tablespoons butter
2   tablespoons flour
⅔   cup light cream
2   chicken bouillon cubes
    Tabasco
1   pound seedless white grapes
1½ cups Swiss cheese, grated
2   egg yolks

1. In a large skillet, combine 1 cup wine, garlic salt, lemon juice, onion, and one tablespoon vegetable oil.

2. Add chicken breasts, cover, bring to boil, and simmer for 20 minutes. Remove chicken breasts from broth and set aside. Reserve the broth, discarding the onion.

3. Melt the butter. Add remaining 2 tablespoons of vegetable oil. Blend in flour and reserved broth, stirring constantly until sauce begins to thicken. Remove from heat and add cream, bouillon cubes, and a dash of Tabasco.

4. Return to heat and simmer briefly before setting aside.

5. Remove the stems from the grapes. Cook grapes in one cup of wine for about 10-15 minutes. Drain and set aside.

6. To assemble, slice the chicken breasts and arrange them in a 9" × 13" greased casserole. Sprinkle lightly with half the cheese. Cover with a layer of grapes.

7. Add the egg yolks to the cream sauce, stir until well blended.

8. Pour sauce over chicken and grapes. Top with another layer of cheese and refrigerate overnight.

9. Before serving, heat in a 350° oven for 20-25 minutes. Garnish with parsley.

Temperature: 350 °
Time: 20-25 minutes

CHICKEN CACCIATORE

Yields: **8 servings**
Preparation Time: 45 minutes

½ cup olive oil
*½ cup corn oil
½ cup flour
*1 teaspoon salt
½ teaspoon black pepper
*5 pounds chicken pieces (your choice-boned if you prefer)
½ teaspoon rosemary, crumbled
½ cup dry sherry
*½ cup butter
1 bunch green onions, chopped
1 green pepper, sliced
1 cup celery, chopped
2 cloves garlic, crushed
1 pound fresh mushrooms
*4 8-ounce cans tomato sauce
*1 10½-ounce can chicken broth
1 teaspoon anchovy paste
½ cup sliced black olives
1 16-20-ounce package thin spaghetti

1. Heat oils in heavy skillet. Mix flour, salt, and pepper. Dredge chicken in flour and brown on all sides. It takes about 20 minutes. Remove chicken from pan.
2. Reduce oil to ½ cup. Add rosemary and sherry. Simmer 15 minutes. Remove this sauce from pan and set aside.
3. Melt butter in pan. Add onions, green pepper, celery, garlic, and mushrooms. Sauté for 5 minutes. Return chicken to pan.
4. Combine tomato sauce, reserved sherry sauce, chicken broth, anchovy paste, and olives. Pour over chicken in pan. Simmer 1 hour.
5. Serve over hot spaghetti.

May be made earlier in the day and reheated for dinner. Very good the second day.

For A Heart Healthy Recipe Make These Substitutions:

*½ cup safflower oil
* omit salt
* use skinless chicken (your choice-boned if you prefer)
*½ cup corn oleo
*4 8-ounce cans low salt tomato sauce
*1 10½-ounce can low salt chicken broth

BREAST OF CHICKEN LOMBARDY

Yields: **4 servings**
Preparation Time: 30 minutes

4	tablespoons cornstarch
1	teaspoon salt
⅛	teaspoon freshly ground nutmeg
⅛	teaspoon white pepper
4	boneless chicken breasts, skin removed
4	tablespoons butter
2	Delicious apples, cored and sliced
1	ounce Benedictine liqueur
1	cup heavy cream watercress to garnish

1. Combine cornstarch, salt, nutmeg, and pepper. Set aside.

2. Wash and dry chicken breasts with paper towels. Dredge chicken with cornstarch mixture. Shake off excess.

3. In large skillet, melt butter and slowly sauté chicken and apple slices, turning often. Remove apple slices and keep warm.

4. In separate saucepan, warm liqueur. Light with match and pour flaming over the chicken. Tilt pan about as flames die out. Remove chicken to another pan and keep warm.

5. With wire whisk, stir pan drippings and remaining butter. Add heavy cream and continue to stir over medium heat until cream is reduced to desired thickness, about 10 minutes. Adjust seasonings if desired.

6. Arrange chicken on platter, separating pieces with apple slices. Pour over chicken and garnish with watercress. Serve at once.

POULET AU CITRON

*Yields: **4 servings***
Preparation Time: 1 hour

4	pounds chicken pieces (your choice)
½	cup butter
1	tablespoon dry sherry
1	tablespoon white wine
1	large lemon
1	small orange
	salt and pepper to taste
1	cup light cream
¼	cup Swiss or Gruyere cheese

1. Brown chicken in foaming butter. Cover and continue to sauté over slow fire until nearly cooked. Remove chicken and stir in sherry and wine.
2. Grate a few pieces of lemon and orange rind. Add 2 teaspoons of lemon juice from lemon. Season with salt and pepper and stir in rind.
3. Turn up heat and stir in cream slowly. Return chicken to pan and cook a few minutes. Sprinkle with grated cheese. Top with a few thin slices of lemon and orange. Put under the broiler for a few minutes. Serve over rice if desired.

TURKEY MORNAY

*Yields: **6 servings***
Preparation Time: 30 minutes

2	10-ounce packages frozen broccoli
12	large slices cooked turkey breast
2	tablespoons butter or margarine
2	tablespoons all-purpose flour
1	cup evaporated milk
8	ounces Velveeta Cheese, cubed
2	ounces sharp Cheddar cheese, cubed
2	ounces Swiss cheese, cubed
1	cup dry white wine
⅓	cup Parmesan cheese, grated
½	teaspoon paprika

1. Cook broccoli according to package directions. Drain.
2. In a 8″ × 12″ baking dish, lay broccoli in bottom, then turkey slices.
3. Melt butter in saucepan. Add flour and cook until bubbly. Slowly add milk and cook until smooth. Boil 1 minute. Remove from heat.
4. Beat cheese into hot cream mixture. Using an electric mixer, beat for a minimum of 15 minutes. Add wine a little at a time while beating.
5. Pour sauce on top. Sprinkle Parmesan cheese and paprika over top of casserole.
6. Bake in 350° oven for 20 minutes until hot and bubbly.

*Temperature: **350** °*
Time: 20 minutes

CHICKEN MONTEREY

Yields: **6 servings**
Preparation Time: 1 hour

½   cup cottage cheese
1   3-ounce package cream cheese, room temperature
½   cup sour cream
1   teaspoon salt
½   teaspoon garlic powder
1   4-ounce can green chilies
3   cups cooked chicken (leave in large pieces)
3   cups cooked rice (cooked in chicken broth)
1   cup Monterey Jack cheese, grated
2   tomatoes, coarsely chopped
1   10¾-ounce can cream of chicken soup
¾   cup corn chips, coarsely crushed.

1. Blend cottage cheese, cream cheese, and sour cream until smooth.
2. Blend in salt, garlic powder, and green chilies.
3. Add chicken, rice, cheese, tomatoes, and soup. Pour into a shallow 2-quart baking dish. Top with crushed corn chips.
4. Bake in 350° oven for 25 minutes uncovered.

Temperature: **350 °**
Time: 25 minutes

For this special look, serve topped with a slice of avocado and sliced tomato.

SHRIMP BOATS

It's estimated that 8,000,000 pounds of shrimp are caught in Galveston Bay annually. No wonder Galveston, one of this country's oldest shrimp ports, is home base for close to 200 shrimp boats which provide a livelihood for the owners and their families. Most visitors consider the armada of intriguing looking commercial watercraft one of their favorite Galveston island spectacles. Certainly there's always a large audience for the blessing of the shrimp fleet, an aquatic parade of decorated boats that takes place every year on the Sunday nearest April 21, San Jacinto Day.

Seafood & Fish

STUFFED FLOUNDER
Must Make Ahead of Time

*Yields: **6 servings***
Preparation Time: 1½ hours

Stuffing:

½	*medium onion, finely chopped*
¾	*cup butter*
1	*egg, well beaten*
1	*tablespoon water*
1	*teaspoon chopped parsley*
3	*tablespoons sherry*
	salt and pepper to taste
1½	*cup shrimp, cooked, peeled, deveined and cut into bite size pieces*
1½	*cups white lump crabmeat*
	toasted bread crumbs

Assembly:

6	*fresh flounder fillets*
	stuffing
2	*tablespoons paprika*
	butter or margarine for greasing baking dish
2	*teaspoons lemon juice*
½	*cup butter or margarine, melted*

Stuffing:

1. Sauté onion in butter until just transparent. Remove from heat and cool to lukewarm. Add next 5 ingredients and stir thoroughly.
2. Then add shrimp and crabmeat and toss gently. Add toasted bread crumbs to make dressing consistency.

Assembly:

1. Spread stuffing on ½ of each fillet and fold over, fastening with metal skewers.
2. Cover with paprika. Wrap immediately in freezer paper and then waxed paper, tying the ends tightly with string. (Be careful not to tie close to fillet ends, as unwrapping will be a problem.)
3. *Freeze these at least one day prior to serving.*
4. When ready to serve, unwrap fillets and place in well-greased baking dish and bake in preheated oven, basting often with butter, lemon juice, and parsley mixture.

Temperature: 375 °
Time: 25-30 minutes

The short fat flounders are best to use so when stuffed and folded over will fit on the dinner plates.

SNAPPER PONTCHARTRAIN

*Yields: **6-8 servings***
Preparation Time: 20-25 minutes

3-4	pounds fresh snapper fillets
1	tablespoon paprika
1	teaspoon garlic salt
½	teaspoon black pepper
2	tablespoons butter or margarine
½	cup butter, melted
1	tablespoon parsley flakes
3	green onions, chopped
10-15	large fresh mushrooms, sliced
3	garlic cloves, minced
1	tablespoon flour
2	tablespoons Parmesan cheese, grated
½	cup cooking sherry
1	pound small shrimp, cooked, cleaned and deveined
½	pound fresh white crabmeat

1. Season fish fillets with paprika, garlic salt, and pepper. Dot with butter and bake in a large shallow pan in a 350° oven for 15-20 minutes (until barely done).
2. Sauté parsley, onions, and mushrooms in butter. Add garlic cloves and brown slightly. Stir in flour to thicken.
3. Add cheese and sherry. Let simmer until it thickens slightly. Add shrimp and crab and mix well.
4. Pour shrimp mixture over baked fish. Broil until browned (approximately 5 minutes).

*Temperature: **350** °*
Time: 15-20 minutes then

Temperature: Broil
Time: 5 minutes

BAKED FISH WITH GRAPES AND ALMONDS

*Yields: **2-4 servings***
Preparation Time: 30 minutes

1	pound skinned fresh fish fillets
3	tablespoons butter
2	tablespoons flour
¾	cup milk
½	cup white wine
1	teaspoon Dijon mustard
1	can green grapes
1	small package slivered almonds
	salt and pepper

1. Place fish in buttered 9″ × 13″ casserole.
2. Make a white sauce with butter, flour, and milk. When thick, add wine, mustard, and grapes. Spoon over fillets and sprinkle with almonds.
3. Bake in 400° oven for 30 minutes.

*Temperature: **400** °*
Time: 30 minutes

RED SNAPPER MOZART

Yields: **4 servings**
Preparation Time: 30 minutes

4   *red snapper fillets (8-ounces each)*
1   *teaspoon salt*
¼   *teaspoon black pepper*
1   *teaspoon lemon juice*
1   *teaspoon Worcestershire sauce*
    flour to coat
½   *cup butter*

Sauce:

4   *tablespoons butter*
1   *cucumber, peeled and diced*
1   *clove garlic, minced*
    salt and pepper to taste
3   *fresh ripe tomatoes, diced*
1   *lemon (juice of) to taste*
2   *teaspoons Worcestershire sauce*
1   *tablespoon fresh parsley*

1. Marinate snapper in a combination of salt, pepper, lemon juice, and Worcestershire in a baking dish for 30 minutes. Remove fish and dip in flour to coat thoroughly.
2. Melt butter in skillet. Brown snapper slowly on both sides. Transfer fish to a 2-quart flat baking dish and bake in 375° oven for 8 minutes. (Total cooking time for skillet and oven is 12-15 minutes).

Sauce:

1. Melt butter in a skillet and sauté cucumbers and garlic with salt and pepper to taste. After 5 minutes, add tomatoes and sauté for 3 minutes more.
2. Add lemon juice (slowly - checking the taste as you might not want the whole lemon). Add Worcestershire sauce.
3. Pour sauce over snapper fillets and sprinkle with fresh parsley.

Temperature: **375 °**
Time: 8 minutes

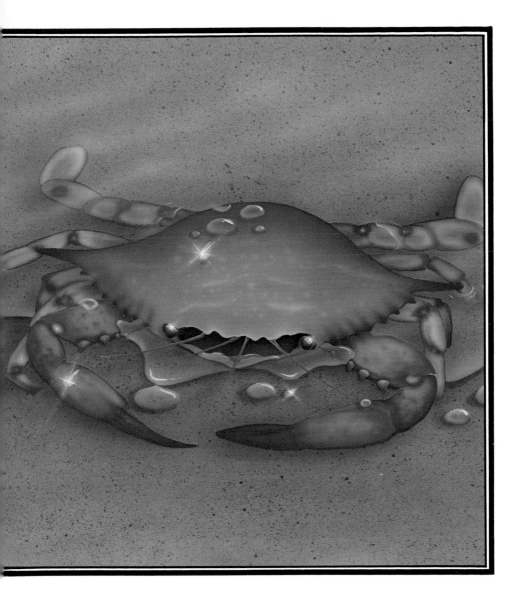

BLUE CRABS

The blue crab exhibits an interesting growth pattern; it alternates between stages of growth and molting until it reaches adult form. The fisherman catches and markets the crab in a soft stage; that's when the crustacean is best for eating. You can catch a blue crab almost anywhere along the rocks or in the surf of Galveston Island. Some people cook the crab while it's still in the shell; others believe the crabmeat should be removed from the shell first. Either procedure is acceptable. The most important rule to remember is to cook the crab as soon as possible since it's a seafood that can spoil quickly.

RED SNAPPER EN PAPILLOTE

Yields: **6 servings**
Preparation Time: 20 minutes

2	pounds Red Snapper Fillets
*¼	cup butter or margarine, melted
*2	teaspoons salt
1	teaspoon paprika
	dash black pepper
1	large green pepper, sliced into rings
1	large onion, sliced into rings
	fresh lemon wedges
1	plastic cooking bag

1. Brush fillets with half the melted butter. Sprinkle with seasoning.
2. Position plastic bag onto a large baking dish (9″ × 13″). Insert remaining butter and vegetables. Place fillets in bag on top of vegetables. Close bag and puncture a few holes according to instructions with bag.
3. Bake in 375° oven for 20-25 minutes. Remove from oven and slit bag and serve directly, or arrange fillets on serving dish and garnish with cooked vegetables and fresh lemon wedges.

Temperature: **375 °**
Time: 20-25 minutes

Other fish fillets may be substituted for the Red Snapper. Also the cooking bag makes this a snap and it looks so pretty when served.

 For A Heart Healthy Recipe Make These Substitutions:

*¼	cup corn oleo, melted
*	omit salt

CURRIED CRABMEAT CREPES

Yields: 12 8" crepes
Preparation Time: 1 hour

Crepe Batter:

2	eggs
1	cup milk
¾	cup flour
	vegetable oil

Crabmeat Filling:

5	tablespoons butter, divided
¼	cup flour
½	teaspoon salt
1½	cups milk
¼-¾	pound fresh crabmeat
1	teaspoon green onion, chopped
½	cup dry white wine
1	teaspoon curry powder
¼	teaspoon Worcestershire sauce
⅛	teaspoon black pepper
1	dash of cayenne
¼	teaspoon salt

Glaze:

1	egg yolk
⅛	teaspoon salt
4	tablespoons butter, melted
2	teaspoons lemon juice
¼	cup heavy cream
	Parmesan cheese, grated

1. Combine eggs, milk, and flour and beat with electric mixer until smooth. Brush crepe pan with oil and pour 1½ tablespoons batter, rotating quickly, to spread batter over bottom of pan.

2. Cook over medium heat until nicely browned on underside; turn; cook until brown on other side. (About 20 seconds on first side, 10-15 on second side. Remove from pan and cool on wire rack. Stack on waxed paper. Repeat with rest of batter. Brush pan with oil on each one.

3. For filling, melt 4 tablespoons of butter in medium saucepan. Remove from heat. Stir in flour and salt. Stir until smooth. Gradually stir in milk, bring to a boil, stirring constantly. Reduce heat, simmer 5 minutes. Remove from heat and set aside.

4. Drain and flake crabmeat. Set aside. Sauté onion in 1 tablespoon butter for 1 minute. Add crabmeat and sauté 2 minutes longer. Add wine, curry powder, Worcestershire, pepper, cayenne, and ¼ teaspoon salt. Cook over medium heat, stirring 3 minutes. Stir in 1 cup of white sauce just until blended.

5. Spoon 1 rounded tablespoon of crabmeat mixture onto each crepe. Fold two opposite sides over filling. Arrange in shallow baking dish. Cover with foil. Bake in 350° oven for 20-25 minutes or until heated through.

6. In small bowl, beat egg yolk for glaze with salt until foamy. Gradu-

ally beat in 2 tablespoons of butter. 7. Mix remaining butter with lemon juice and gradually beat into egg yolk mixture. Fold in remaining white sauce until it is combined. Fold in whipped cream. Spoon glaze over hot crepes, then sprinkle with Parmesan cheese. Broil 4-6 inches from heat, until nicely browned.

Temperature: 350 °
Time: 20-25 minutes

Temperature: Broil
Time: 3-5 minutes

GALVESTON CRAB CAKES

Yields: 6 cakes
Preparation Time: 25 minutes

1	*pound fresh lump crabmeat*
¾	*cup Italian flavored breadcrumbs*
1	*large egg, beaten*
¼	*cup good quality mayonnaise*
1	*teaspoon Worcestershire sauce*
1	*teaspoon dry mustard*
½	*teaspoon salt*
¼	*teaspoon pepper*
½	*teaspoon parsley*
	oil for frying
	lemon wedges (optional)

1. Place crabmeat in large bowl and, without breaking up the lumps too much, carefully remove cartilage and shell.
2. Add breadcrumbs and mix *gently*.
3. In a separate bowl, combine egg, mayonnaise, Worcestershire sauce, mustard, salt, pepper, and parsley. Gently blend with crabmeat mixture.
4. Form mixture into 6 patties.
5. In a large skillet, fry the cakes in oil until golden brown. (About 3 minutes on each side.) Serve with lemon wedges.

May be made ahead of time and reheated. May also be frozen.

CRAB OR SHRIMP MORNAY

Best If Made Ahead Of Time

Yields: **8 servings**
Preparation Time: 45 minutes

½	cup butter
½	cup flour
¼	cup onion, grated
½	cup green onion, chopped
⅛	cup parsley
2	cups heavy cream
1	cup dry white wine
2½	teaspoons salt
½	teaspoon white pepper
¼	teaspoon cayenne pepper
2½	ounces Swiss cheese, grated
8	fresh artichokes, boiled, leaves scraped, bottoms quartered
2	tablespoons fresh lemon juice
2	pounds lump crabmeat or 3 pounds shrimp, boiled and peeled
½	pound fresh mushrooms, sliced thick
3	tablespoons Romano cheese, grated

1. In a 2-quart saucepan, melt butter. Stir in flour and cook 5 minutes over medium heat, stirring often. Add onions and cook 2-3 minutes without browning.

2. Stir in parsley. Gradually add cream and allow to get hot. Then add wine, salt, white pepper, and cayenne. Blend well and bring to a simmer, stirring occasionally.

3. Add Swiss cheese. Stir, cover, remove from heat, and allow to cool. When sauce has cooled to lukewarm, stir in scrapings from artichoke leaves and lemon juice.

4. In a 3-quart casserole, make alternate layers of crabmeat (or shrimp), quartered artichoke bottoms, sliced raw mushrooms, and sauce (using sauce between layers and on top).

5. Sprinkle with Romano cheese over all. Cover and refrigerate until ready to bake. (Allow casserole to reach room temperature before heating.)

6. Bake uncovered in 350° oven for 30-45 minutes. If top is not brown, turn under broiler and brown 3-5 minutes.

Temperature: **350 °**
Time: 30-45 minutes

May use canned artichoke bottoms rather than fresh artichokes.

CRAB SMOTHERED SHRIMP

Yields: **4-6 servings**
Preparation Time: 30 minutes

2	dozen fresh jumbo shrimp, shelled and deveined
*2	tablespoons butter or margarine
1	small onion, finely minced
½	cup green pepper, finely minced
1	tablespoon parsley, chopped
*1	pound fresh white crabmeat
*1	teaspoon salt
1	teaspoon Worcestershire sauce
¼	teaspoon thyme
1	dash of Tabasco
½	cup seasoned bread crumbs
*1	egg, beaten
*1	cup light cream
*½	cup butter (DO NOT SUBSTITUTE)
2	cloves garlic, minced
	paprika

1. Split the raw shrimp lengthwise so they can be opened flat, but DO NOT CUT ALL THE WAY THROUGH.

2. Spread the shirmp flat in a 9" × 13" shallow baking dish and set aside.

3. In medium skillet, melt 2 tablespoons butter. Sauté onion, celery, and green pepper until onion is transparent. Remove from heat.

4. Add parsley. Toss this mixture with crabmeat. Add seasonings, breadcrumbs, egg, and cream. Toss gently but thoroughly. Mound crab mixture on shrimp. Pour ½ cup butter over all.

5. Sprinkle top with paprika and bake in 400° oven for 20 minutes.

Temperature: **400 °**
Time: 20 minutes

For A Heart Healthy Recipe Make These Substitutions:

*2	tablespoons corn oleo
*1	pound Crabmeat Delight
*	omit salt
*¼	cup cholesterol free egg substitute
*1	cup skim evaporated milk
*½	cup corn oleo (DOES NOT CHANGE TASTE)

W.F.C.C. WORLD'S FINEST CRAB CASSEROLE

"The Name Says It All"

Yields: 8-10 servings
Preparation Time: 30 minutes

2	cups medium white sauce
2	tablespoons Worcestershire sauce
1	teaspoon Tabasco
	salt
	lemon pepper
¼	cup butter or margarine, divided
½	green pepper, minced
1	cup celery, minced
1	large onion, minced
2	cloves garlic, minced
½	pound fresh mushrooms, sliced
¼	cup dry sherry
1	lemon (juice of)
2	pounds of fresh lump crabmeat
½	cup fresh parsley, chopped
1	cup medium or sharp Cheddar cheese, grated
1	cup Parmesan cheese, grated divided
1	cup saltine cracker crumbs, crushed
1½	teaspoons paprika

1. Make white sauce (using your own recipe). Flavor with Worcestershire sauce, salt, and pepper.
2. In medium skillet, melt 2 tablespoons of butter. Sauté green pepper, celery, onion, and garlic. Add this mixture to cream sauce.
3. Sauté mushrooms in another 2 tablespoons of butter. Mix this also with cream sauce.
4. Add sherry, lemon juice, crabmeat, parsley, cheddar cheese, and ½ cup Parmesan cheese to cream sauce. Mix thoroughly but gently.
5. Pour into greased 9" × 13" casserole. Sprinkle top with Parmesan cheese and cracker crumbs. Top with paprika.
6. Bake in 350° oven for 45 minutes or until bubbly.

Temperature: 350 °
Time: 45 minutes

If you prefer a hotter flavor, add more Tabasco. Shrimp may be substituted for crab.

SEAFOOD CASSEROLE

Yields: 4
Preparation Time: 30 minutes

1	cup Pepperidge Farm cornbread stuffing mix
¾	cup green pepper, chopped
¾	cup onion, chopped
2	cups celery, chopped
2	cups fresh crabmeat
1	cup shrimp, cooked, cleaned, and deveined
1	cup good quality mayonnaise
2	tablespoons butter or margarine
¼	cup dry bread crumbs

1. Prepare stuffing mix according to package directions.
2. Add green pepper, onion, and celery. Mix well.
3. Add crabmeat, shrimp and mayonnaise. Mix well again.
4. Transfer to a 2½-quart casserole dish. Mix butter and bread crumbs. Sprinkle on top of casserole.
5. Bake in 325° oven for 30 minutes.

Temperature: 325 °
Time: 30 minutes

CRAB STUFFED POTATOES

Yields: 6 servings
Preparation Time: 1 hour

6	medium baking potatoes
½	cup butter, softened
½	cup light cream
1	teaspoon salt
⅛	teaspoon white pepper
3½	teaspoons onion, grated
1	cup sharp Cheddar cheese, grated
½	pound fresh lump crabmeat
½	teaspoon paprika

1. Scrub potatoes and bake for 30 minutes. Pierce potatoes with fork and turn over. Bake another 20-30 minutes or until done. Remove from oven and cool briefly.
2. Cut each potato in half lengthwise and scoop potato from the skin into a medium-size mixing bowl.
3. Add butter, cream, salt, pepper, and onion. Whip with electric mixer until smooth. Fold in cheese and crabmeat.
4. Fill each potato half with mixture, mounding slightly. Sprinkle with paprika.
5. Bake in 450° oven for 15 minutes.

Temperature: 450 °
Time: 15 minutes

MEETING STREET CRAB AND SHRIMP

Yields: **8-10 servings**
Preparation Time: 45 minutes

¼   cup butter
¼   cup all-purpose flour
1   cup light cream
¼   cup plus 2 tablespoons dry sherry
½   teaspoon salt
¼   teaspoon black pepper
1   pound fresh crabmeat, cartilage and shell removed
1   pound shrimp, cooked, cleaned and deveined
½   pound sharp Cheddar cheese, grated

1. Melt butter in medium saucepan. Add flour and blend in thoroughly. Gradually add the cream, stirring constantly over medium heat until thickened.
2. Add sherry and spices. Mix well. Remove from heat. Add crab and shrimp and mix thoroughly.
3. Pour into 1½-quart buttered casserole. Top with grated cheese.
4. Bake in 350° oven for 30 minutes.

Temperature: **350 °**
Time: 30 minutes

May be made the night before. DO NOT freeze.

LINGUINI WITH WHITE CLAM SAUCE

Yields: **4 servings**
Preparation Time: 15 minutes

1   medium onion, chopped
1   clove garlic, finely chopped
3   tablespoons butter or margarine
1   tablespoon flour
3   6½-ounce cans of minced clams
½   teaspoon salt
½   teaspoon dried basil leaves
⅛   teaspoon pepper
1   tablespoon salt
3   quarts water
1   8-ounce package linguini
¼   cup fresh parsley, snipped
     Parmesan cheese, grated

1. In large skillet, cook onions and garlic in butter until onion is tender. Stir in flour.
2. Add clams (plus liquid), ½ teaspoon salt, basil, and pepper. Heat to boiling. Reduce heat. Cover and simmer five minutes.
3. In a 4-quart saucepan, bring water to a boil. Add 1 tablespoon salt. Add linguini gradually.
4. Boil linguini, stirring occasionally until tender (approximately 7-10 minutes).
5. Drain quickly in colander or sieve.
6. Add parsley to clam sauce. Serve over hot linguini. Sprinkle with Parmesan cheese.

LOBSTER THERMIDOR

*Yields: **4 servings***
*Preparation Time: **45 minutes***

2	*6-ounce lobster tails or 1 large 12-ounce tail*
4	*tablespoons butter*
½	*pound fresh mushrooms, sliced*
4	*tablespoons flour*
1	*teaspoon dry mustard*
1	*teaspoon salt*
	dash of cayenne pepper
⅛	*teaspoon nutmeg*
1	*cup milk*
1	*cup light cream*
2	*egg yolks, slightly beaten*
1	*tablespoon lemon juice*
3	*tablespoons dry sherry*
½	*cup plain dry bread crumbs*
2	*tablespoons fresh Parmesan cheese, grated (do not use canned)*
2	*tablespoons melted butter*

1. Cook lobster by placing in 3-quart saucepan and cover with water. Bring to a boil and cook for 5 minutes. Simmer 15 minutes.
2. Remove immediately and run it under cold water to stop the cooking process.
3. Dice lobster and set aside.
4. Melt the 4 tablespoons of butter. Sauté mushrooms until brown. Remove mushrooms and set aside. Blend in flour, mustard, salt, cayenne, and nutmeg. Gradually stir in milk and cream. Cook and stir over medium heat until mixture thickens and comes to a boil.
5. Stir 2 tablespoons of this mixture into egg yolks. Add egg yolk mixture to sauce and remove from heat. Add mushrooms to sauce. Stir in lemon juice, sherry, and lobster meat.
6. Pour into individual ramekins or into a 10″ × 10″casserole.
7. Combine bread crumbs, cheese, and melted butter. Sprinkle over all.
8. Bake in a 400° oven for 15 minutes.

*Temperature: **400** °*
*Time: **15 minutes***

If using a large casserole, serve over white rice or in pastry shells.

BUTTERED LOBSTER WITH BACON

Yields: **4 servings**
Preparation Time: 25 minutes

*4 frozen lobster tails
*½ cup butter
5 green onions, chopped
*3 strips of bacon, fried and crumbled
4 ounces fresh mushrooms, sliced
4 cloves garlic, finely chopped
1 teaspoon Worcestershire sauce
* seasoned salt to taste
*¼ cup fresh Parmesan cheese, grated

1. Place lobster tails in boiling water to cover tails. Boil 12-15 minutes. Remove from water, cool and then remove meat from tails and cube.
2. Melt butter. Sauté onions and garlic until soft. Add mushrooms, Worcestershire, and seasoned salt. Simmer 5 minutes.
3. Meanwhile, fry bacon. Drain and crumble.
4. Place cubed lobster in a shallow 2 quart baking dish. Pour butter mixture over lobster. Top with Parmesan cheese. Bake in 350° oven for 20 minutes.
5. Remove from oven and add crumbled bacon. Bake 5 minutes more.

Temperature: **350** °
Time: 20 minutes
Temperature: **350** °
Time: 5 minutes

For A Heart Healthy Recipe Make These Substitutions:

* may use equal amount Louis Kemp Lobster Delight
*½ cup corn oleo
*3 strips cholesterol free breakfast strips, fried and crumbled
* omit salt
*¼ cup fresh (a must) Parmesan cheese, grated

SHRIMP AND OYSTER JAMBALAYA

Yields: *6 servings*
Preparation Time: 1½ hours

1	pound medium shrimp, shelled and deveined
1	dozen large oysters
½	cup butter, margarine or vegetable oil
1	cup white onions, finely chopped
½	cup celery, chopped
½	cup green pepper, chopped
4	cloves garlic, minced
2	teaspoons tomato paste
2	cups water, divided
½	teaspoon salt
¼	teaspoon black pepper dash of cayenne pepper
1	teaspoon sugar
½	teaspoon cornstarch
4	cups cooked rice
½	cup green onions (tops only), finely chopped

1. Chop shrimp and oysters into bite-size pieces and set aside.

2. In large skillet, heat butter or oil. Add white onions, celery, pepper, and garlic. Cook uncovered over medium heat until onions are transparent. Add tomato paste and cook, stirring constantly for about 15 minutes.

3. Add 1½ cups water. Stir until well blended. Season with salt, pepper, and cayenne. Adjust seasonings to desired taste.

4. Add sugar and heat covered over medium heat 40 minutes or until oil floats to the top. Spoon off the excess oil.

5. Add shrimp and oysters. Cook 20 minutes.

6. Dissolve cornstarch in ½ cup water. Add to shrimp mixture. Cook 5 minutes.

7. Stir in cooked rice, green onion tops, and parsley. Mix thoroughly. Simmer until ready to serve

Can make early in the day and heat when ready to serve. Serve with green salad and hot rolls.

FRENCH BROILED OYSTERS

Yields: **4 servings**
Preparation Time: 15 minutes

1   quart fresh oysters
1   cup flour
1   cup butter
2   lemons (juice of)
2   tablespoons Worcestershire
    sauce

1. Dredge oysters in flour. Melt butter in large skillet. Sauté oysters until just slightly curled (about 1 minute).
2. Combine lemon juice and Worcestershire sauce. Sprinkle over oysters. Turn oysters. Sprinkle again with sauce. Cook another minute or two.
3. Serve hot.

Can be kept warmed until serving time in a chafing dish. Great also for cocktail parties.

CHARCOALED PAELLA ON A STICK

Yields: **6-8 servings**
Preparation Time: 1½ hours

1½ pounds sirloin tips
4   boned chicken breasts
2   links smoked sausage
2   green bell peppers
40 shrimp, peeled
2   boxes whole, fresh
    mushrooms
2   packages boiling onions
20 small oysters

Sauce:

½   cup olive oil
½   cup butter
2   tablespoons garlic powder
1   tablespoon black pepper
2   tablespoons lemon juice

Serve over saffron rice.

1. Cube sirloin tip steaks, chicken breasts, sausage, and bell pepper.
2. Place on skewers in this order: sausage, chicken, pepper, shrimp, mushroom, onion, oyster, pepper, and steak, etc.
3. Place skewers over charcoal grill. Baste with sauce made of butter, olive oil, garlic powder, pepper, and lemon juice, that has been previously warmed.
4. Cook 45 minutes to 1 hour. Baste and turn frequently.

charcoal grill
Time: 45 minutes—1 hour

OYSTERS BIENVILLE

Yields: 1 dozen
Preparation Time: 25 minutes

1   *dozen oysters on half shell*
      rock salt
1   *bunch green onions, finely*
      chopped
1   *tablespoon butter*
1   *tablespoon flour*
½   *cup chicken broth*
½   *cup shrimp, cooked and*
      chopped
⅓   *cup fresh mushrooms,*
      chopped and drained
1   *egg yolk*
⅓-½ *cup dry white wine*
      salt and pepper to taste
1   *cup buttered breadcrumbs*

1. Bake oysters on a tray covered with rock salt in a 350° oven for 6-8 minutes (until partly done). Set aside.
2. Sauté onions in butter until brown. Add flour and stir until brown. Add chicken broth, shrimp, and mushrooms.
3. Beat egg yolk with wine and slowly add to sauce. Season to taste with salt and pepper. Simmer for 10 minutes.
4. Spoon mixture on top of oysters. Sprinkle lightly with buttered bread crumbs. Bake in 350° oven for 10 minutes or until bubbly and brown.

*Temperature: **350** °*
Time: 6-8 minutes
*Temperature: **350** °*
Time: 10 minutes

BAKED OYSTERS

Yields: **2 servings**
Preparation Time: 15 minutes

1   *dozen large oysters*
2   *cups Progresso Italian*
     Flavored Bread Crumbs
½   *teaspoon garlic salt*
½   *teaspoon onion salt*
     dash cayenne pepper
½   *cup butter or margarine,*
     divided

1. Pat oysters dry with paper towel.
2. Combine bread crumbs and seasonings. Dip oysters in bread crumbs. Let set 5-10 minutes.
3. Place on greased cookie sheet. Melt butter. Dribble butter over oysters and bake in 400° oven for 12-15 minutes. Baste a couple of times while cooking.
4. Serve with rest of butter on the side for dipping.

Temperature: **400 °**
Time: 12-15 minutes

The amount of oysters is an arbitrary amount. If you would eat more than 6 apiece, just use more bread crumbs and butter.

SHRIMP CREOLE

Yields: **4 servings**
Preparation Time: 30 minutes

⅓   *cup shortening*
¼   *cup flour*
1   *cup hot water*
1   *8-ounce can tomato sauce*
1   *pound medium shrimp,*
     cleaned and deveined
½   *cup green onions and tops,*
     chopped
4   *cloves garlic, pressed*
½   *cup fresh parsley, chopped*
¼   *cup green pepper, chopped*
1½   *teaspoon salt*
2   *whole bay leaves*
½   *teaspoon crushed thyme*
1   *lemon slice*
     cayenne pepper
2-3 *cups cooked rice (prepared*
     according to package
     directions)

1. In a large skillet, melt shortening. Blend in flour, stirring constantly until mixture is brown (about 5-10 minutes). Add water and cook until thick, stirring constantly.
2. Add tomato sauce and mix thoroughly.
3. Add remaining ingredients, using cayenne pepper to personal taste. Serve over rice.

SEAFOOD LA JOLLA
"Absolutely Superb"

Yields: 8 servings
Preparation Time: 2-3 hours

2-2½ *pounds scallops*
2-2½ *pounds fresh shrimp*
2   *cups Chablis wine*
¼   *cup fresh lemon juice*
1   *pound fresh mushrooms,*
      sliced
2   *green peppers, diced*
6   *tablespoons butter*
¾   *teaspoon salt*
      dash pepper to taste
6-7   *tablespoons flour*
3   *cups Swiss cheese, grated*
1   *cup Romano or Parmesan*
      cheese, grated, or ½ cup each
½-1   *pint heavy cream, whipped*
      butter for topping
      paprika

1. Wash and drain scallops. Clean and devein shrimp. Bring wine and lemon juice to boil. Add scallops, shrimp, mushrooms, and green peppers. (If needed, use additional wine to be sure that ingredients are just barely covered.) Simmer slowly for 6-8 minutes. Drain and save liquid.

2. Melt butter. Blend in flour until bubbly and smooth. Gradually blend in 2 cups of reserved liquid. Stir constantly and cook over medium heat until sauce is smooth and thickened.

3. Add salt, pepper, Swiss cheese, and ½ cup Parmesan cheese or Romano cheese. Stir over lowest heat until well blended. Remove from heat and cool to room temperature.

4. Whip cream until very stiff and fold into cooled sauce. Stir in shrimp and scallop mixture. If using large shrimp, cut in half.

5. Divide mixture into individual ramekins. Top with remaining cheese. Dot with butter. Sprinkle with paprika if desired.

6. If serving immediately, brown under broiler until brown and bubbly. If serving later in the day, bake in 350° oven for 20 minutes or until thoroughly heated and bubbly.

Temperature: 350 °
Time: 20 minutes

This is best served with just a fruit salad and garlic bread. Freezes very well.

175

COQUILLES ST. JACQUES

Yields: **4 servings**
Preparation Time: *45 minutes*

½   cup dry sherry
1½ cups water
1   pound bay scallops washed
    (if you use sea scallops,
    quarter them)
½   teaspoon salt
⅛   teaspoon black pepper
1   medium onion, chopped
1   tablespoon parsley
2½ tablespoons butter
    juice of ½ a lemon
½   pound fresh mushrooms,
    sliced
2   tablespoons flour
½   cup heavy cream, heated
    paprika

1. Bring sherry and ½ cup water to a boil in a 2-quart saucepan.
2. Add scallops, salt, and pepper. Poach for 5-7 minutes. Remove scallops to 2-quart casserole or individual ramekins. Reserve liquid.
3. Sauté onion and parsley in ½ tablespoon butter 5-7 minutes. Boil remaining cup of water. Add lemon juice and mushrooms. Simmer for 5 minutes. Drain.
4. Melt remaining butter. Add the flour, stirring constantly and cook for 1-2 minutes. With a wire whisk, blend in reserved poaching liquid and cook until sauce thickens.
5. Add onions, parsley, mushrooms, and hot cream. Season to taste if necessary. Pour sauce over scallops and sprinkle with paprika.
6. Cover and refrigerate or bake immediately in 350° oven for 25-30 minutes.

Temperature: **350 °**
Time: *25-30 minutes*

SHRIMP FLORENTINE

*Yields: **4-6 servings***
Preparation Time: 1 hour

3   *10-ounce packages frozen chopped spinach*
2   *tablespoons onion, grated*
1   *lemon (juice of)*
    salt and pepper to taste
2   *pounds shrimp, cooked, cleaned, and deveined*
    Parmesan cheese, grated

Cream Sauce:

6   *tablespoons butter*
¼   *cup flour*
2   *cups heavy cream*
2   *cloves garlic, minced*
1   *tablespoon Worcestershire sauce*
3   *drops Tabasco*
¼   *teaspoon paprika*
1   *tablespoon dry sherry*

1. Cook spinach as directed on package. Drain and squeeze dry. Season with onion, lemon, salt, and pepper. Set aside.
2. In a saucepan, combine butter, flour, and cream. Blend in garlic, Worcestershire sauce, Tabasco, paprika, and sherry. Stir until thickened.
3. In a shallow casserole, layer shrimp, spinach, and cream sauce alternately. Sprinkle cheese on top. Bake in 325° oven for 30 minutes.

*Temperature: **325** °*
*Time: **30 minutes***

Can be made a day ahead or frozen for later use.

GALVESTON SHRIMP CREOLE

*Yields: **4-6 servings***
Preparation Time: 1 hour

3   *tablespoons butter or margarine*
1   *green pepper, chopped*
1   *large onion, chopped*
½   *pound fresh okra, cut in bite size pieces*
1   *10-ounce can chicken broth*
2½   *cups stewed tomatoes*
1½   *pounds shrimp*
    salt
    black pepper
    cayenne pepper
3-4   *cups white rice, cooked*

1. Melt butter in heavy (4-6 quart) iron pot or heavy saucepan. Sauté vegetables until onion is transparent.
2. Add chicken broth, plus 2 soup cans of water. Add stewed tomatoes and stir thoroughly. Adjust seasonings to taste. Simmer for 1½ hours.
3. Add shrimp and cook for 15 minutes. Remove from stove and let cool. Adjust seasonings again if desired.
4. When ready to serve, reheat but do not boil. Serve over white rice.

Freezes very well.

SHRIMP DE JONGHE

Yields: **4-6 servings**
Preparation Time: 1 hour

2 **pounds large shrimp, peeled and deveined**
¼ **cup dry white wine**
   white pepper
4 **tablespoons butter, softened**
4 **slices French bread, finely crumbled**
2 **cloves garlic, crushed**
4 **tablespoons green onion tops**
¼ **teaspoon salt**

1. Place raw shrimp in a flat 9" × 13" baking dish.
2. Sprinkle with white wine and white pepper over all.
3. Combine butter and crumbled bread. Add rest of ingredients.
4. Distribute butter mixture evenly over the shrimp.
5. Bake in 350° oven for 20 minutes.

Temperature: **350 °**
Time: 20 minutes

SEAFOOD STUFFED BELL PEPPERS

Yields: **4-6 servings**
Preparation Time: 30 minutes

8 **medium size bell peppers**
½ **cup butter or margarine**
½ **cup onions, chopped**
½ **cup celery, chopped**
1 **teaspoon tomato paste**
½ **pound shrimp, peeled and deveined**
1 **cup raw rice, cooked according to package directions**
1 **cup fresh crabmeat**
   salt and pepper to taste
   cayenne pepper to taste
½ **cup dry bread crumbs**
3 **tablespoons butter, melted**

1. Remove tops and centers from bell peppers and put in cold water. Bring to a boil and boil for ten minutes. Drain and set aside.
2. Melt ½ cup butter. Sauté onions and celery until soft. Add tomato paste and mix well. Add shrimp and cook 6 minutes or until shrimp are almost cooked.
3. Add rice, crabmeat, and seasonings. Mix thoroughly. Fill each pepper with mixture. Cover with bread crumbs and dribble butter on top.
4. Bake uncovered in 350° oven for about 15 minutes.

Temperature: **350 °**
Time: 15 minutes

SNOWFLAKE SHRIMP AND SAUCE

Yields: **6 servings**
Preparation Time: 1 hour

Must Make Ahead Of Time

Batter:

1   egg, beaten
¼   cup milk
¼   cup water
½   cup flour
⅛   teaspoon salt
1   tablespoon butter, melted

Shrimp:

2½   cups vegetable oil
1½   pounds medium shrimp,
     peeled and deveined
1   7-ounce can unsweetened
     flaked coconut

Sauce:

½   cup orange marmalade
2   tablespoons dry sherry
1   tablespoon horseradish
1-2 drops Tabasco, optional

1. In a small bowl, combine beaten egg with liquids a little at a time, beating well after each addition. Stir in flour and salt and blend until smooth. Stir in butter. Cover and refrigerate at least 2 hours.
2. Heat oil in large skillet over medium heat until very hot. (You want the oil to be about 1½ inches thick. So depending on the size of your skillet, you may need more oil).
3. Coat shrimp with batter and roll in coconut. Fry in batches until golden about 2-3 minutes. Remove and drain on paper towels.
4. Place marmalade in blender and mix until smooth. Pour into small saucepan. Stir in sherry, horseradish, and Tabasco. Blend well. Warm gently over low heat. Serve warm or cool with shrimp.

CHILI FLAVORED SHRIMP

Yields: **6 servings**
Preparation Time: 5 minutes

½   cup butter, melted (no
     substitutes)
1   tablespoon chili powder
¼   teaspoon garlic powder
1   pound medium sized shrimp,
     cleaned and deveined
     bacon slices

1. In a medium size mixing bowl, combine butter, chili powder, and garlic powder. Mix well.
2. Dip shrimp into mixture and wrap each with ¼ slice of bacon. Secure with toothpick.
3. Cook on barbeque grill, 5 minutes on each side.

SHRIMP ARTICHOKE SPECIAL

Yields: **6-8 servings**
Preparation Time: 30-40 minutes

2   **15-ounce cans artichoke hearts**
3   **pounds shrimp, cooked, cleaned, and deveined**
½   **pound fresh mushrooms, sliced**
1   **tablespoon butter**
2   **tablespoons Worcestershire sauce**
½   **cup dry sherry**
½   **cup fresh Parmesan cheese, grated**
     paprika

White Sauce:

6   **tablespoons butter**
6   **tablespoons flour**
3   **cups milk**
¾   **teaspoon salt**
¼   **teaspoon white pepper**

1. Arrange artichoke hearts in a buttered 3-quart casserole. Layer shrimp and mushrooms on top.
2. Add Worcestershire and sherry to white sauce. Pour this over all in baking dish. Sprinkle with Parmesan cheese on top. Sprinkle lightly with paprika.
3. Bake in 375° oven 35-40 minutes.

Sauce:

1. Melt butter in saucepan. Gradually blend in flour. Slowly add milk and cook, stirring constantly, until mixture thickens. Season with salt and pepper.

Temperature: **375 °**
Time: **35-40 minutes**

SHRIMP VICTORIA

Yields: **4-6 servings**
Preparation Time: 30 minutes

1½   **pounds raw shrimp, peeled and deveined**
1   **small onion, finely chopped**
¼   **cup green pepper, finely chopped**
½   **pound fresh mushrooms or 2 4-ounce cans sliced mushrooms**
½   **cup butter or margarine**
2   **tablespoons flour**
¼   **teaspoon salt**
     dash cayenne pepper
2   **cups sour cream**
3   **cups cooked rice**

1. Sauté shrimp, onion, green pepper, and mushrooms in butter for 10 minutes or until tender.
2. Sprinkle with flour, salt, and pepper. Stir in sour cream and cook gently for 10 minutes. Do not boil.
3. Serve over rice.

HERBED SHRIMP

*Yields: **4-6 servings***
Preparation Time: 1 hour

36   *large shrimp, cleaned and deveined*
1   *teaspoon salt*
1   *teaspoon oregano*
1   *teaspoon thyme*
8   *tablespoons of butter, divided*
4   *cloves of garlic, crushed*
1   *tablespoon parsley, minced*
¼   *pound fresh mushrooms, sliced*

1. Toss shrimp with salt, oregano, and thyme in a large bowl. Chill for at least 20 minutes in the refrigerator.
2. Cream 4 tablespoons of the butter with garlic and parsley. Set aside.
3. In a small skillet, melt the other 4 tablespoons of butter. Sauté mushrooms until softened.
4. Divide shrimp into 4 individual ramekins or shells. Top with mushrooms. Dot each ramekin with garlic butter.
5. Bake in 375° oven for 15-20 minutes.

*Temperature: **375** °*
Time: 15-20 minutes

CHARCOALED SHRIMP

Must Make Ahead Of Time

*Yields: **4 servings***
Preparation Time: 30 minutes

1¼   *pounds large shrimp (allow approximately 12 per person)*
1   *8-ounce bottle Italian salad dressing*
3-4   *cloves garlic*
   paprika

1. Clean shrimp. Place in a large shallow baking dish and pour Italian dressing over until shrimp are covered. Add garlic cloves. Chill for 2-24 hours.
2. Place shrimp on metal skewers. Sprinkle with paprika.
3. When coals are very hot, cook shrimp approximately 7-8 minutes on each side. The cooking depends on the size of the shrimp.
4. You may serve immediately or you can put them back into dish with marinade and place in oven to keep warm.

The paprika will make them brown nicely.

SHRIMP AND OYSTER CASSEROLE

Yields: **4**
Preparation Time: 25 minutes

1   **pound medium shrimp, cleaned and deveined**
1½   **pints oysters, drained (optional)**
½   **pound fresh mushrooms, sliced**
½   **cup butter or margarine**
1   **10¾-ounce can cream of shrimp soup**
1   **10¾-ounce can golden mushroom soup**
¼   **cup dry white wine**
1   **cup dry bread crumbs**
2   **tablespoons butter or margarine**
2   **tablespoons Parmesan cheese**

1. Sauté shrimp, oysters, and mushrooms in ½ cup butter until shrimp are a light pink. Remove from heat. Drain off any excess butter.
2. Combine soups and wine. Add to shrimp mixture. Blend thoroughly. Pour into a 2-quart baking dish.
3. Combine 2 tablespoons butter, bread crumbs, and cheese. Sprinkle on top of shrimp mixture.
4. Bake in 350° oven for 30 minutes.

Temperature: **350 °**
Time: **30 minutes**

You may eliminate oysters and add another pound of shrimp. This can be easily doubled, but don't double the wine, use ⅓ cup.

SHRIMP SCAMPI

Yields: **2 servings**
Preparation Time: 30 minutes

¾-1 **pound medium size fresh shrimp, shelled and deveined**
6   **tablespoons butter**
1   **tablespoon green onion, minced**
1   **tablespoon olive oil or vegetable oil**
4-5 **cloves garlic, minced**
2   **teaspoons lemon juice**
¼   **teaspoon salt**
2   **tablespoons minced parsley**
¼   **teaspoon lemon peel**
     dash of Tabasco

1. Pat shrimp dry with paper towel and set aside.
2. Melt butter in a wide frying pan over medium heat. Stir in green onion, oil, garlic, lemon juice, and salt.
3. Cook until bubbly. Add shrimp to pan and cook, stirring occasionally until shrimp turns pink (4-5 minutes).
4. Stir in parsley, lemon peel and Tabasco.
5. Serve with rice.

SHRIMP AND WILD RICE

Yields: **4 servings**
Preparation Time: 45 minutes

½   cup onion, thinly sliced
½   cup mushrooms, sliced
¼   cup butter or margarine
1   tablespoon Worcestershire sauce
    Tabasco to taste
2   cups cooked wild rice (or 2 cups cooked long grain and wild rice)
1   pound shrimp, cooked, cleaned, and deveined
2   cups thin cream sauce
2   tablespoons butter or margarine
2   tablespoons flour
2   cups chicken broth

1. Sauté onions and mushrooms in ¼ cup butter until soft.
2. Add Worcestershire, Tabasco, rice, and shrimp. Set aside.
3. Melt 2 tablespoons butter. Blend in flour, stirring well. Slowly add broth—stirring well. Cook over medium heat, stirring constantly, until of a thin sauce consistency (not real watery).
4. Add cream sauce to shrimp mixture. Pour into 2-quart buttered casserole.
5. Bake in 300° for 20 to 25 minutes (until hot and bubbly).

*Temperature: **300** °*
Time: 20 to 25 minutes

MR. MOORE'S SHRIMP PIE

Yields: **4 servings**
Preparation Time: 30 minutes

1¼   pounds fresh shrimp
2   teaspoons crushed red pepper
2   whole bay leaves
2   teaspoons salt
1   cup toasted bread crumbs, divided
½   cup butter, melted, divided
1   egg, beaten
¼   teaspoon Tabasco
1   tablespoon Worcestershire sauce
½   cup milk
2   teaspoons dry mustard
     salt and pepper to taste

1. Cook shrimp in boiling water to which you have added red pepper, bay leaves, and salt. Boil 1 minute. Drain, peel, and devein.
2. Combine 4 tablespoons of the butter with egg and milk. Set aside.
3. Combine ½ cup bread crumbs, shrimp and spices. Mix together the egg mixture with the shrimp. Place in a greased shallow 2-quart baking dish. Top with remaining crumbs and butter.
4. Bake in 350° oven for 25-30 minutes or until crisp and brown.

*Temperature: **350** °*
Time: 25-30 minutes

SHRIMP SUPREME
"A Lovely Stroganoff Flavor"

Yields: **4 servings**
Preparation Time: **20 minutes**

1	medium onion, finely chopped
1	clove garlic, crushed
*1	tablespoon butter or margarine
*¼	cup ketchup
*2	cups cooked shrimp
*½	teaspoon salt
1	10¾-ounce can cream of mushroom soup
½	pound fresh mushrooms, sliced and stems removed
½	teaspoon black pepper
*1	cup sour cream
	hot cooked rice

1. Sauté onion and garlic in butter or margarine. Cook until onions are tender.
2. Stir in ketchup, shrimp, salt, soup, mushrooms, and pepper. Mix thoroughly. Simmer for 15 minutes.
3. Stir in sour cream. Heat thoroughly—but DO NOT bring to a boil.
4. Serve over hot cooked rice.

 For A Heart Healthy Recipe Make These Substitutions:

*1	tablespoon corn oleo
*¼	cup low calorie ketchup
*2	cups cooked imitation shrimp
*	omit salt
*	use Mock Sour Cream Recipe, page 224

TRUEHEART-ADRIANCE BUILDING

In 1882 the Trueheart-Adriance Building, a design of famed architect Nicholas Clayton, was opened on Galveston's 22nd Street just a half a block from the primary mercantile avenue the Strand. By purchasing the building and then refurbishing it, the Junior League of Galveston, Inc. initiated the historical restoration of that important section of the city. The Trueheart-Adriance Building boasts an exceptionally illustrious history since during its lifetime it housed the state's first and largest real estate firm and one of the city's oldest and most respected law offices.

Great Accompaniments

SCALLOPED ARTICHOKES

Yields: 4 servings
Preparation Time: 15 minutes

1	small onion, finely chopped
½	medium green pepper, finely chopped
2	tablespoons vegetable oil
8	artichoke hearts
1	egg
¾	cup sour cream
⅛	teaspoon thyme
⅛	teaspoon sweet basil or rosemary
¼	teaspoon salt
¼	teaspoon Tabasco (optional)
10	small butter crackers

1. Cook onion and green pepper in oil until tender.
2. Turn into 1½-quart casserole dish and add artichokes.
3. Beat egg slightly and combine with sour cream.
4. Add seasonings and pour over artichoke mixture.
5. Crush crackers and sprinkle on top.
6. Bake in 350° oven for 20-25 minutes.

Temperature: 350 °
Time: 20-25 minutes

STUFFED ARTICHOKES

Yields: 4 servings
Preparation Time: 20 minutes

4	fresh artichokes
1½	cups dry bread crumbs
½	cup fresh Parmesan or Romano cheese, grated
1½	tablespoons garlic powder
1	teaspoon salt
2	tablespoons dry parsley
½	teaspoon black pepper
1-1½	cups olive oil

1. Wash artichokes and cut all pointed tips — straight across as many leaves as possible. Do not remove center, but cut stem off so artichoke sits flat on the bottom.
2. Combine all dry ingredients. Mix well. Fill as many leaves as possible with mixture and place in large roasting pan.
3. Pour olive oil over all of the artichokes and fill pan with 1-1½ inches of water.
4. Cover tightly and steam in 350° oven 1-1½ hours or until leaves open and can be easily pulled off.
5. Baste with oil and water often. Add more water if necessary.

Temperature: 350 °
Time: 1-1½ hours

SPINACH STUFFED ARTICHOKE BOTTOMS

Yields: **6 servings**
Preparation Time: 15 minutes

1	10-ounce package chopped spinach
1	tablespoon onion, chopped
1/4	cup sour cream
6	artichoke bottoms
2	tablespoons butter or margarine, melted
	freshly ground black pepper

1. Cook spinach according to package directions. Drain thoroughly.
2. Combine spinach and onion in food processor. Add sour cream. Process until thoroughly mixed. Add salt now if desired.
3. Mound spinach mixture on each artichoke bottom. Drizzle melted butter over each one. Add pepper.
4. Heat in 350° oven until piping hot. About 10-15 minutes.

Temperature: **350 °**
Time: 10-15 minutes

Freshly grated Parmesan cheese could be added to mixture or spinkled on top.

SCALLOPED GREEN BEANS

Yields: **6-8 servings**
Preparation Time: 15 minutes

2	tablespoons butter
3	tablespoons flour
1	tablespoon prepared mustard
1/2	teaspoon salt
1/8	teaspoon pepper
1/2	cup milk
1/2	cup sharp Cheddar cheese, grated
2	16-ounce cans whole green beans, well drained
1/4	cup buttered bread crumbs

1. In small saucepan, melt butter. Blend in flour, mustard, salt, and pepper. Slowly add milk, stirring constantly. Blend well and cook over medium heat until thick. Fold in cheese and beans.
2. Pour mixture into a 2-quart greased casserole. Top with bread crumbs.
3. Bake in 350° oven for 1 hour.

Temperature: **350 °**
Time: 1 hour

ARTICHOKE LEAVES AND MY WAY SAUCE

Must Make Ahead Of Time

Yields: 8 servings
Preparation Time: 30 minutes

4	*globe artichokes, medium size*
1	*lemon, cut in half*
¼	*cup olive oil*

Sauce:

1½	*cups good quality mayonnaise*
¼	*teaspoon garlic powder*
1	*teaspoon seasoned salt*
2	*dashes ground cloves*
1	*tablespoon plus 1 teaspoon chives, finely chopped*

1. Wash artichokes in cold running water and pull off small bottom leaves.
2. With serated knife, "saw" off 1-inch of top and trim stem evenly so artichokes sit flat.
3. Cut off thorny tip of outer leaves with kitchen scissors. Rub cut edges with juice of lemon.
4. In dutch oven, stand artichokes upright in 2-3 inches of boiling water. Add olive oil to water. Cover and reduce heat.
5. Simmer 45 minutes, or until a leaf may be pulled off easily. Turn artichokes upside down to drain. Chill.
6. Arrange artichokes on platter with sauce in center bowl for dipping.

Sauce:

1. Combine all ingredients. Mix thoroughly and refrigerate 6 hours before serving.

COLORFUL PEAS

Yields: 6-8 servings
Preparation Time: 15 minutes

2	*tablespoons butter or margarine*
1	*teaspoon onion, minced*
¼	*teaspoon oregano*
3	*tablespoons chopped pimiento*
¼	*cup ripe olives, chopped*
1	*16-ounce package frozen peas salt and pepper to taste*

1. Melt butter. Add onions and oregano. Sauté 5 minutes. Add pimiento and olives. Stir in peas and heat thoroughly over low heat.
2. Adjust seasonings.

ASPARAGUS-MUSHROOM CASSEROLE

*Yields: **4 servings***
Preparation Time: 30 minutes

1	10-ounce package frozen asparagus
½	cup mushrooms, sliced and drained
2½	tablespoons butter
¼	cup onion, chopped
2½	tablespoons flour
1	cup milk
¼	teaspoon salt
¼	teaspoon black pepper
2	hard boiled eggs, chopped

1. Cook asparagus in ¼ cup salted water for 8-10 minutes. Drain and set aside.
2. Sauté onions and ¼ cup mushrooms in butter.
3. Remove saucepan from heat and mix in flour and milk gradually, stirring until smooth. Cook and stir over medium heat until thickened. Add salt and pepper. Mix well.
4. Arrange layers of asparagus, eggs, and remaining mushrooms in casserole.
5. Cover with sauce and bake in 300° oven for 10-12 minutes.

*Temperature: **300** °*
Time: 10-12 minutes

ASPARAGUS PARMESAN

*Yields: **6 servings***
Preparation Time: 20 minutes

1½	pounds fresh asparagus or 3 10-ounce packages frozen asparagus (Do not use canned)
¾	cup butter, melted
¾	cup Parmesan cheese, grated
1	teaspoon salt
½	teaspoon pepper

1. Cook asparagus until just tender. Drain and set aside.
2. Pour ⅓ butter into 1½-quart casserole, then ⅓ each of asparagus, cheese, salt, and pepper.
3. Repeat layers, ending with cheese, salt, and pepper.
4. Bake in 400° oven for 10 minutes or until cheese melts.

*Temperature: **400** °*
Time: 10 minutes

BLACK BEANS AT THEIR VERY BEST

Yields: **10-15 servings**
Preparation Time: 20 minutes

1	*pound dried black beans*
1½	*cups chopped onion*
2	*large cloves of garlic, minced*
3	*ribs of celery, coarsely chopped*
1	*medium carrot, coarsely chopped*
1½	*teaspoons salt*
½	*teaspoon freshly ground black pepper*
2	*bay leaves*
¼	*teaspoon oregano*
1	*tablespoon fresh parsley dash cayenne*
4	*tablespoons butter or margarine*
1½	*ounces dark rum*
4	*cups cooked white rice*
2	*cups sour cream*

1. Rinse the beans thoroughly.
2. In a large heavy 6-quart saucepan, place beans and enough water to cover them. Cover and quickly bring to a full boil on high heat.
3. Remove from heat and let stand covered for 1 hour. Do not remove top. Add onion, garlic, celery, carrot, salt, pepper, bay leaves, oregano, and parsley. Add more water to cover beans again.
4. Bring back to a rolling boil and then simmer, covered over low heat for 2 hours, stirring occasionally. Add cayenne and more seasoning to taste.
5. Remove bay leaves and transfer beans to a 3-quart casserole. Stir in butter and rum, mixing thoroughly.
6. Cover and bake in 350° oven for 1 hour or until beans are tender.
7. Serve over white rice and top with a dollop of sour cream.

Temperature: **350 °**
Time: 1 hour

FRIED RED CABBAGE

Yields: **4-5 servings**
Preparation Time: 1 hour

1	*small head red cabbage, shredded*
1	*large onion, diced*
2	*slices bacon*
1	*teaspoon salt*
¼	*teaspoon pepper*
1	*tablespoon wine vinegar*
1	*teaspoon sugar*

1. Fry bacon until crisp.
2. Add cabbage in small amounts to bacon fat. Add onions, salt, and pepper. Fry slowly over low heat, covered, about ½ hour.
3. Add sugar, vinegar, and crumbled bacon. Simmer 5-10 minutes or longer.

Add more water if cabbage begins to get dry.

BEANS MEZZINO

Yields: **12 servings**
Preparation Time: 1½ hours

1	*large onion, chopped*
1	*green pepper, chopped*
1	*clove garlic, minced*
3	*tablespoons bacon drippings*
½	*cup chili sauce*
2	*tablespoons brown sugar*
1	*tablespoon Grey Poupon or 1 teaspoon dry yellow mustard*
1	*14-16-ounce can lima beans*
1	*14-16-ounce can white navy beans, drained and rinsed*
1	*14-16-ounce can pork and beans*

1. Sauté onion, pepper, and garlic in bacon drippings.
2. Add remaining ingredients. Mix thoroughly and transfer to a 9" × 13" baking dish.
3. Cover and bake in 300° oven for one hour.
4. Remove cover. If too soupy, bake another 15 minutes.

Temperature: **300 °**
Time: *one hour*

May use red kidney beans instead of white navy beans.

TEXAS STYLE GREEN BEANS AND NEW POTATOES

Yields: **6-8 servings**
Preparation Time: 15 minutes

2	*pounds fresh green beans*
6	*slices bacon*
1	*large onion, sliced or chopped*
1½	*tablespoons Worcestershire sauce*
1	*tablespoon salt*
6-8	*small new potatoes, unpeeled Tabasco to taste*

1. Wash and snap beans.
2. In large pot or dutch oven, combine all ingredients and cover with water.
3. Simmer until beans and potatoes are tender.

FRIJOLES DE TIEMPOS PASADOS

Yields: **2 quarts**
Preparation Time: *20-25 minutes*

"Beans from the Past"
Must Make Ahead Of Time

4	cups dried pinto beans
10	cups water
2	cups onions, chopped
3	cloves garlic, crushed
2	teaspoons ground cumin
6	tablespoons bacon drippings
6	tablespoons chili powder
2	teaspoons salt
1	cup butter or margarine
½	pound medium or mild Cheddar cheese
1	tablespoon Mexican salsa

1. Wash beans thoroughly, removing only foreign particles.
2. EITHER soak beans overnight in large heavy pot (enamel or pottery is better than metal) OR boil for 2 minutes in 10 cups of water. Remove from heat, cover and let stand for 1 hour (or boil an hour or two longer than specified).
3. Add onions, garlic, cumin, and bacon drippings.
4. Simmer until beans are very soft stirring occasionally with a wooden spoon, 3 to 4 hours, until most liquid is absorbed.
5. Add salt (salting too soon hardens the beans).
6. Remove from heat and transfer to electric mixing bowl and beat in butter, cheese, and Mexican sauce on a low speed.
7. Continue beating until fairly smooth.

For dip: serve warm in chafing dish with large fritos.

For refried beans: heat 1 stick margarine in iron skillet on low for 10 minutes. Add beans and cook, stirring for 15 minutes. Or put in pyrex dish and heat, covered in oven.

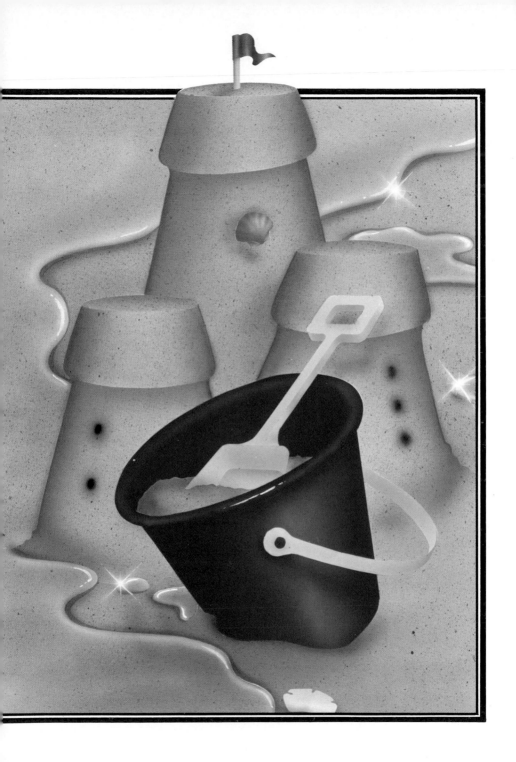

BEACHES

Galveston's 32 miles of sandy beaches are a year-long enticement for people to swim, to sun, to surf, to fish, to boat, to parasail, to water ski and to search for sea shells. The 17-mile seawall that acts as a barrier against the water provides a scenic setting for bicycling, rollerskating, jogging or simply strolling.

BROCCOLI ONION DELUXE

*Yields: **6-8 servings***
Preparation Time: 30-45 minutes

2	10-ounce packages frozen chopped broccoli
1½	cups frozen whole small onions
4	tablespoons butter or margarine, divided
2	tablespoons all-purpose flour
¼	teaspoon salt
⅛	teaspoon black pepper
1	cup milk
1	3-ounce package cream cheese
1	cup soft bread crumbs
¼	cup Parmesan cheese, grated

1. Cook broccoli according to package directions. Drain thoroughly. Set aside.
2. Cook onions in boiling salted water (about 10 minutes). Drain and set aside.
3. In medium saucepan, melt 2 tablespoons butter. Blend in flour, salt, and pepper. Add milk all at once. Cook and stir over medium heat until thick and bubbly.
4. Reduce heat. Blend in cream cheese. Stir until smooth.
5. Add vegetables. Mix well. Pour into 1½-quart casserole. Bake uncovered in 350° oven for 20 minutes.
6. Melt remaining butter. Toss with bread crumbs and Parmesan cheese. Sprinkle over casserole.
7. Bake in 350° oven for 35-40 minutes.

*Temperature: **350** °*
Time: 20 minutes
*Temperature: **350** °*
Time: 35-40 minutes

SWEET POTATOES SNOWBALLS

*Yields: **16 balls***
Preparation Time: 20 minutes

2	23-ounce cans sweet potatoes
½	cup butter, melted
1	dash cinnamon
16	large marshmallows
1	3½-ounce can flake coconut

1. Mash potatoes. Add butter and cinnamon. With 1 large heaping tablespoon of mixture, form ball around each marshmallow.
2. Roll each ball in coconut. Arrange in a 9″ × 13″ baking dish. Bake in 350° oven for 5-10 minutes.

*Temperature: **350** °*
Time: 5-10 minutes

DILLED CARROTS
Must Make Ahead Of Time

Yields: **4 servings**
Preparation Time: 30 minutes plus
4-6 hours chill time

8	*carrots, peeled and julienned*
¼	*cup water*
4	*tablespoons tarragon vinegar*
4	*tablespoons vegetable oil*
1	*teaspoon salt*
⅛	*teaspoon pepper*
1	*tablespoon dried dill*
1	*teaspoon sugar*
½	*teaspoon lemon juice*
2	*tablespoons green onions, chopped*

1. Place carrots in water, cover, and cook over low heat 15-20 minutes until crisp. Drain.
2. Combine remaining ingredients and add carrots. Mix well.
3. Cover and chill several hours, tossing occasionally.

COPPER PENNIES
Must Make Ahead Of Time

Yields: **6-8 servings**
Preparation Time: 30 minutes

2	*pounds carrots, sliced*
1	*medium onion, chopped*
¾	*cup butter-flavored vegetable oil*
1	*teaspoon dry mustard*
1	*10½-ounce can tomato soup*
1	*cup sugar*
¾	*cup apple cider vinegar*
1	*tablespoon Worcestershire sauce*
	salt and pepper to taste
1	*small green pepper, diced*

Can be made the night before.

1. Cook carrots until tender, drain.
2. Add remaining ingredients and bring to a boil.
3. Remove from heat and store in refrigerator a minimum of 6 hours before serving.

BAKED CARROTS JULIENNE

Yields: **4 servings**
Preparation Time: 20 minutes

¼	cup butter or margarine
1	tablespoon lemon juice
½	teaspoon salt
½	teaspoon sugar
6	medium carrots
1	medium onion, sliced
2	tablespoons water
1	tablespoon parsley, chopped

1. Melt butter and stir in lemon juice, salt, and sugar.
2. Pare carrots and cut into ¼ inch strips, about 3 inches long.
3. Arrange carrots in layers in 8″ × 8″ baking dish with onions, pouring some butter mixture over each layer and all remaining mixture over the top. Add water and cover.
4. Bake in 350° oven for 50 minutes to 1 hour.
5. Sprinkle with parsley before serving.

Temperature: **350 °**
Time: 50-60 minutes

HOLIDAY GLAZED CARROTS

Yields: **6 servings**
Preparation Time: 45 minutes

1½	pounds carrots, peeled and sliced ¼ inch thick
1¼	cups water
1	tablespoon sugar
¼	cup butter, divided
¾	teaspoon salt, divided
⅓	cup apricot preserves
¼	teaspoon nutmeg
	dash of white pepper
1	small orange peel, grated
	fresh lemon juice

1. Cook carrots in water, sugar, 1 tablespoon butter, and ½ teaspoon salt until tender — crisp. Drain.
2. Heat and strain apricot preserves.
3. In a skillet, melt 3 tablespoons butter and stir in preserves, nutmeg, ¼ teaspoon salt, pepper, orange peel, and lemon juice to taste. Cook until glaze consistency.
4. Return carrots to pan and coat with glaze.

CARROT-CHEESE SCALLOP

Yields: 6 servings
Preparation Time: 20 minutes

4   cups carrots, sliced
½   cup water
½   teaspoon salt
2   tablespoons butter
2   tablespoons flour
1   cup milk
1   cup medium Cheddar cheese, grated
1   3½-ounce can french-fried onions

1. In a medium saucepan, cook carrots 5 minutes in salted water. Drain well. Set aside.
2. In a saucepan over medium heat, melt butter and stir in flour slowly. Gradually add milk, stirring constantly until sauce thickens. Add cheese and stir until melted.
3. Put ⅓ of the carrots in a 1½-quart casserole and cover with ⅓ onions. Repeat, saving ⅓ onions for top. Pour sauce over all.
4. Bake in 350° oven for 15 minutes. Sprinkle with remaining onions and bake for 5 minutes more.

Temperature: 350 °
Time: 15 minutes
Temperature: 350 °
Time: 5 minutes

CORN CASSEROLE

Yields: 4 servings
Preparation Time: 15 minutes

2½   cups fresh corn kernels, divided
½   cup butter, melted
2   eggs
1   cup sour cream
1   cup Monterey Jack cheese, diced
½   cup yellow corn meal
1   4-ounce can green chilies, diced
1½   teaspoons salt

1. Purée 1 cup of corn with butter and eggs in food processor or blender.
2. Combine remaining ingredients. Add to puréed mixture and blend well.
3. Pour into a 1-quart buttered casserole and bake uncovered in a 350° oven for 50-60 minutes.

Temperature: 350 °
Time: 50-60 minutes

FOURTH GENERATION EGGPLANT

Yields: **6-8 servings**
Preparation Time: 30 minutes

2	large eggplants, peeled and cubed
1	teaspoon salt
¼	cup cooking oil or olive oil
¼	pound lean ham
2	ribs celery, finely chopped
10	green onions, finely chopped
½	large green pepper, finely chopped
2	cloves garlic, finely chopped
½	teaspoon Tabasco
1	cup Progresso seasoned bread crumbs

1. Boil salt and eggplant in a 2-quart saucepan, until very tender.
2. Sauté ham and the other vegetables in the oil over medium heat until limp.
3. Thoroughly drain eggplant and combine with sautéed vegetables until well blended.
4. Add garlic, Tabasco, and bread crumbs. Adjust seasonings.
5. Place in a 2-quart casserole dish and top with remaining bread crumbs. Bake in 350° oven for 10 minutes.

Temperature: **350 °**
Time: 10 minutes

ONION CASSEROLE

Yields: **4 servings**
Preparation Time: 20 minutes

7-8	cups onion, cut in thick, uneven slices
4	tablespoons butter
1	cup rice, cooked
1	cup Swiss cheese, grated
1	cup light cream
	salt and pepper to taste
	cracker crumbs, optional

1. Sauté onion in butter until transparent.
2. Mix all ingredients.
3. Bake uncovered in 350° oven until onions are tender.
4. Cracker crumbs may be sprinkled on top.

Temperature: **350 °**
Time: 30-40 minutes

APPLES AND ONIONS

Yields: **6-8 servings**
Preparation Time: 25 minutes

2	medium onions, sliced and separated into rings
½	cup butter or margarine
4	large apples, cored, peeled, and sliced
½	cup cold water
2	tablespoons light brown sugar
½	cup seedless golden white raisins
	cloves to taste
	nutmeg to taste
	cinnamon to taste
	dash of salt
	dash of pepper

1. Slice onions. Separate into rings, then sauté in butter.
2. Add water before onions brown. Add apples, sugar, and raisins. Cover and steam about 3 minutes.
3. Sprinkle lightly with spices, very light sprinkle of salt and a bare taste of pepper.

COMPANY PEAS

Yields: **8 servings**
Preparation Time: 20 minutes

2	medium onions, chopped
4	tablespoons olive oil
2	10-ounce packages frozen peas
½	teaspoon thyme
1	15-ounce can artichoke hearts, drained and quartered
1	7-ounce can water chestnuts, drained and sliced
	salt and pepper to taste

1. Sauté onions in oil until tender. Add peas and thyme, cover, and simmer until peas are separated (about 5 minutes or a little longer).
2. Add artichoke hearts, water chestnuts, and seasonings. Cook another 2 minutes or until hot throughout.
3. Stir very gently and be careful not to break up artichokes.

GOLDEN POTATO CASSEROLE

*Yields: **6-8 servings***
Preparation Time: 45 minutes plus 30 minutes set time.

6   large potatoes, washed and peeled
¼   cup butter or margarine
2   cups sharp Cheddar cheese, grated
2   cups sour cream
⅓   cup green onion, chopped
1   teaspoon salt
⅛   teaspoon black pepper

1. Cut potatoes in half. Place in a 2-quart saucepan and cover with water. Cook over medium high heat until fork tender. Drain.
2. Set potatoes in freezer for a half hour.
3. Remove potatoes from freezer and grate them. Set aside.
4. Combine butter and cheese in a saucepan. Cook over a low heat until almost melted. Remove from heat and blend in sour cream, onions, salt, and pepper.
5. Pour sauce over potatoes in a 2-quart casserole. Mix *gently* so potatoes are not mashed.
6. Bake in 350° oven for 45 minutes.

*Temperature: **350** °*
Time: 45 minutes

HASH BROWN POTATO BAKE

*Yields: **12 servings***
Preparation Time: 1 hour

1   2-pound bag frozen hash brown potatoes
¾   cup butter or margarine melted, divided
1   10¾-ounce can cream of chicken soup
1   cup sharp Cheddar cheese, grated
½   cup onion, chopped
1   cup sour cream
2   cups corn flakes, crushed
     parsley (optional)

1. Combine potatoes, ½ cup butter, soup, cheese, onion, and sour cream. Mix well and place in 11" × 7" baking dish.
2. Crush cereal and stir in remaining butter. Sprinkle over potato mixture.
3. Bake in 350° oven for 50 minutes. Garnish with parsley, if desired.

*Temperature: **350** °*
Time: 50 minutes

SPINACH SOUFFLÉ

Yields: **8-10 servings**
Preparation Time: 15 minutes

2 10-ounce packages frozen spinach, defrosted and well drained
2 pints small curd cottage cheese, creamed
¾ pound Cheddar cheese, diced (any sharpness that you prefer)
3 eggs, beaten
¼ teaspoon salt
½ cup butter, slightly softened and cubed
3 tablespoons flour

1. Mix first 5 ingredients together. Blend in butter, then add flour.
2. Place in well-greased 9" × 13" baking dish. Bake in 350° oven for 1 hour or until brown.

Temperature: **350** °
Time: 1 hour

SQUASH SOUFFLÉ

Yields: **4-6 servings**
Preparation Time: 20 minutes

2 pounds yellow squash
¼ cup onion, chopped
½ teaspoon salt
2 eggs, beaten
½ pound Cheddar cheese, grated
1 cup cracker crumbs
2 tablespoons butter or margarine
   pepper to taste

1. Cook squash and onion in salted water. Drain. Cool a few minutes.
2. Add beaten eggs and mix well. Add half of the grated cheese and salt and mix well.
3. Place in 1½-quart casserole and sprinkle rest of cheese on top. Put crumbs on top, dot with butter, and sprinkle with pepper. Bake in 350° oven for 20 minutes.

Temperature: **350** °
Time: 20 minutes

SPINACH "A LA CREME"

Yields: **6 servings**
Preparation Time: 30 minutes

1   10-ounce package frozen
     chopped spinach
⅛   teaspoon salt
1   tablespoon butter
1   tablespoon chicken bouillon
     powder
3   tablespoons sour cream
¼   cup Jarlsberg cheese,
     shredded
½   tablespoon Aromat
3   large tomatoes, cut in half
     and remove seeds
     paprika

1. Boil spinach with salt, butter, and bouillon 10-15 minutes. Drain and rinse with water.
2. Add sour cream, Aromat, and cheese. Stir until cheese is melted.
3. While still on low heat, arrange tomatoes on platter. Pour spinach in tomatoes and sprinkle with paprika. Serve while hot.

Can be made ahead of time and warmed in 375° oven for not more than 10 minutes. Do not freeze. Aromat is a Swiss seasoning.

WHITE CAP TOMATOES

Yields: **8 servings**
Preparation Time: 25 minutes

½   cup sour cream
¼   cup good quality mayonnaise
½   teaspoon instant minced
     onion
¼   teaspoon dill seed
½   teaspoon salt
4   large tomatoes
     salt and pepper to taste
4   tablespoons butter of
     margarine
     fresh dill (optional)

1. Twenty minutes before serving, combine first 5 ingredients.
2. Mix thoroughly and refrigerate.
3. Cut tomatoes in half crosswise, and sprinkle with butter.
4. Broil on lower rack 2-3 minutes until heated through. Top each with dressing and a dash of fresh dill.

Temperature: Broil
Time: 2-3 minutes

STUFFED TOMATOES WITH SQUASH

Yields: **6 servings**
Preparation Time: *15 minutes*

6	*large firm tomatoes*
6-8	*yellow squash*
1	*bunch green onions, finely chopped*
¾	*pound bacon, fried crisp*
¼	*teaspoon salt*
⅛	*teaspoon black pepper*
¼	*cup Progresso Italian bread crumbs*
¼	*cup Parmesan cheese*
3	*tablespoons butter or margarine*
	paprika

1. Scoop insides from tomatoes leaving thick walls.
2. Boil squash 5 minutes or until tender. Cut squash into chunks.
3. Mix chunky pieces of squash, onion, and bacon. Salt and pepper to taste. Fill tomatoes with squash mixture.
4. Combine bread crumbs and cheese. Sprinkle liberally on top of tomatoes. Dot with butter and sprinkle with paprika.
5. Bake in 350° oven for 20-30 minutes. (Tender, but not falling apart).

Temperature: **350 °**
Time: *20-30 minutes*

GRILLED STUFFED TOMATOES

"A Great Outdoor Dish"

Yields: **6 servings**
Preparation Time: *15 minutes*

6	*large tomatoes*
½	*cup butter or margarine*
1¾	*cups plain dry bread crumbs*
1½	*cups sharp Cheddar cheese*
	snipped parsley

1. Cut tops of tomatoes off and scoop out half of the pulp. (Use this pulp for a salad or save for a vegetable soup, etc).
2. Melt butter and blend in bread crumbs and cheese. Blend thoroughly. Stuff tomatoes with this cheese mixture. Top with a few snips of parsley.
3. Wrap each tomato in foil and set on grill over hot coals for about 25 minutes. Check after 15 minutes to make sure they are not getting too soft.

May be baked in the oven in a baking dish. Bake in 400° oven for 20-25 minutes.

GARDEN VEGETABLE CASEROLE

Yields: **6-8 servings**
Preparation Time: 30 minutes

1	cup almonds, slivered
1/2	pound bacon, cut into 1-inch lengths
1	pound zucchini squash, sliced
1	pound eggplant, diced
1	large onion, cut into wedges
1	tablespoon flour
2	cups fresh tomatoes, diced or 1 one-pound can tomatoes, undrained
1	teaspoon garlic, minced
1 1/2	teaspoons salt
1/4	teaspoon black pepper
1	teaspoon basil
1	6-ounce package Swiss cheese

1. Brown almonds with bacon. Remove with slotted spoon. Add zucchini, eggplant, and onion. Cover and cook over medium low heat 15 minutes, stirring often to prevent sticking.
2. Add flour. Next add tomatoes, breaking into chunks with a spoon. Stir in garlic, salt, pepper, and basil.
3. Layer vegetable mixture, almonds, bacon, and cheese slices in a baking dish, ending with bacon and almonds in a ring on top.
4. Bake uncovered in a 400° oven 15-20 minutes or until bubbly throughout.

Temperature: **400 °**
Time: 15-20 minutes

If you do not wish to use bacon, use 3 tablespoons oil instead.

BOURBON SWEET POTATOES

Yields: **8-10 servings**
Preparation Time: 30 minutes

4	1-pound cans sweet potatoes
1	cup sugar
1/4	cup butter
1/4	cup milk, more if needed
1/4	cup bourbon
1/2	cup pecans, chopped
1	7-ounce jar marshmallow cream

1. Heat potatoes in juice. Drain and mash well.
2. Add sugar, butter, milk, and bourbon, then blend well.
3. Fold in pecans.
4. Bake in 350° oven for 15 minutes or until bubbling. Cover with marshmallow cream and brown in oven again.

Temperature: **350 °**
Time: 15 minutes

ZUCCHINI CASSEROLE

Yields: **8-10 servings**
Preparation Time: 1 hour

4	cups zucchini, thinly sliced
1	cup onion, chopped
½	cup butter
2	tablespoons parsley flakes
1	teaspoon salt
½	teaspoon pepper
¼	teaspoon garlic powder
½	teaspoon basil
¼	teaspoon oregano
2	eggs, well beaten
2	cups Mozzarella cheese, grated
1	8-ounce can crescent rolls
2	teaspoons Dijon mustard

1. Cook or steam zucchini and onions until tender. Add butter, parsley flakes, salt, pepper, garlic powder, basil, and oregano.
2. Blend eggs and cheese together. Stir zucchini mixture into egg and cheese mixture.
3. Place crescent rolls dough flat onto ungreased pizza pan or baking pan. Spread with mustard and top with zucchini mixture.
4. Bake in 325° oven for 18-20 minutes. Let stand 10 minutes before serving.

Temperature: **325 °**
Time: 18-20 minutes

SAVORY ZUCCHINI

Yields: **4-6 servings**
Preparation Time: 15 minutes

2	pounds zucchini, thinly sliced
½	cup onions, chopped
2	tomatoes, peeled and chopped
1½	teaspoons salt
½	teaspoon pepper
½	teaspoon oregano
2	tablespoons butter

1. Place zucchini, onions, and chopped tomatoes in center of a large piece of heavy duty foil. Sprinkle with salt, pepper, and oregano. Dot with butter. Bring foil over vegetables and seal tightly.
2. Put foil container in a heavy skillet and cook over moderate heat, shaking occasionally.
3. Cook 10 minutes, then check for doneness. If it needs more cooking, reseal foil tightly and cook until tender.

ZUCCHINI MINI-PANCAKES

Yields: **4-6 servings**
Preparation Time: 15 minutes

3	cups zucchini, grated
1/2	cup flour, sifted
1	teaspoon baking powder, sifted
1/4	teaspoon onion powder
	salt and pepper to taste
1/8	teaspoon garlic powder
1	egg, beaten
	oil for frying
	butter, melted
	Parmesan cheese, grated

1. Combine first 6 ingredients in a medium size bowl. Add egg and stir until blended.
2. Drop mixture by large tablespoonfuls onto a very hot oiled griddle. Cook until brown on both sides.
3. Serve with melted butter and Parmesan cheese.

ARGENTINE RICE

Yields: **8 servings**
Preparation Time: 45 minutes

1	14½-ounce can asparagus
1	onion, coarsely chopped
1	green pepper, chopped
3	cloves garlic, minced
1½	cups raw long grain rice
2	tablespoons butter
1/2	cup Parmesan cheese
	salt and pepper to taste
2¼	cups water
1	8-ounce carton sour cream
1	8-ounce package Monterey Jack cheese

1. Drain asparagus and save juice. Set aside.
2. Cook onion, green pepper, and garlic in a small amount of oil until onions are clear.
3. Add rice, butter, and Parmesan cheese. (Toss so cheese doesn't gum up). Add salt and pepper to taste.
4. Using the drained asparagus juice, add water to make 2½ cups. Blend into rice mixture.
5. Cook covered until rice is done and all juices are absorbed (about 25 minutes). Add sour cream and mix well.
6. Butter a 2-quart casserole dish and layer rice mixture, asparagus, and cheese, ending with cheese on top.
7. Bake in 350° oven for 30 minutes.

Temperature: **350 °**
Time: 30 minutes

If you would like to add more asparagus, another can would fit in nicely.

HERBED SPINACH RICE

Yields: **6 servings**
Preparation Time: 30 minutes

1	10-ounce package frozen spinach, cooked and drained
1	cup rice, cooked
1	cup sharp American cheese, shredded
2	eggs, slightly beaten
2	tablespoons butter or margarine, softened
1/3	cup milk
2	tablespoons onions, chopped
1/2	teaspoon Worcestershire sauce
1	teaspoon salt
1/4	teaspoon rosemary or thyme, crushed

1. Mix all ingredients and pour into 10" × 6" baking dish.
2. Bake in 350° oven for 20-25 minutes or until knife inserted in center comes out clean.
3. Cut into squares.

Temperature: **350 °**
Time: **20-25 minutes**

WILD RICE AND ALMOND CASSEROLE

Yields: **8 servings**
Preparation Time: 30 minutes

1/2	cup butter or margarine, melted
1/2	pound mushrooms, sliced
1	clove garlic
2	tablespoons green onions, chopped
1/2	cup almonds, blanched and slivered
1	cup wild rice
3	cups chicken broth
	salt and pepper to taste

1. In skillet, melt butter. Add mushrooms, garlic, green onions, almonds, and wild rice.
2. Cook, stirring continually until rice begins to turn yellow, 5-10 minutes.
3. Add broth and season with salt and pepper to taste. Turn into dish and cover tightly. Bake in 325° oven for 1 hour.

Temperature: **325 °**
Time: **1 hour**

RICE MUSHROOM MEDLEY

Yields: **6-8 servings**
Preparation Time: 30 minutes

1	*6-ounce package long grain and wild rice mix*
1¼	*cups condensed beef broth*
1¼	*cups water*
½	*cup onion, chopped*
½	*cup celery, chopped*
4	*tablespoons butter or margarine*
1	*4-ounce can sliced mushrooms, drained*

1. Prepare rice mix according to package directions, substituting the beef broth and 1¼ cup water for the liquid called for.
2. Sauté onion and celery in butter until tender, but not brown.
3. Five minutes before end of cooking time for rice, stir onions, celery, and mushrooms into rice. Continue cooking until liquid is absorbed.

Delicious as a dressing for Thanksgiving! Easy to make the day of the dinner.

TOMATO FRIED RICE

Yields: **4-6 servings**
Preparation Time: 15 minutes

2	*tablespoons vegetable oil*
2	*tablespoons butter*
1	*small onion, finely chopped*
3	*cups rice, cooked and cold*
½	*teaspoon salt*
½	*teaspoon sugar*
1	*2-ounce can pimiento, diced and drained*
¼	*teaspoon pepper*
2	*tablespoons dry sherry*
2	*medium tomatoes, chopped chopped parsley or green onion for garnish (optional)*

1. Heat large frying pan or wok to medium high heat. Add oil and butter and sauté onion until golden, about 2 minutes.
2. Add rice and continue stirring until golden, about 7 minutes. Add salt, pepper, pimiento, and wine. Cook 1 minute. Add tomatoes and cook 2 minutes.
3. Garnish with chopped parsley or green onions, if desired.

ROSSINE STEAK SAUCE

Yields: **3 cups**
Preparation Time: 30 minutes

½	cup butter
6	green onions, chopped
½	cup onion, chopped
½	pound fresh mushrooms, sliced
¾	cup Bordeaux Wine
1	cup beef broth
1½	tablespoons flour
¼	teaspoon salt
	dash of pepper
1	2¾-ounce can liver pâté or 1 3-ounce can pâté de fois gras

1. Melt butter in medium saucepan. Sauté onions and mushrooms, stirring occasionally until tender — about 5 minutes.
2. Add wine and simmer uncovered 15 minutes.
3. Combine beef broth, flour, salt, and pepper. Mix well. Stir into wine mixture. Cook, stirring until slightly thickened.
4. In small skillet, over low heat, melt pâté. Add to sauce. Mix well. Serve with steaks.

SWEET DIP MUSTARD SAUCE

Yields: **1½ cups**
Preparation Time: 5 minutes

Must Make Ahead Of Time

1	cup mayonnaise
½	cup sour cream
¼	cup prepared mustard
1	tablespoon onion flakes
2	tablespoons horseradish
	dash of salt
	juice of ½ lemon

1. Mix all ingredients.
2. Refrigerate several hours before serving.

PEPPER JELLY

Yields: **6-8 servings**
Preparation Time: 15 minutes

3	bell peppers (or 1 cup)
6	hot jalapeño peppers
6½	cups sugar
1½	cups vinegar
1	bottle Certo
6-9	drops green food coloring

1. Grind peppers, sugar, and vinegar. Boil for 3 minutes, then strain.
2. Bring strained juice to a boil. Add Certo and coloring. Boil one minute.
3. Remove from heat and skim off any foam. Pour into hot, sterile glasses. Seal with melted paraffin.

VELVET RUM SAUCE

Yields: **2-4 servings**
Preparation Time: 10 minutes

2	tablespoons butter
1/2	cup light brown sugar
2 1/2	jiggers light rum
1/8	teaspoon cinnamon

1. Melt butter over low heat in sauce pan. Add sugar and stir well until dissolved.
2. Pour in rum. Add cinnamon and heat thoroughly. Serve with fruit.

Add sliced bananas at end and simmer until limp for a special treat. Pour over ice cream or use sauce as a dip for fruit.

CREAMY MUSHROOM SAUCE

Yields: **1 1/2 cups**
Preparation Time: 15 minutes

1/4	cup onion, chopped
4	ounces fresh mushrooms, sliced
2	tablespoons butter
1	tablespoon flour
1 1/2	cups light cream
1/2	teaspoon salt
1/4	teaspoon pepper
1/2	cup dairy sour cream

1. Sauté onions and mushrooms in butter.
2. Add next 4 ingredients.
3. Heat to boiling, stirring constantly.
4. Stir in sour cream and heat thoroughly.

REMOULADE SAUCE FOR SHRIMP SALAD

Yields: **1 cup**
Preparation Time: 10 minutes

Must Make Ahead Of Time

1	cup good quality mayonnaise
1	teaspoon tarragon, chopped
1	clove garlic, minced
1	teaspoon dry mustard
1	teaspoon parsley, minced
2	small sour pickles, grated

1. Combine all ingredients in a small bowl. Mix thoroughly.
2. Refrigerate overnight or at least 4-6 hours.
3. Serve over your choice of seafood.

WALNUT AND BRANDY SAUCE

Yields: **4-6 servings**
Preparation Time: 10 minutes

1	cup light brown sugar, packed
1/4	cup butter
1/4	cup heavy cream
2	tablespoons light corn syrup
1/4	cup brandy
1/2	cup walnut pieces

1. Combine first four ingredients in a medium saucepan and bring to boil over moderate heat, stirring constantly.
2. Reduce heat and continue cooking and stirring 5 more minutes.
3. Remove pan from heat and stir in brandy and nuts.
4. Return pan to heat and simmer 1 minute.
5. Serve warm over ice cream or frozen soufflé.

Can make ahead and reheat slowly in microwave.

JOHN'S HERB BUTTER FOR GRILLED STEAK

Yields: **4 servings**
Preparation Time: 5 minutes

1/4	cup butter, softened
2	tablespoons green onions, chopped
1	tablespoon chives, chopped
2	tablespoons parsley, chopped
1/2	teaspoon dill weed
1/2	teaspoon salt
1/4	teaspoon Tabasco
1	tablespoon lemon juice

1. Combine all ingredients, gradually beating until blended.
2. Cook steaks to taste.
3. Spread herb butter and serve immediately.

SPICED PEACHES

Yields: **4 pints**
Preparation Time: 5 minutes

2	29-ounce cans cling peach halves
1 1/3	cups sugar
1	cup cider vinegar
4	cinnamon sticks
2	teaspoons whole cloves

1. Drain peaches, reserving syrup.
2. Combine syrup with last 4 ingredients in a 2-quart saucepan.
3. Bring mixture to a boil. Reduce heat and simmer 10 minutes.
4. Pour hot syrup over peach halves and let cool. Chill thoroughly in refrigerator before serving.

JOE'S MUSTARD SAUCE

Yields: 2 pints
Preparation Time: 15 minutes

1	2-ounce can dry English mustard
2	cups good quality mayonnaise
¼	cup A-1 sauce
¼	cup Worcestershire sauce
1	cup light cream

1. Mix all ingredients, except cream. Beat slowly. Gradually add the cream while beating.
2. Continue beating at slow speed until it thickens to a consistency you like.

Great served with crab or any cold fish.

SHRIMP SAUCE

Yields: 1 cup
Preparation Time: 5 minutes

3	tablespoons chili sauce
½	cup ketchup
1	tablespoon horseradish
2	tablespoons lemon juice
½	teaspoon Worcestershire sauce
1	drop Tabasco sauce
½	teaspoon salt

1. Blend all ingredients thoroughly and chill at least ½ hour before serving.

Keeps well in refrigerator for several weeks.

CANDIED CRANBERRIES

Yields: 4 servings
Preparation Time: 5 minutes

1	12-ounce package of cranberries or 2 cups cranberries
1½	cups sugar
	butter or margarine

1. Butter 9-inch square pan very generously.
2. Add washed and dried cranberries. Cover with sugar. Cover tightly with foil. Bake in 350° oven for 1 hour.

Temperature: 350°
Time: 1 hour

211

FLUFFY BANANA TOPPING

*Yields: **3 cups***
Preparation Time: 15 minutes

1	ripe banana
1	egg white, unbeaten
⅓	cup sugar
⅛	teaspoon salt
½	teaspoon vanilla
1	teaspoon lemon juice

1. Mix all ingredients in a small bowl.
2. Using an electric mixer, begin on low speed, gradually moving up to high. Beat until fluffy and thickened.

Great topping for gingerbread or spice cake.

HOT FUDGE ICE CREAM TOPPING

*Yields: **10-15 servings***
Preparation Time: 30-40 minutes

⅓	cup whole milk
1	16-ounce package caramels
1	4-ounce package milk chocolate, chopped
½	pint vanilla ice cream, softened
1	teaspoon vanilla

1. In a double boiler, place milk and caramels. Heat and stir until smooth and creamy and mixture is quite hot.
2. Add chopped chocolate to caramel mixture. Stir until melted.
3. Mix in soft ice cream and vanilla to the chocolate mixture. Stir until smooth.

Can be stored in a tightly covered jar. Serve over ice cream. For variation: Use ⅔ cup strong coffee or whole milk and use Baker's chocolate for semi-sweet topping.

ELISSA

The *Elissa* is a square-rigged sailing ship built in 1878 and lovingly restored by the citizens of Galveston. A project of the Galveston Historical Foundation, the *Elissa* was chosen to be part of a permanent exhibit at the Galveston wharves. Today visitors tour the *Elissa* and watch a film, describing the tall ship's dramatic adventures on the high seas.

Perfect Endings

🐚 HUMDINGERS

Yields: 5 dozen
Preparation Time: 50 minutes

1   cup butter
1½   cups sugar
1   pound dates, chopped
2   eggs
2   tablespoons milk
1   cup nuts, chopped
1   teaspoon vanilla
4   cups Rice Krispies
1   14-ounce package flaked
      coconut

1. Melt butter and sugar in a skillet, stirring for 2 minutes. Add chopped dates. Set aside.
2. In a small bowl, beat 2 eggs and milk. Slowly add a small amount of hot mixture to eggs and milk. Pour entire egg mixture into skillet. Cook mixture 2 minutes, stirring constantly. Add nuts, vanilla, and cereal.
3. Roll small amount (about 1 large heaping tablespoon) into a ball (it will be hot) and roll ball in coconut.

This freezes well.

🐚 ALMOND RASPBERRY TASSIES

Yields: 2 dozen
Preparation Time: 30 minutes

Pastry Dough:

½   cup butter or margarine,
      softened
1   3-ounce package cream cheese
1   cup flour

Filling:

¼   cup raspberry preserves
½   cup sugar
½   cup (2-ounces) almond paste
2   egg yolks
3   tablespoons flour
2   tablespoons milk
1   tablespoon orange juice

Pastry Dough:

1. Blend softened butter and cream cheese. Stir in flour. Cover and chill.
2. Divide dough into 24 balls. Press into sides and bottom of small muffin tins. Fill with almond-raspberry filling.

Filling:

1. Put ½ teaspoon raspberry preserves into each unbaked shell.
2. Use your fingers to combine sugar and almond paste. Add egg yolks one at a time. Beat well as you add each yolk. Blend in other ingredients. Spoon into shells.
3. Bake in a 400° oven for 15 minutes.
4. Cool before removing from pan.

Temperature: 400 °
Time: 15 minutes

Store in refrigerator or freeze.

ANISE COOKIES
"An Italian Biscuit Cookie"

Yields: 3½ dozen
Preparation Time: 1 hour

½   *cup butter*
1   *cup sugar*
2   *eggs*
3   *cups flour*
½   *cup chopped almonds or*
     pecans
¼   *teaspoon salt*
2   *teaspoons baking powder*
¼   *teaspoon cinnamon*
½   *teaspoon anise oil or 1*
     teaspoon anise seeds,
     pulverized

1. Cream butter and sugar. Then add eggs one at a time. If using anise oil, add it now.
2. Mix thoroughly the flour, salt, and baking powder. Add cinnamon and the anise seeds if using them. Add the flour mixture to the butter mixture and mix thoroughly.
3. Place dough on a lightly floured pastry board and add the almonds or pecans. Knead until the nuts have been distributed through the dough. (You may have to use a little more flour.)
4. Divide the dough into 4 parts. Form into rolls about 1½" in diameter. Put each roll about 5" apart on a greased cookie sheet. Bake in 350° oven for 30 minutes, turning once after 15 minutes.
5. Remove from oven and cut into diagonal slices about ½" thick. Immediately put back on cookie sheet and return to oven to brown each side slightly.

Temperature: 350 °
Time: 30 minutes
Just to brown

APRICOT NUT BARS

Yields: **20 2-inch bars**
Preparation Time: 45 minutes

2	sticks butter
1⅓	cups sugar, divided
5	eggs, separated
1	tablespoon vanilla
2½	cups flour
2	cups apricot jam
	pinch of salt
2	cups pecans or walnuts, chopped
1	tablespoon bourbon or vanilla

1. Cream butter with ⅓ cup of the sugar until light and fluffy.
2. Beat in 5 egg yolks, one at a time, beating well after each addition. Add vanilla.
3. Add flour, ½ cup at a time, to make a smooth dough.
4. Pat dough evenly into a buttered 16" × 11" pan, then spread with apricot jam.
5. Beat 5 egg whites with a pinch of salt until they hold soft peaks.
6. Add 1 cup sugar, 2 tablespoons at a time, and 1 teaspoon vanilla or bourbon, then beat until meringue is stiff and shiny.
7. Fold in chopped nuts and spread meringue evenly over jam.
8. Bake in 350° oven for 40-45 minutes or until meringue is lightly browned.
9. Chill thoroughly in refrigerator before cutting into bars.

Temperature: **350** °
Time: 40-45 minutes

VIENNA DREAM BARS

Yields: **3 dozen**
Preparation Time: 25 minutes

1	cup flour
½	cup butter or margarine
1¼	cups brown sugar
2	eggs, beaten
1	cup brown sugar
¼	cup flour
½	teaspoon baking powder
1	cup coconut
1	cup pecans, chopped
1	teaspoon vanilla

Frosting:

1	lemon (juice of)
1	teaspoon lemon rind
3	tablespoons butter or margarine
2	cups powdered sugar

1. In medium size mixing bowl, combine first three ingredients. Mix well by hand. Press dough into ungreased 9″ × 13″ pan.
2. Bake 15 minutes at 350°.
3. While baking, combine eggs, brown sugar, flour, baking powder, coconut, vanilla, and pecans.
4. Remove dough pan from oven and add coconut mixture on top. Spread evenly. Bake 20 minutes at 350°.
5. For frosting, combine lemon juice, rind, butter, and sugar. Pour on cookies while still warm.
6. Cut into square.

Temperature: **350 °**
Time: 15 minutes
Temperature: **350 °**
Time: 20 minutes

DECORATED SUGAR COOKIES

Yields: **3-4 dozen**
Preparation Time: 1 hour

1	cup butter
1	cup corn oil
2	cups sugar
2	eggs
1	teaspoon salt
1	teaspoon vanilla
2	teaspoons baking soda
2	teaspoons cream of tartar
5	cups flour
	assorted decorations

1. Cream butter, oil, and sugar. Beat in eggs and then add vanilla.
2. Gradually blend in dry ingredients. Roll out on floured surface and cut out cookies. (Dough should be about ⅜″ thickness.)
3. Bake on ungreased cookie sheet in 350° oven for approximately 10 minutes (until barely brown).
4. Decorate with assorted sprinkles, M & M's or leave plain.

Temperature: **350 °**
Time: 10 minutes

SCOTCH SHORTBREAD

Yields: 6-8 dozen
Preparation Time: 30 minutes

1   pound butter (do not
     substitute)
½   cup brown sugar (light or
     dark)
½   cup powdered sugar
5½   cups flour
½   teaspoon vanilla

1. Cream butter. Add sugars. Blend in flour and vanilla.
2. Roll out on pastry cloth or board to ¼ inch thickness or less.
3. Cut into 2-inch squares or use 2-3 inch round cookie cutter.
4. Place on ungreased cookie sheets and bake 30-40 minutes at 275°.

Temperature: 275 °
Time: 30-40 minutes

Freezes well for up to six months.

ORANGE DROP COOKIES

Yields: 5 dozen
Preparation Time: 45 minutes

1½   cups brown sugar
1   cup shortening
2   eggs, unbeaten
     grated rind of 1 orange
1   cup buttermilk
3½   cups flour (sift before
     measuring)
2   teaspoons baking powder
½   teaspoon soda
1   teaspoon salt

Frosting:

2   cups powdered sugar
2   tablespoons butter, melted
     orange juice

1. Cream sugar and shortening. Add eggs and beat well.
2. Add remaining ingredients and mix thoroughly.
3. Drop by rounded teaspoon onto greased cookie sheet.
4. Bake in a 375° oven for 12-15 minutes. Frost when cooled completely.

Frosting:

1. Combine sugar and butter. Add enough orange juice to make a spreading consistency.
2. Frost cooled cookies.

Temperature: 375 °
Time: 12-15 minutes

MACADAMIA NUT COOKIES

Yields: **80 servings**
Preparation Time: 20 minutes

Cookie Crust:

½   *cup butter, softened*
¼   *cup sugar*
1   *cup flour, sifted*

Nut Filling:

2   *eggs*
½   *cup coconut*
1½   *cups light brown sugar*
1   *cup chopped macadamia nuts*
    (3½ ounce jar)
2   *tablespoons flour*
1   *teaspoon vanilla*
1   *teaspoon salt*
¼   *teaspoon baking powder*

Frosting:

2   *tablespoons butter, softened*
1¼   *cups powdered sugar*
1½-2 *tablespoons milk*
½   *cup coconut, toasted*

1. To make crust, cream butter and sugar. Work in flour until smooth. Pat ingredients into bottom of 9" × 9" pan. Bake 18 minutes or until golden.
2. To make nut filling, beat eggs slightly. Add coconut, brown sugar, nuts, flour, vanilla, salt, and baking powder. Stir until well blended.
3. Spread filling over crust. Bake in a 350° oven for 25 minutes, or until browned and firm to the touch.
4. Let cool in pan.
5. To make frosting, beat butter, sugar, and milk until smooth. Spread evenly over filling as desired. Garnish with toasted coconut.
6. Cut into 1 inch squares.

Temperature: **350 °**
Time: 18 minutes
Time: 25 minutes

219

ORANGE OATMEAL COOKIES

*Yields: **4 dozen***
Preparation Time: 20 minutes

1	cup butter
1	cup firmly packed brown sugar
1	egg
1	tablespoon grated orange peel
2	tablespoons orange juice
1	cup all purpose flour
½	teaspoon soda
1	teaspoon salt
1	cup quick cooking oats
½	cup raisins
½	cup salted, roasted sunflower seeds or pecans

1. In a large mixing bowl, cream butter and sugar until light and fluffy.
2. Add egg, orange peel, and juice. Beat thoroughly.
3. With an electric mixer, blend in flour, soda, and salt. Blend well.
4. Stir in oats, raisins and sunflower seeds.
5. Drop by teaspoon, 2 inches apart on a greased cookie sheet. Bake in a 350° oven for 15-18 minutes or until golden brown.
6. After baking, remove to a wire rack and cool. Store in an air-tight container.

*Temperature: **350 °***
Time: 15-18 minutes

MOON ROCKS

*Yields: **8 dozen***
Preparation Time: 20 minutes

1	6-ounce can frozen orange juice
1	14-ounce can shredded coconut
1	14-ounce box vanilla wafers
1	cup pecans, finely chopped
1	16-ounce box powdered sugar
½	cup butter, softened
1	teaspoon grated orange peel

1. Thaw orange juice and set aside. Reserve half of coconut. Set aside.
2. With a food processor, crush vanilla wafers.
3. In a large mixing bowl, combine orange juice, coconut, vanilla wafers, pecans, sugar, butter, and orange peel and mix thoroughly.
4. Shape into 1-inch balls. Roll into remaining coconut. Store in an air-tight container.

220

ORANGE WALNUT DATE BARS

Yields: **42 bars**
Preparation Time: 30 minutes

1	cup unsifted flour
½	teaspoon baking soda
½	teaspoon cinnamon
¼	teaspoon nutmeg
¼	teaspoon salt
⅓	cup butter or margarine, softened
¾	cup packed brown sugar
1	egg
1	tablespoon orange rind, grated
2	tablespoons orange juice
½	cup chopped pitted dates
¾	cup walnuts, coarsely chopped

Frosting:

¼	cup butter
1	teaspoon orange rind, grated
1	egg yolk
½	teaspoon vanilla
2	cups sifted powdered sugar
2	tablespoons orange juice

1. Sift together dry ingredients.
2. Beat butter and brown sugar in large bowl until light and fluffy. Beat in egg, orange rind, and orange juice. Then beat in flour mixture until smooth. Stir in dates and walnuts.
3. Spread evenly in greased and floured 13" × 9" baking pan. Bake 25-30 minutes in 350° oven until brown.
4. Spread with frosting. Cut into 2" × 1" bars.

Frosting:

1. Cream butter, egg, orange rind, and vanilla until fluffy.
2. Gradually add confectioners sugar. Mix in 2 tablespoons orange juice. Add more if necessary to make frosting spreading consistency.

Temperature: **350** °
Time: 25-30 minutes

If cookies are not to be used at once, do not frost. Cover whole pan with moisture-proof wrap and store in refrigerator. Frost before serving. Frosted cookies keep well in the freezer, but do not ship well.

DOUBLE CHOCOLATE BROWNIES

Yields: 1½-2 dozen
Preparation Time: 15 minutes

*⅓	cup butter
¾	cup sugar
2	tablespoons water
1	12-ounce package semi-sweet chocolate chips, divided
¾	cup flour
¼	teaspoon baking soda
*¼	teaspoon salt
1	teaspoon vanilla
*2	eggs
*½	cup nuts, chopped (your choice)
¾	cup powdered sugar
*1	1-ounce square unsweetened chocolate
*2	tablespoons butter, melted
*1	teaspoon milk

1. Combine ⅓ cup butter, ¾ cup sugar, water, and 1 cup of chocolate chips in a saucepan. Cook over low heat until chocolate and butter are thoroughly mixed and melted.
2. Stir in flour, soda, salt, vanilla, eggs, and nuts. Add remaining chocolate chips. Stir until well blended.
3. Spread mixture in a greased and floured 8-inch square pan. Bake in 325° oven for 30-35 minutes. Remove from oven.
4. Melt chocolate square. Combine chocolate and butter. Stir in powdered sugar and milk. Add a few more drops of milk if necessary until smooth. Spread over warm brownies. Cool before cutting into squares.

Temperature: 325 °
Time: 30-35 minutes

Recipe can be doubled and then use a 9" x 13" pan. They freeze beautifully. Works best if left in pan for 3 hours.

For A Heart Healthy Recipe Use These Substitutions:

*⅓	cup corn oleo
*	omit salt
*½	cup cholesterol free egg substitute
*½	cup nuts, chopped, almonds or walnuts
*3	tablespoons cocoa + 1 tablespoon safflower oil
*2	tablespoons corn oleo, melted
*1	teaspoon skim milk

ENGLISH ROCKS

Yields: **10-12 dozen**
Preparation Time: *20 minutes*

1   *cup butter*
1½   *cups light brown sugar*
3   *eggs*
3   *cups sifted flour*
1   *teaspoon soda*
½   *teaspoon salt*
2   *teaspoons cinnamon*
½   *teaspoon ground cloves*
½   *teaspoon allspice*
½   *cup buttermilk*
4-6 *cups chopped pecans*
1   *pound candied cherries,
       chopped*
2   *cups dates, chopped*
6   *sliced candied pineapples,
       chopped*

Can be frozen.

1. Cream butter and sugar until light and fluffy. Beat in eggs and sifted dry ingredients. Add buttermilk and mix well.
2. Pour batter over nuts and fruit. Mix thoroughly.
3. Drop by the teaspoon on greased cookie sheet.
4. Bake in 325° oven for 18-20 minutes.

*Temperature: **325** °
Time: 18-20 minutes*

SURPRISE KISS TEACAKES

Yields: **4 dozen**
Preparation Time: *30 minutes*

1   *cup butter or margarine*
½   *cup granulated sugar*
1   *teaspoon vanilla*
2⅓   *cups flour*
¾   *cup nuts, finely chopped*
1   *9-ounce package chocolate
       kisses
       powdered sugar*

1. In large mixing bowl, cream butter, sugar, and vanilla until fluffy. Stir in flour and nuts.
2. Remove foil from kisses.
3. Shape about 1 tablespoon of dough around each kiss, covering chocolate completely.
4. Place on ungreased cookie sheets. Bake in preheated 375° oven for 8-10 minutes or until set, not browned.
5. Remove to cooling rack.
6. Roll in powdered sugar.

*Temperature: **375** °
Time: 8-10 minutes*

CARROT COOKIES

*Yields: **3-4 dozen***
Preparation Time: 20 minutes

1	**cup carrots**
¾	**cup sugar**
¾	**cup shortening**
1	**egg, well beaten**
2	**cups flour**
1	**teaspoon baking powder**
1	**teaspoon salt**
½	**teaspoon vanilla**

Frosting:

3	**cups powdered sugar**
¼	**cup orange juice**
1	**teaspoon butter or margarine, melted**
¼	**teaspoon orange rind, grated**

1. Cook carrots. Mash well and set aside.
2. In a large mixing bowl, cream sugar, and shortening. Add egg, carrots, flour, baking powder, salt, and vanilla. Mix thoroughly.
3. Drop by teaspoon on an ungreased cookie sheet. Bake in 350° oven for 10-12 minutes, or until golden brown.
4. Combine icing ingredients. Ice cookies while still warm.
5. Store in a covered container.

*Temperature: **350 °***
Time: 10-12 minutes

♥ **For A Heart Healthy Substitute For Sour Cream, Try This Recipe:**

2	**tablespoons skim milk**
1	**tablespoon lemon juice**
1	**cup low-fat cottage cheese**

1. Place all ingredients in a blender and mix on medium-high speed until smooth and creamy.

*Yields: **about 1¼ cups***

The American Heart Association Cookbook, Fourth Edition, p. 209.

SEAHORSE

The clever little seahorse possesses a fascinating array of individual characteristics: it can look up and down at the same time and it is able to protect itself by changing colors or taking on the appearance of a piece of weed. People have always described the creature's head as horselike in appearance, but the seahorse is indeed a fish that has dwelled in the seas and oceans of the world for centuries. Because the seahorse is such an unusual looking creature, people have always thought that it manifests wondrous magical and medical powers.

CHOCOLATE FINNS
You will need a candy thermometer.

Yields: 2½ dozen
Preparation Time: 30-45 minutes

1st Layer:

2   ounces unsweetened baking chocolate
½   cup butter (do not substitute)
2   eggs, beaten
1   cup sugar
½   cup flour
1   cup nuts, chopped
1   teaspoon vanilla extract

2nd Layer:

1½   cups powdered sugar
½   cup butter, softened (do not substitute)
½   cup heavy cream

3rd Layer;

2   ounces unsweetened baking chocolate
1   tablespoon butter (do not substitute)

1st Layer:

1. In saucepan over a *very* low heat, melt the chocolate and butter.
2. Set aside to cool slightly.
3. Add the eggs, then sugar, flour, nuts, and vanilla.
4. Spread evenly in a 9″ × 13″ pan.
5. Bake in a 350° oven for 10 minutes.

2nd Layer:

1. In another saucepan, combine ingredients and cook over low heat to the soft ball stage about 20-25 minutes. Spread over baked layer.

3rd Layer:

1. In a small saucepan over low heat melt together the chocolate and butter.
2. Drizzle over the top of the layer.
3. Cool until set, then cut into squares.

Temperature: 350 °
Time: 10 minutes

WEST VIRGINIA'S FINEST

Yields: **8 dozen**
Preparation Time: 40 minutes

1   cup butter (no substitutions)
1   cup sugar
1   cup light brown sugar, firmly packed
1   egg
1   cup oil
1   cup rolled oats, regular
1   cup cornflakes, crushed
½   cup shredded coconut, optional
½   cup walnuts, chopped
3½ cups sifted all purpose flour
1   teaspoon soda
1   teaspoon salt
1   teaspoon vanilla

1. In a large mixing bowl, cream butter and sugars until light and fluffy.
2. To the creamed mixture, add egg, mixing well. Then add oil. Mix thoroughly. Add oats, cornflakes, coconut, and nuts. Stir well.
3. To the same mixture, add flour, soda, salt, and vanilla. Mix well.
4. Form into balls the size of small walnuts. Place on an ungreased cookie sheet. Flatten each ball with a fork dipped in water.
5. Bake in 350° oven for 12 minutes.
6. Allow to cool on the cookie sheet for a few minutes before removing.

Temperature: **350 °**
Time: 12 minutes

RUN AWAY GINGERBREAD BOYS

Yields: **3 dozen**
Preparation Time: 45 minutes

1   cup shortening (not butter or margarine)
1   cup brown sugar
1   cup molasses
1   egg, beaten
4   cups flour
1   teaspoon cinnamon
2   teaspoons ginger
1   teaspoon baking soda
½   teaspoon salt
½   teaspoon ground cloves
½   teaspoon nutmeg
    raisins
    almonds
    red hots

1. Cream shortening and brown sugar. Add molasses and beaten egg.
2. Gradually add flour, spices, and other dry ingredients. Chill 2½ hours.
3. Roll dough on floured surface to about ⅜ inch thickness. Cut out cookies and place on greased cookie sheets. Decorate with raisins, almonds, and red hots.
4. Bake in a 325° oven for 10-15 minutes.

Temperature: **325 °**
Time: 10-15 minutes

ORANGE GRANOLA COOKIES

Yields: **3 dozen**
Preparation Time: 20 minutes

1½ **cups granola with nuts (almonds are good)**
¼   **cup orange juice**
1   **cup sugar**
½   **cup shortening**
1   **egg, beaten**
1   **cup sifted flour**
2   **teaspoons baking powder**
½   **teaspoon salt**
½   **teaspoon nutmeg**
1   **tablespoon grated orange peel**

1. In a small mixing bowl, place granola and pour orange juice over all. Set aside.
2. In separate bowl, cream sugar and shortening. Add beaten egg.
3. In separate bowl, combine flour, baking powder, salt, nutmeg, and orange peel. Add to creamed mixture and blend thoroughly.
4. Stir in granola and orange juice. Drop by teaspoon onto greased cookie sheet, 2 inches apart.
5. Bake in a 375° oven for 10 minutes (chewy) to 15 minutes (crunchy).
6. Cool on wire rack.

Temperature: **375 °**
Time: **10-15 minutes**

GO TEXAN DINNER

Sally's Wine Cooler   page 42

Texas Caviar   page 20

Deluxe Cherry Brisket   page 117

Cowboy Slaw   page 73

Corn on the Cob

French Bread

Texas Style Green Beans and New Potatoes   page 191

Aunt Julia's Buttermilk Ice Cream   page 283

Double Chocolate Brownies   page 222

When the Houston Livestock Show and Rodeo comes to town in late February, everyone in the Houston/Galveston area can dress and act western and really Go Texan in honor of our rich heritage of the old west.

PEANUT BUTTER CREAMS

Yields: **6-7 dozen**
Preparation Time: 30 minutes

1   pound peanut butter (smooth
     or crunchy)
1½   pounds powdered sugar
½   pound butter
2-3 teaspoons coffee grains
1   6-ounce package semi-sweet
     chocolate pieces
½   block Gulf wax

1. Cream peanut butter, butter, and sugar together. Add 2 or 3 tablespoons coffee as needed to hold together.
2. After mixed, roll into little balls the size of walnuts.
3. Place on a cookie sheet and chill in refrigerator for 1 hour.
4. Melt chocolate pieces and wax in double boiler. Using a fork, dip balls in chocolate. Set on wax paper.

EASY PECAN TOFFEE BARS

Yields: **4 dozen**
Preparation Time: 15 minutes

1   cellophane package of
     graham crackers
1   cup sugar
½   cup butter
½   cup margarine
1   cup pecans, chopped

1. Cover a cookie sheet with the graham crackers.
2. In a small saucepan, combine the sugar, butter, and margarine. Cook for 2 minutes or until dissolved.
3. Sprinkle chopped pecans over graham crackers. Pour sugar mixture over pecans and graham crackers.
4. Bake in 350° oven for 10 minutes.
5. Cool slightly, then cut into bars. When toffee bars have cooled completely, break up into pieces and store in tightly covered container or freeze until ready to eat.

Temperature: **350 °**
Time: 10 minutes

228

BUTTER PECAN TURTLES

*Yields: **3-4 dozen***
Preparation Time: 15 minutes

Crust:

2 *cups flour*
1 *cup light brown sugar*
½ *cup butter*
1 *16-ounce package pecan halves*

Caramel Mixture:

⅔ *cup butter*
½ *cup light brown sugar*
½ *pound Hershey bars, broken into pieces*

Crust:

1. With an electric mixer, mix flour, brown sugar, and butter until mixture is crumbly.
2. Press mixture into 9" × 13" greased pan.
3. Cover crust with rows of pecan halves.

Caramel Mixture:

1. In a saucepan, stir butter and brown sugar until it bubbles. Boil for ½ to 1 minutes. Pour over crust.
2. Bake 18-22 minutes at 350° until caramel bubbles and browns. Remove from oven. Sprinkle cooked ingredients with milk chocolate pieces.
3. Let stand for 3 minutes for chocolate to melt, then swirl chocolate.
4. Cut in squares while warm and serve.

*Temperature: **350** °*
Time: 18-22 minutes

GRANDMA'S MOLASSES COOKIES

Yields: **75 cookies**
Preparation Time: 30 minutes

2	cups sugar
¾	cups shortening
½	cup molasses
2	eggs, beaten
3	cups flour
2	teaspoons soda
¼	teaspoon allspice
¼	teaspoon ginger
¼	teaspoon cinnamon
¼	teaspoon ground cloves
	additional sugar for rolling cookies

1. Beat sugar and shortening. Add molasses, then eggs, beating well. Add flour, soda, and seasonings. Mix well.
2. Form small balls and roll in sugar.
3. Place on greased cookie sheet 2" apart. Bake in 350° oven for 8-10 minutes. Do not overbake.

Temperature: **350 °**
Time: 8-10 minutes

CHOCOLATE CHIP BRITTLE

Yields: **¼ pound**
Preparation Time: 15-20 minutes

1	cup butter or margarine, softened
1½	teaspoons vanilla
1	teaspoon salt
1	cup sugar
2	cups flour
1	6-ounce package semi-sweet chocolate chips
½	cup walnuts or pecans, chopped

1. Blend butter, vanilla, salt, and sugar. Add flour, one cup at a time, mixing well after each addition. Stir in chocolate chips.
2. Press into ungreased cookie sheet *very* thin with fingers. Sprinkle nuts over top and press in with rolling pin.
3. Bake 25 minutes in 375° oven. Cool completely, then break into pieces like you would peanut brittle.

Temperature: **375 °**
Time: 25 minutes

Store in an air-tight container.

CHOCOLATE BOURBON BALLS

Yields: 5 dozen
Preparation Time: 45 minutes

1	*6-ounce package semi-sweet chocolate pieces*
3	*tablespoons corn syrup*
½	*cup bourbon*
1	*11-ounce package vanilla wafers, crushed*
½	*cup powdered sugar*
1	*cup pecans, finely chopped*
	granulated sugar for coating

1. In a double boiler or microwave, melt chocolate.
2. Add corn syrup and remove from heat. Add bourbon and blend well. Set aside.
3. In a large mixing bowl, combine vanilla wafers, sugar, and nuts. Add chocolate mixture and blend well. Let stand 30 minutes.
4. Form into small balls and roll in granulated sugar.
5. Let season in covered container for several days before serving.

Make several days ahead of time.

NUTTY FUDGE
Must Make Ahead Of Time

Yields: 5 pounds
Preparation Time: 1 hour

½	*pound miniature marshmallows*
3	*6-ounce packages of semi-sweet chocolate chips*
2	*cups nuts, chopped*
1	*cup butter, **not** softened*
1	*teaspoon vanilla*
4½	*cups sugar*
1	*13-ounce can evaporated milk*

1. Mix marshmallows, chocolate chips, nuts, butter, and vanilla in large bowl. Set aside.
2. Mix sugar and evaporated milk in large (12-inch) saucepan. Boil for 12 minutes, stirring constantly.
3. Pour over marshmallow mixture. Stir until well mixed and chocolate chips, butter, and marshmallows are melted.
4. Place in a 9" × 13" pan. May be decorated with frosting. Chill for at least 24 hours.

PEANUT BUTTER CHOCOLATE CANDY

Yields: **3½ dozen**
Preparation Time: 20-25 minutes

1	1-pound box powdered sugar
1-1½	cups graham cracker crumbs
12	ounces peanut butter
1	cup butter, melted
1	12-ounce package chocolate chips, melted

1. Mix sugar and graham cracker crumbs. Add peanut butter and melted butter. Put in a 9" × 13" pan and pack down.
2. Top with melted chocolate chips. Refrigerate.
3. Cut into squares or any desired shape.

SOUTHERN PRALINES

Yields: **3 dozen**
Preparation Time: 15 minutes

½	cup white sugar
1	cup brown sugar
⅓	cup evaporated milk
1	cup pecans
1	teaspoon vanilla

1. In a saucepan, bring sugars and milk to a boil. Remove from stove.
2. Fold in 1 cup pecans.
3. Return to heat and boil mixture for 3 minutes.
4. Remove from stove and stir in 1 teaspoon vanilla.
5. With an electric mixer, beat until thick.
6. Spoon out on waxed paper. Let set until hard.

HAWAIIAN DIVINITY

Yields: **2 dozen**
Preparation Time: 1 hour

3	cups granulated sugar
¾	cup white corn syrup
¾	cup water
3	egg whites
¼	cup concentrated Hawaiian Punch
1	cup nuts, chopped
1	cup maraschino cherries, chopped coarsely

1. Combine sugar, corn syrup, and water. Boil until mixture beads.
2. Beat egg whites until stiff. Slowly add syrup mixture and concentrated punch to egg whites and continue to beat until thick.
3. When mixture is thick, stop beating and fold in nuts and cherries.
4. Drop mixture by the tablespoon on wax paper. Let dry.

Make this only on dry days. If humidity is high, the candy will not be stiff.

CARROT CAKE DELICIOUS

Yields: **12 servings**
Preparation Time: 1¼ hours

2	cups flour
2	cups sugar
2	teaspoons baking powder
2	teaspoons baking soda
⅔	teaspoon cinnamon
1	teaspoon salt
4	eggs
1½	cups vegetable oil
3	cups carrots, grated
½	cup nuts, chopped

1. Mix all dry ingredients together.
2. Beat eggs and add oil to them, beating well. Add egg mixture to dry ingredients. Mix thoroughly. Stir in grated carrots and chopped nuts.
3. Pour into 3 greased 9-inch round pans and bake in 300° oven for 45 minutes.
4. Frost when cooled.

Frosting:

½	cup butter or margarine, softened
8	ounces cream cheese, softened
1	16-ounce box powdered sugar
1	teaspoon vanilla
1	8-ounce can pineapple chunks, drained
1	cup pecans, finely chopped

Frosting:

1. Cream together butter and cream cheese. Gradually add sugar, then vanilla, pineapple, and pecans. Mix well by hand and frost carrot cake.

Temperature: **300°**
Time: **45 minutes**

COCONUT OATMEAL CAKE

Yields: **12 servings**
Preparation Time: 30 minutes

1½   cups boiling water
1   cup regular oats
1   cup brown sugar
1   cup sugar
½   cup butter or margarine
2   eggs
1½   cups flour
1   teaspoon baking soda
1   teaspoon cinnamon
½   teaspoon salt

Frosting:

9   tablespoons butter or
      margarine
1   cup brown sugar
1   7-ounce can flaked coconut
1   teaspoon vanilla
½   cup evaporated milk
½   cup pecans, chopped

1. Pour boiling water over oatmeal and set aside to cool.
2. Combine brown sugar, sugar, and butter. Mix well. Add eggs and flour. Mix thoroughly. Add soda, cinnamon, and salt. Fold in oatmeal mixture.
3. Pour into well-greased and floured 9" × 13" baking dish. Bake in 325° oven 50-60 minutes (until cake pulls away from sides of pan).
4. Combine all ingredients for frosting. Mix thoroughly.
5. Remove cake from oven when done. Pour frosting over cake. Place under broiler for 3 minutes.

Temperature: **325 °**
Time: **50-60 minutes**

PURPLE, GREEN AND GOLD OF MARDI GRAS

Champagne or Wine Coolers
Caviar and Egg Hor D'Oeuvres   page 23
Crunchy Spinach Dip   page 17 (serve in purple cabbage)
Shrimp Creole   page 174
Fruit Kabobs with Kiwi, Red Grapes, and Pineapple
Caesar Salad with Dressing   page 82
Grasshopper Crêpes   page 294
Lemon Pie Bars   page 264

Galveston Mardi Gras began in 1871 and is celebrated every February. Krewes, such as the Knights of Momus, have "Grand" Balls, and day and night parades. The town is decorated in purple, green and gold.

SHEER FANTASY CAKE
"Love That Chocolate"

*Yields: **10-12 servings***
Preparation Time: 20 minutes

*¾	cup butter
¼	cup sugar
2¼	cups light brown sugar, firmly packed
*2	eggs
*3	1-ounce squares unsweetened chocolate, melted and cooled
1	teaspoon vanilla
2¼	cups cake flour
1½	teaspoons baking powder
*½	teaspoon salt
1	teaspoon baking soda
*1	cup milk

Frosting:

*1	8-ounce package cream cheese, softened
*½	cup butter, softened
*2-3	tablespoons milk
1	16-ounce package powdered sugar
*2	1-ounce squares unsweetened chocolate, melted
2	teaspoons vanilla
*1	dash of salt
*1	cup pecans, chopped

1. Cream butter and sugars. Beat in eggs, one at a time. Blend in chocolate and vanilla.
2. Sift together flour, baking powder, salt, and soda. Add flour mixture alternately with milk to chocolate mixture.
3. Pour into two 8-inch, greased and floured cake pans. Bake in 350° oven for 25-30 minutes. Cool completely before frosting.
4. Cream together cream cheese, butter and milk for frosting. Gradually beat in sugar. Add more milk if too thick. Blend in chocolate, vanilla, and salt.
5. Spread frosting on top, between layers, and on sides. Sprinkle pecans on top.

*Temperature: **350 °***
Time: 25-30 minutes

For A Heart Healthy Recipe Make These Substitutions:

*¾	cup corn oleo
*½	cup cholesterol free egg substitute
*9	tablespoons cocoa + 3 tablespoons safflower oil
*	omit salt
*1	cup skim milk

*1	8-ounce package Neufchâtel cream cheese, softened
*½	cup corn oleo, softened
*2-3	tablespoons skim milk
*6	tablespoons cocoa + 2 tablespoons safflower oil
*	omit salt
*1	cup almonds or walnuts, chopped

PUMPKIN CRUNCH PUDDING CAKE

*Yields: **15 servings***
Preparation Time: 25 minutes

1   16-ounce can pumpkin
1   13-ounce can evaporated
     milk
1   cup sugar
3   eggs
2   tablespoons cinnamon
1   18½-ounce yellow pudding
     cake mix
1   cup butter, melted
¼   cup nuts, chopped
1   8-ounce package cream cheese
¾   cup frozen whipped topping
     coconut, grated

1. Mix pumpkin, milk, sugar, eggs, and cinnamon. Mix thoroughly. Pour into a 9" × 13" pan lined with wax paper. Sprinkle the box of dry cake mix on pumpkin mixture. Pat nuts on top.
2. Spoon the cooled melted butter over nuts evenly. Bake in 350° oven for 50-60 minutes. Let cook and then invert onto a large tray.
3. Combine cream cheese and whipped topping. Spread on cake. Sprinkle with coconut on top.

*Temperature: **350 °***
Time: 50-60 minutes

SOUR CREAM POUND CAKE

*Yields: **10-15 servings***
Preparation Time: 30 minutes

1   cup butter or margarine,
     softened
3   cups sugar
6   eggs
¼   teaspoon soda
3   cups flour
1   pint sour cream

1. Cream butter and sugar thoroughly. Add eggs one at a time, beating thoroughly after each addition.
2. Mix flour and soda. Add flour mixture and sour cream alternately to creamed mixture, mixing well after each addition.
3. Bake at 300° for 1½ hours in a greased and sugared tube pan. Crust should be brown on top. Let stand 15 minutes before removing from pan.

*Temperature: **300 °***
Time: 1½ hours

Freezes beautifully. The cake gets more moist the longer you keep it!

GOLDEN CALIFORNIA ICE BOX CAKE

Yields: **6 servings**
Preparation Time: 1½ hours

Sponge Cake:

8	*egg yolks*
2	*cups sugar*
2	*tablespoons hot water*
1	*teaspoon vanilla*
1	*cup boiling water*
1	*teaspoon baking powder*
½	*teaspoon salt*
2½	*cups flour*
6	*egg whites*

Custard:

6	*egg yolks*
¾	*cups sugar*
6	*tablespoons pineapple juice*
1½	*cups butter*
2¼	*cups powdered sugar*
6	*egg whites*
1/16	*teaspoon salt*
2¼	*cups crushed pineapple, drained*

1. Cream yolks, sugar, and water for 15 minutes.
2. Add vanilla and hot water, all at once. Add sifted dry ingredients. Mix well until smooth.
3. Fold in egg whites and bake in 325° oven in ungreased 8-inch round pans for 20-25 minutes. Invert pans until cool. Split each layer into two, forming 4 layers.

Custard:

1. Beat egg yolks and add ¾ cup sugar, gradually.
2. Add pineapple juice and cook in double boiler until thick, stirring constantly. Cool.
3. In bowl, cream butter and powdered sugar until light and fluffy. Add to cooled custard.
4. Beat egg whites with salt. Fold into custard mixture. Add pineapple (drained).
5. Spread mixture between the four layers of sponge cake. Cover with wax paper and refrigerate overnight.
6. Spread with whipped cream before serving.

Temperature: **325 °**
Time: 20-25 minutes

BIRTHDAY BUTTERMILK CAKE AND POSIE CREAM ICING

*Yields: **8-10 servings***
Preparation Time: 1 hour

2½   cups sugar
1   cup shortening
½   cup butter or margarine
5   eggs
3   cups flour
1   cup buttermilk
½   teaspoon soda dissolved in 2
      tablespoons hot water
1   teaspoon almond extract

1. Cream first 3 ingredients.
2. Add eggs, one at a time, continuing to beat. Add flour and milk alternately, using lower speed. Add soda mixture and extract.
3. Bake in 325° oven for 50 minutes in lightly greased and floured pans.
4. Cool cake and ice with Posie Cream Icing.

Posie Icing:

1   cup shortening
⅛   teaspoon salt
3   cups powdered sugar
¼   cup butter, softened
1½   teaspoons vanilla or almond
      extract

Icing:

1. Combine shortening, salt, 1 cup sugar, butter and vanilla until smooth, using low speed on mixer.
2. Gradually beat in rest of sugar and beat until spreading consistency.

*Temperature: **325 °***
Time: 50 minutes

Icing stays soft for several days if stored covered.

MEXICAN EXCELLANTE CAKE

Yields: 15 servings
Preparation Time: 1 hour

7	eggs, separated
1½	cups sugar
1	teaspoon vanilla
½	teaspoon baking powder
2	tablespoons flour
3	cups pecans, finely ground

Frosting:

1	pint whipping cream, whipped
½	cup powdered sugar
1	teaspoon vanilla

1. Cream sugar with egg yolks. Add vanilla, baking powder, and flour, mixing thoroughly. Stir in pecans.
2. Beat egg whites until stiff. Fold into cake mixture.
3. Bake at 350° for 30 minutes in 3 well greased 8-inch round pans.

Frosting:

1. Whip cream until soft peaks form. Add powdered sugar and vanilla. Beat again until spreading consistency. Ice cake.

Temperature: 350 °
Time: 30 minutes

This is very pretty when iced only between layers and on top, then sprinkled with more finely chopped pecans.

COINTREAU CAKE

Yields: 16-20 servings
Preparation Time: 30 minutes

1	18¼-ounce box yellow cake mix
1	3½-ounce package instant vanilla pudding mix
4	eggs
½	cup vegetable oil
½	cup orange juice
½	cup Cointreau or Curãcao

Glaze:

1	cup sugar
½	cup butter
¼	cup orange juice
¼	cup Cointreau

1. In a large mixing bowl, combine cake mix, pudding mix, eggs, oil, orange juice, and Cointreau. Beat well for 10 minutes with an electric mixer.
2. Pour into a lightly greased Bundt pan.
3. Bake in a 325° oven for 45-60 minutes. Let stand 10 minutes; turn out.

Glaze:

1. While cake is baking, boil sugar, butter, orange juice and Cointreau for a few minutes. Pour over cake while cake is still warm.

Temperature: 325 °
Time: 45-60 minutes

Freezes well. Remains moist at room temperature for a week.

PINEAPPLE CAKE

*Yields: **15 servings***
Preparation Time: 15 minutes

2   *cups flour*
2   *cups sugar*
2   *eggs*
1   *teaspoon baking soda*
⅛   *teaspoon salt*
1   *20-ounce can crushed pineapple*
¼   *cup vegetable oil*

Frosting:

¾   *cup sugar*
½   *cup butter or margarine*
½   *cup evaporated milk*
½   *cup pecans **OR** ½ cup coconut*

1. Mix all of ingredients together in a large mixing bowl until well blended.
2. Pour batter into a greased 9" × 13" pan. Bake in a 325° oven for 35 minutes.

Frosting:

1. To make icing, cook sugar, butter, and milk over medium heat until thick and bubbly (about 5 minutes). Add pecans or coconut, then stir well. While icing is hot, spread on cake.

*Temperature: **325** °*
Time: 35 minutes

CHOCOLATE LADYFINGER CAKE
Must Make Ahead Of Time

*Yields: **12 servings***
Preparation Time: overnight

½   *pound butter*
3   *cups powdered sugar*
6   *eggs, separated*
3   *squares unsweetened chocolate, melted*
½   *teaspoon almond extract*
1   *teaspoon vanilla*
2   *dozen ladyfingers, split*
1   *pint heavy cream, whipped*

1. Cream butter and sugar thoroughly with mixer. Add yolks, one at a time, beating well after each addition. Blend in melted chocolate, almond extract, and vanilla. Set aside.
2. Beat egg whites until stiff and fold into chocolate mixture slowly.
3. Line 12-inch springform pan with ladyfingers. Spoon in some chocolate mixture, then more ladyfingers. Continue alternating layers until mixture is gone. Refrigerate overnight.
4. Before serving, unmold and top with whipped cream.

MARR FAMILY CHRISTMAS CAKE

*Yields: **8-10 servings***
Preparation Time: 2½ hours

½   cup butter
2   cups sugar
3   cups applesauce
3½ cups flour, reserve ½ cup for fruit
1   teaspoon nutmeg
1   teaspoon ground cloves
1   teaspoon cinnamon
3   teaspoons soda
1   cup dates, chopped
1   cup raisins, chopped
1   cup pecans, chopped

Frosting:

½   cup butter
½   cup whipping cream
1   package light brown sugar
1   teaspoon vanilla

1. Cream butter and sugar, add 3 cups sifted flour.
2. Mix soda and spices alternately with applesauce to flour mixture.
3. Dredge fruit and nuts in flour and add to cake batter. Fold into a greased tube pan.
4. Bake in 300° oven for 1½-2 hours.

Frosting:

1. Melt butter, cream, and sugar over low heat.
2. Bring to a boil for 5 minutes to soft ball stage. Add vanilla and let set until cool. Beat until thick enough to spread.

*Temperature: **300 °***
Time: 1½-2 hours

Freezes well.

CELEBRATING THE OLEANDER

Chutney Cheese Ball   page 31
Assorted Crackers
Oven-Smoked Brisket   page 112
Company Peas   page 198
Golden Potato Casserole   page 199
Squash Soufflé   page 200
Bourbon Chocolate Pie   page 263

The Oleander Festival is an annual event which honors the blossoming of the oleander, a shrub which permeates and decorates the island of Galveston nearly year round. Festivities have included beauty contests, sports tournaments, home and garden tours and much more.

CHERRY WAFER CHEESECAKE

*Yields: **6-8 servings***
Preparation Time: 1-1½ hours

Crust:

3   *cups vanilla wafers, crushed*
5   *tablespoons sugar*
1   *teaspoon cinnamon*
½   *cup butter, melted*

Filling:

24   *ounces cream cheese*
1½   *cups sugar*
4   *eggs*
1   *teaspoon vanilla*

Topping:

1   *cup sour cream*
4   *tablespoons sugar*

Optional:
1   *can cherry pie filling*

Crust:

1. Combine all ingredients and press into bottom of springform pan.

Filling:

1. Mix all ingredients and pour into unbaked crust.
2. Bake on bottom shelf of oven for 45-60 minutes at 300°.

Topping:

1. Stir sour cream and sugar together. Pour topping on cheesecake and return to oven for 10 minutes at 350°. Chill.

*Temperature: **300** °*
Time: 45-60 minutes
*Temperature: **350** °*
Time: 10 minutes

Serve plain or top with cherry pie filling just before serving.

OATMEAL CAKE

*Yields: **6-8 servings***
Preparation Time: 45 minutes

1¼	cups boiling water
½	cup butter
1	cup rolled oats
2	eggs
1	cup sugar
1	cup brown sugar
1¼	cups sifted flour
1	teaspoon baking soda
½	teaspoon cinnamon
½	teaspoon salt

Frosting:

1	pound powdered sugar
2	3-ounce packages cream cheese
1	teaspoon vanilla
	water to make smooth

1. Combine first 3 ingredients, let stand for 20 minutes.
2. Add eggs, mix well.
3. In separate bowl, combine remaining ingredients and add to oat mixture, mix well. Pour into well greased and floured 9" x 13" pan.
4. Bake in 350° oven for 30 minutes.
5. Cool before adding topping.

Frosting:

1. Mix all ingredients well and spread over cooled cake.

*Temperature: **350 °***
Time: 30 minutes

CHOCOLATE CINNAMON CAKE

*Yields: **16 servings***
Preparation Time: 10 minutes

1	cup water
4	tablespoons cocoa
½	cup butter or margarine
2	cups flour
2	cups sugar
½	cup buttermilk
1	teaspoon soda
1	teaspoon vanilla
1	teaspoon cinnamon
2	eggs

Frosting:

½	cup butter or margarine
8	tablespoons milk
4	tablespoons cocoa
1	pound box powdered sugar

Top with pecans if desired.

1. Boil water, cocoa, and butter in a small saucepan.
2. Add immediately to flour and sugar in a large bowl. Beat well. Stir in buttermilk, soda, vanilla, and cinnamon. Mix thoroughly.
3. Bake in a greased 9" × 13" pan in 350° oven for 20-30 minutes.

Frosting

1. Bring butter, milk, and cocoa to a boil in saucepan over medium heat. Add powdered sugar, stirring vigorously to remove lumps. Pour over *hot* cake.

*Temperature: **350 °***
Time: 20-30 minutes

ITALIAN CREAM CAKE

Yields: **12 servings**
Preparation Time: **30 minutes**

1   cup butter (no substitution)
2   cups sugar
5   egg whites, stiffly beaten
5   egg yolks, beaten well
2   cups flour
1   teaspoon soda
1   cup buttermilk
1   teaspoon vanilla
1   small can chopped coconut
1   cup nuts, chopped

Frosting:

1   8-ounce package cream
     cheese, softened
¼   cup butter
1   box powdered sugar
1   teaspoon vanilla
1   cup pecans, chopped
     (optional)
1   cup coconut (optional)

1. Cream butter and sugar. Add beaten egg yolks to creamed mixture. Mix well.
2. Combine flour and soda. Set aside.
3. Combine buttermilk, vanilla, coconut, and nuts. Set aside.
4. Alternately add flour mixture and buttermilk to creamed mixture, mixing well after each addition.
5. Beat egg whites until stiff. Fold into mixture.
6. Pour into three greased and floured 8-inch cake pans. Bake in 350° oven for 20 minutes.

Frosting:

1. In a mixing bowl, beat cream cheese and butter.
2. Add powdered sugar and vanilla. Beat until smooth.
3. Add pecans and coconut if desired.
4. Ice cake when cool.

Temperature: **350** °
Time: **20 minutes**

GERMAN CHOCOLATE CHEESE CAKE

Better If Made Ahead Of Time

Yields: **8 servings**
Preparation Time: *25 minutes*

Crust:

1	package German chocolate cake mix
½	cup shredded coconut
⅓	cup butter or margarine, softened
1	egg

Filling:

16	ounces cream cheese
2	eggs
¾	cup sugar
2	teaspoons vanilla

Topping:

2	cups sour cream
1	teaspoon vanilla
¼	cup sugar

Crust:

1. Mix all ingredients for crust at low speed until crumbly.
2. Press lightly into ungreased 13" × 9" pan.

Filling:

1. Beat all ingredients until smooth and fluffy. Spread over crust.
2. Bake in 350° oven for 25-30 minutes. Cool.

Topping:

1. Combine all ingredients and spread over top of cooled filling.
2. Refrigerate for several hours or days.

Temperature: **350 °**
Time: *25-30 minutes*

Sprinkle with grated chocolate, if desired.

CHOCOLATE POUND CAKE AND FROSTING

*Yields: **12-16 servings***
Preparation Time: 30 minutes

Cake:

1	cup butter or margarine, softened
½	cup shortening
3	cups sugar
5	eggs
3	cups flour
¼	teaspoon salt
½	teaspoon baking powder
½	cup cocoa
1¼	cups milk
1	teaspoon vanilla

Frosting:

2	cups sugar
½	cup butter
2	squares unsweetened chocolate
⅔	cups evaporated milk
1	teaspoon vanilla

Cake:

1. In a mixing bowl, cream butter with shortening and sugar. Add eggs one at a time, beating well after each addition.
2. Sift flour, salt, baking powder, and cocoa. Add this mixture to creamed mixture, alternating with milk. Add vanilla. Mix thoroughly.
3. Pour mixture into a large greased tube pan and bake in 325° oven for 1½ hours.

Frosting:

1. In a medium saucepan, combine sugar, margarine, unsweetened chocolate, evaporated milk, and vanilla. Bring to a boil and cook 2 minutes. Cool and beat until smooth enough to spread.

*Temperature: **325 °***
Time: 1½ hours

Sprinkle white sugar around bottom and edges. This will release the cake easier.

PAUL REVERE COCONUT CAKE

*Yields: **15-20 servings***
Preparation Time: 1½ hours

Cake:

1	*package yellow cake mix*
1	*3¾-ounce package vanilla instant pudding mix*
1⅓	*cup water*
4	*eggs*
¼	*cup oil*
2	*cups coconut, shredded*
1	*cup pecans, chopped*

Frosting:

4	*tablespoons butter or margarine, divided*
2	*cups coconut, shredded*
1	*8-ounce package cream cheese, softened*
2	*tablespoons milk*
½	*teaspoon vanilla*
3½	*cups powdered sugar, sifted*
1	*cup pecans, halved or chopped*

1. Blend cake and pudding mixes with water, eggs, and oil in a large mixing bowl. Beat at medium speed for 4 minutes. Stir in coconut and pecans.
2. Bake in greased and floured 13" × 9" pan in 350° oven for 40-50 minutes. Cool completely.

Frosting:

1. Prepare icing by melting 2 tablespoons butter in skillet. Add coconut and stir constantly over low heat until golden brown. Spread on paper towels to cool.
2. Cream 2 tablespoons butter with cream cheese. Add milk and sugar alternately, beating well after each addition. Add vanilla. Stir in 1½ cups coconut and pecans.
3. Frost cake. Sprinkle with remaining coconut.

*Temperature: **350** °*
Time: 40-50 minutes

HEATH TORTE

Yields: **15 servings**
Preparation Time: 1 hour

6   egg whites
2   cups sugar
1   teaspoon vinegar
1   teasoon vanilla
⅛   teaspoon salt

Filling:

1   pint heavy cream, whipped
10-15 Heath bars, finely ground
1   tablespoon vanilla
2   tablespoons powdered sugar
    nuts, chopped

1. Beat egg whites with vinegar, salt, and vanilla until very stiff.
2. Add sugar and beat until very stiff.
3. Pour into two 9-inch cake pans, buttered on sides and greased brown paper on bottom.
4. Bake in 300° oven for 1 hour. Cool.

Filling:

1. Whip cream and add sugar and vanilla. Fold in ground Heath bars.
2. Place half of filling between layers and other half on top.
3. Cover top with chopped nuts. Cover with plastic wrap. Refrigerate overnight.

Temperature: **300** °
Time: 1 hour

HERSHEY BAR BUNDT CAKE

Yields: **24 slices**
Preparation Time: 30 minutes

7   1.45-ounce Hershey bars
    (melted)
2   cups sugar
4   eggs
1   teaspoon vanilla
1   cup buttermilk
1   cup butter
1   pound can chocolate syrup
2½ cups cake flour
1   teaspoon salt
¼   teaspoon baking soda

1. Blend all ingredients thoroughly.
2. Pour into well-greased and floured, large bundt pan.
3. Bake in 350° oven for 1¼ hours.

Temperature: **350** °
Time: 1¼ hours

This cake is especially good served with vanilla ice cream.

MINIATURE CHEESE CAKES

Yields: 24
Preparation Time: 45 minutes

"Great For A Luncheon"

3	*3-ounce package cream cheese, divided*
½	*cup butter or margarine*
1	*cup flour*
2	*tablespoons sugar*
1	*teaspoon vanilla*
1	*egg*
1½	*cups cherry or blueberry pie filling*

1. Cream together one 3-ounce package cream cheese and butter. Blend in flour. Divide into 24 small (about 1-inch) balls. Put one in each of 24 small muffin tins. Press against sides with fingers to line cup evenly.
2. Beat remaining cheese until smooth. Add sugar and vanilla. Beat well. Add egg and beat with electric mixer until creamy.
3. Spoon cheese filling into each tin until filled. Bake in 350° oven for 20 minutes. Cool and remove. Top with pie filling. Refrigerate until ready to serve.

Temperature: 350 °
Time: 20 minutes

Your favorite jam may be substituted for the pie filling.

MAY FÊTE BRUNCH

Strawberry Daiquiri   page 37   *Banana-Orange Punch   page 36*
Bacon Crisps   page 28   *Sausage Cheese Dip   page 32*
Raspberry-Cranberry Salad   page 65
Spiced Apple Muffins   page 84   *Blueberry Coffeecake   page 95*
Italian Sausage Quiche   page 108
Humdingers   page 214
Almond Raspberry Tassies   page 214

May Fête is a rich southern tradition. Debutantes or duchesses are presented to the King and Queen of the May. The ladies and their flowergirls are dressed in formals done in all colors of the rainbow. The escorts or Dukes are dressed in white tuxedoes. After the court is presented there is entertainment.

DUTCH APPLE PIE CAKE

"Delicious a la Mode"

*Yields: **10 servings***
Preparation Time: 20 minutes

2	*cups flour*
3	*teaspoons baking powder*
¾	*cup sugar*
1	*teaspoon salt*
1	*teaspoon cinnamon*
1	*egg, beaten*
¾	*cup milk*
⅓	*cup shortening, melted*
1½	*cups apples, chopped*

Topping:

½	*cup sugar*
3	*tablespoons flour*
2	*tablespoons butter, softened*
½	*teaspoon cinnamon*

1. Sift the flour, baking powder, sugar, salt, and cinnamon. Set aside.
2. Combine beaten egg and milk. Add shortening. Add egg mixture all at once to dry ingredients. Fold in apples and mix thoroughly. Turn into a greased 8-inch baking pan.
3. Combine remaining ingredients for topping and sprinkle over top of batter.
4. Bake in 400° oven for 25-30 minutes.

*Temperature: **400** °*
Time: 25-30 minutes

Walnuts or pecans, chopped, may be added to batter before baking.

HISTORICAL HOMES TOUR BRUNCH

Milk Punch   page 37
Rainbow Compote   page 66
Banana Nut Bread   page 88
South of the Border Egg Casserole   page 105

The Galveston annual Tour of Homes is held two weekends in May always including Mother's Day. Locals and tourists alike take this opportunity to visit some of the most beautiful historical homes in Galveston.

UPSIDE DOWN APPLE CAKE

Yields: **8 servings**
Preparation Time: **20 minutes**

¼   cup butter or margarine,
    melted
½   cup brown sugar
½   teaspoon cinnamon
½   cup pecans
3   apples, cored and thinly
    sliced
¼   cup butter or margarine
1   cup flour
½   cup brown sugar
1   egg, slightly beaten
½   teaspoon vanilla
1½ teaspoons baking powder
½   teaspoon salt

1. Grease sides of 10-inch pie dish and pour in melted butter. Sprinkle brown sugar and cinnamon evenly on top. Add pecans and then layer apple slices.
2. Cream butter and brown sugar. Add egg and vanilla, set aside.
3. Mix flour, baking powder, and salt. Add to egg mixture and mix until well blended. Pour over apples and spread evenly.
4. Bake in 350° oven for 40-45 minutes until center springs back when lightly touched. Loosen sides with knife and invert onto plate.

Temperature: **350 °**
Time: **40-45 minutes**

CINCO DE MAYO

Jalapeño Mushrooms   page 11
Ninfa's Avocado Sauce   page 22
Tortilla Chips
Mexican Salad   page 70
Mexican Quesadillas   page 110
Sour Cream Chicken Enchiladas   page 144
Mexican Excellante Cake   page 239

The Texas Gulf Coast is rich in Hispanic heritage. Many groups celebrate Cinco de Mayo or Mexican Independence Day in this area. There are parades and fiestas and lots of good Mexican food.

TURTLE CAKE

*Yields: **20-25 servings***
Preparation Time: 20 minutes

1	14-ounce caramel candies
½	cup evaporated milk
1	18½-ounce package German Chocolate cake mix
1⅓	cups water
¾	cup butter, softened
3	eggs
1	cup pecans, chopped
1	cup chocolate chips

1. Melt caramels with milk in top of double boiler or in microwave.

2. Combine cake mix with water, butter, and eggs in large mixing bowl. Blend on low speed 30 seconds, then at medium speed for 2 minutes. Pour half the batter in a greased 13" × 9" pan.

3. Bake in 350° oven for 10 minutes or until cake puffs up and is "gooey". Pour caramel-milk mixture over partially baked layer to within ½" of edge. Sprinkle nuts and chocolate chips evenly over caramel. Pour remaining batter over all and bake in 350° oven 25-30 minutes until top springs back when touched lightly in center.

4. Cool in pan. Cut into squares.

*Temperature: **350** °*
Time: 10 minutes
*Temperature: **350** °*
Time: 25-30 minutes

It can be served with ice cream or whipped topping.

BLACKBERRY WINE CAKE

"You'll Always Want More"

1	*18½-ounce white cake mix*
1	*3-ounce package blackberry jello*
4	*eggs*
½	*cup vegetable oil*
1	*cup blackberry wine*
½	*cup pecans, chopped*

Glaze:

1⅓	*cups powdered sugar, sifted*
½	*cup butter or margarine*
½	*cup blackberry wine*

1. Combine cake mix and jello. Add eggs, oil, and wine. Beat with electric mixer in bowl on low speed until moistened. Beat on medium speed for 2 minutes, scraping the sides of bowl frequently.
2. Sprinkle bottom of greased and floured bundt pan with pecans. Pour batter on top. Bake in 350° oven for 45-50 minutes. Remove from oven.
3. Combine ingredients for glaze using only 1 cup of powdered sugar, and bring to a boil. Pour half the glaze over cake while still in pan.
4. Let cake cool 30 minutes. Turn cake out of pan to finish cooling.
5. Add rest of powdered sugar to glaze. Mix well. Dribble over cake.

ISLAND SPLASH DAY

Fresh Strawberry Soup   page 44
Super Seafood Salad   page 71
Cheese Bread   page 84
Miniature Cheese Cakes   page 249

An old Galveston tradition now being revived, Splash Day was the official opening of the 120 day Galveston tourist season which ended with Labor Day. Usually held in late April or early May and originally sponsored by Southern Select Beer, Splash Day activities such as beauty contests and parades were attended by people from all over the United States.

HUMMINGBIRD CAKE

Yields: **12-15 servings**
Preparation Time: 20 minutes

3 cups flour
2 cups sugar
1 teaspoon soda
1 teaspoon salt
1 teaspoon cinnamon
3 eggs, beaten
1½ cups vegetable oil
1½ teaspoons vanilla
1 8-ounce can crushed pineapple
2 cups pecans, divided
2 cups bananas, chopped

Cream Cheese Frosting:

2 8-ounce packages cream cheese, softened
1 cup butter, softened
2 pounds powdered sugar
2 teaspoons vanilla

1. In a large mixing bowl, combine flour, sugar, soda, salt, and cinnamon. Stir well.
2. Add eggs and salad oil. Stir only until dry ingredients are moistened. DO NOT BEAT. Stir in vanilla, pineapple, pecans, and bananas.
3. Spoon batter into three well greased and floured 9-inch pans or one 9" × 13" pan.
4. Bake in 350° oven for 25-30 minutes or until done. Cool in pans 10 minutes. Remove and cool completely. Spread with cream cheese frosting.

Frosting:

1. In a large mixing bowl, combine cream cheese, butter, powdered sugar, and vanilla. Beat until light and fluffy.
2. Spread on cake and between layers.

Temperature: **350 °**
Time: 25-30 minutes

AMARETTO CHEESECAKE

Make 24-48 Hours Ahead Of Time.

Yields: *12 servings*
Preparation Time: *1½-2 hours*

Crust:

1½	*cups graham cracker crumbs*
2	*tablespoons sugar*
1	*teaspoon ground cinnamon*
¼	*cup plus 2 tablespoons melted butter or margarine*

Filling:

3	*8-ounce packages cream cheese, softened*
1	*cup sugar*
4	*eggs*
⅓	*cup Amaretto*

Topping:

1	*8-ounce carton sour cream*
1	*tablespoon plus 1 teaspoon sugar*
1	*tablespoon Amaretto*
¼	*cup toasted sliced almonds*
1	*1.2-ounce chocolate candy bar, grated*

Crust:

1. Combine all ingredients for crust, mix well.
2. Firmly press mixture into bottom and ½-inch up the sides of an ungreased 9-inch springform pan.

Filling:

1. Beat cream cheese with electric mixer until light and fluffy.
2. Gradually add sugar, mixing well.
3. Add eggs, one at a time, beating well after each addition.
4. Stir in Amaretto.
5. Pour into pan and bake in 375° oven for 45-50 minutes.

Topping:

1. Combine sour cream, sugar, and Amaretto.
2. Stir well.
3. Spoon over cheesecake.
4. Bake in 500° oven for 5 minutes.
5. Cool to room temperature.
6. Refrigerate 24-48 hours.
7. Garnish with almonds and grated chocolate.

*Temperature: **375** °*
Time: 45-50 minutes
*Temperature: **500** °*
Time: 5 minutes

CHOCOLATE FUDGE CAKE

Yields: **15 servings**
Preparation Time: 20 minutes

½   *cup butter, softened*
1   *16-ounce package light brown sugar*
3   *eggs*
3   *1-ounce squares unsweetened chocolate, melted*
2¼   *cups cake flour, sifted*
2   *teaspoons soda*
½   *teaspoon salt*
1   *cup sour cream*
1   *cup hot water*
1½   *teaspoons vanilla*

Frosting:

4   *1-ounce squares unsweetened chocolate*
½   *cup butter*
1   *16-ounce box powdered sugar, sifted*
½   *cup milk*
2   *teaspoons vanilla*

1. Cream butter. Gradually add sugar, beating well. Add eggs, one at a time, beating well after each addition. Add chocolate, mixing thoroughly.
2. Combine flour, soda, and salt. Alternately add flour and sour cream to chocolate mixture, beating well after each addition.
3. Add water and vanilla. Mix thoroughly. Batter will be thin.
4. Pour batter evenly into 2 greased and floured 9-inch round cake pans. Bake in 350° oven for 45 minutes or until cake tests done. Let cool in pans 10 minutes. Remove from pan and place on wire racks to complete cooling.

Frosting:

1. Combine chocolate and butter for frosting. Place over low heat until melted, stirring constantly.
2. Combine sugar, milk, and vanilla in a medium mixing bowl. Mix well. Set bowl in large pan of ice cold water and stir in chocolate mixture. Then beat at high speed until of spreading consistency (about 2 minutes).
3. Spread frosting between layers and on top and sides of cake.

Temperature: **350 °**
Time: 45 minutes

OLEANDERS

Based on the abundance of blossoms during certain times of the year, Galvestonians like to say they live in the Oleander City, but, in all honesty, the flower isn't truly native to the city. When the plants began to be grown in Galveston in abundance was after the Great Storm of 1900. The Women's Health Protective Association, in an attempt to revitalize Galveston after the devastation, initiated a beautification project by planting oleanders in every section of the city.

CHERRY SPICE CAKE
"Recipe is over 100 years old"

Yields: 15 servings
Preparation Time: 30 minutes

1	*cup butter*
2	*cups sugar*
3	*egg yolks, well beaten*
1	*cup apples, cooked and refrigerated*
1	*teaspoon baking soda*
½	*cup buttermilk*
3¼	*cups flour*
1	*cup candied cherries, cut in pieces*
1	*cup pecans, left whole*
1	*teaspoon vanilla*
½	*teaspoon salt*
2	*teaspoons cinnamon*
1	*teaspoon nutmeg*
3	*egg whites, stiffly beaten powdered sugar*

1. Cream butter and sugar. Add egg yolks and beat well. Add apples.
2. Combine baking soda and buttermilk. Add 3 cups flour and buttermilk alternately to egg mixture, beating after each addition.
3. Dip cherries and pecans in ¼ cup flour. Add pecans, cherries, vanilla, salt, cinnamon, and nutmeg. Fold in egg whites. Bake in 350° oven in a greased and floured bundt pan for 50-60 minutes.
4. Sprinkle with powdered sugar when removed from pan.

Temperature: 350 °
Time: 50-60 minutes

This is a great Christmas dessert. It looks so pretty.

BLESSING OF THE FLEET BRUNCH

Spiced Apple Muffins   page 84
Brunch Pie   page 103
Fresh Pineapple and Melon Chunks
Tomato Frappés   page 38
Molly Hogans   page 35

The Blessing of the Fleet is an annual event during which local shrimpers decorate and parade their boats in and around Galveston's harbor. During this celebration, a blessing is delivered by local clergy to the shrimpers praying that they have a safe and successful harvest.

RUM CAKE

*Yields: **10-12 servings***
Preparation Time: 15 minutes

3	cups flour
¼	teaspoon salt
1	teaspoon baking powder
½	teaspoon baking soda
1	cup butter
2	cups sugar
4	eggs
1	cup buttermilk
2	tablespoons rum

Rum Icing:

1	cup sugar
½	cup water
2	tablespoons rum

Cake:

1. Sift flour, salt, baking powder, and baking soda together. Set aside.
2. Cream butter and sugar together. Add eggs one at a time. Mix thoroughly. Add the flour and buttermilk alternately. Stir in the rum. Pour batter into a small bundt pan. Bake in 350° oven for 1 hour.

Rum Icing:

1. Combine sugar and water. Bring to a rolling boil. Remove from heat and add rum. Pour over cake and let sit until cool.

*Temperature: **350** °*
Time: 1 hour

A 1-ounce bottle of rum flavoring may be substituted for the rum.

ALOHA BUFFET

KENTUCKY JAM CAKE

*Yields: **16-20 servings***
Preparation Time: 30 minutes

1	**cup butter**
2	**cups sugar**
1	**cup buttermilk**
4	**eggs**
3	**cups flour**
1	**teaspoon baking soda**
2	**teaspoons allspice**
3	**teaspoons cinnamon**
2	**tablespoons cocoa**
1	**cup nuts**
1½	**cups jam (blackberry with seeds is best)**
½	**cup peach preserves**
1	**cup raisins**
½	**cup red or rosé wine**

Frosting (Optional):

1½	**cups brown sugar**
⅓	**cup buttermilk**
2	**tablespoons butter**

1. Cream butter and sugar. Add beaten eggs. Set aside.
2. Sift flour, baking soda, allspice, cinnamon and cocoa.
3. Mix nuts, raisins, jam, and preserves.
4. Mix all ingredients alternately with buttermilk. Add wine.
5. Bake in 300° oven for 1 hour in a tube pan, or 1½ hours in a greased and floured bundt pan.

Frosting:

1. Boil sugar and milk over medium heat to the soft boil stage.
2. Remove and add butter.
3. Cool and spread when it has reached a spreadable consistency.

*Temperature: **300** °*
Time: 1 hour

DICKENS ON THE STRAND
FORMAL DINNER

King Arthur's Oysters   page 28
Marinated Tomatoes   page 69
Beef Wellington   page 120
Wild Rice and Almond Casserole   page 206
Buttered English Peas
Diana Tort   page 280

Dickens on the Strand, a project of Galveston Historical Foundation, is held the first weekend in December. This major fundraiser is attended by over 100,000 people each year. Visitors are encouraged to dress in the Victorian style as are the vendors and shopowners on the Strand.

FRESH APPLE SPONGE CAKE

"So Simple, Yet So Good"

*Yields: **15 servings***
Preparation Time: 20 minutes

3   cups flour
2   cups granulated sugar
¼   teaspoon salt
1   teaspoon baking soda
2   teaspoons cinnamon
1   cup vegetable oil
3   eggs, well beaten
3   cups apples, peeled and diced
2   teaspoons vanilla
1   cup nuts, chopped (optional)

1. In a large mixing bowl, combine all ingredients. Mix thoroughly.
2. Pour into greased and floured tube pan. Bake in 300° oven for 1½-2 hours. Cool 15 minutes in pan. Remove from pan. Cool completely.

*Temperature: **300** °*
Time: 1½-2 hours

APPLE SURPRISE

*Yields: **10-12 servings***
Preparation Time: 20 minutes

3   cups flour
½   teaspoon baking soda
½   teaspoon salt
1   tablespoon cinnamon
1   tablespoon nutmeg
1   tablespoon allspice
3   eggs
2   cups sugar
1   cup vegetable oil
½-¾ cup milk
1   tablespoon vanilla
1   tablespoon rum flavoring
1   tablespoon black walnut flavoring
3   cups apples, peeled and chopped
1   cup raisins
1   cup pecans, chopped

1. Mix all ingredients and put in floured, and greased bundt pan.
2. Bake in 350° oven 45 minutes to an hour.

*Temperature: **350** °*
Time: 45 minutes-1 hour

Start with the ½ cup of milk. Use the other ¼ cup if too dry.

CZECH LEMON MERINGUE CHEESE CAKE

Yields: 15 servings
Preparation Time: 1 hour

Dough:

½   *cup unsalted butter or*
     margarine, softened
½   *cup sugar*
2   *egg yolks*
1   *cup flour*
     ring of 1 lemon, grated

Filling:

1   *8-ounce package cream cheese*
     or DRY cottage cheese
6   *tablespoons sugar*
2   *egg yolks*
3   *tablespoons sour cream*
     juice of 1 large lemon
¼   *cup raisins (optional)*

Topping:

4   *tablespoons sugar*
4   *egg whites*

1. Make dough by blending the first 5 ingredients in a medium-size mixing bowl and work them into a dough. Let dough rest for ½ hour, wrapped in the refrigerator.
2. Butter a 10-inch "deep dish" pie plate. Roll out the dough to fit pie pan. Prick all over with a fork. Bake in 350° oven for 10 minutes.

Filling:

1. To make filling, beat together cream cheese, sugar, egg yolks, sour cream, and lemon juice until very light and fluffy. Fold in the raisins and put the filling into the baked pie crust.

Topping:

1. Make meringue by beating egg whites until stiff, then gradually adding sugar a tablespoon at a time. Beat at high speed of mixer until forming stiff peaks. Spread over filling, smoothing it with a wet knife.
2. Bake in middle of a very hot oven (475°) for about 5 minutes or until golden brown.

Temperature: 350 °
Time: 10 minutes
Temperature: 475 °
Time: 5 minutes

CHOCOLATE AMARETTO CHEESECAKE

*Yields: **12-15 servings***
Preparation Time: 20 minutes

2½ cups chocolate cookie crumbs,
    finely crumbled
½ cup butter or margarine,
    melted
3 8-ounce packages cream
    cheese, softened
¾ cup sugar
4 eggs
6 ounces milk chocolate, melted
2 cups sour cream
½ cup plus 2 tablespoons
    Amaretto liqueur, divided
¾ cup butter or margarine,
    melted and divided
1 teaspoon vanilla
    sliced almonds, toasted

1. Mix cookie crumbs and ½ cup melted butter. Press into a 2-quart or 9-inch springform pan.
2. Mix cream cheese with sugar until fluffy. Add eggs, melted chocolate, 1 cup sour cream, ½ cup Amaretto, ¼ cup butter, and vanilla. Pour into crust.
3. Bake in 350° oven for 60-65 minutes. Mix remaining 1 cup of sour cream with 2 tablespoons Amaretto. Spread over cheese cake. Return to oven for only 3 minutes.
4. Cool, cover, and chill. Garnish with toasted almonds before serving.

*Temperature: **350** °*
Time: 60-65 minutes
*Temperature: **350** °*
Time: 3 minutes

You can make half of the recipe in an 8-inch or 9-inch square pan.

MOTHER'S BEST BUTTER CAKE

Yields: **15 servings**
Preparation Time: 25 minutes

1   *18-ounce yellow cake mix*
½   *cup butter, melted*
3   *eggs, divided*
1   *16-ounce box powdered sugar*
1   *8-ounce package cream cheese*
1   *cup pecans, halved*

1. Combine cake mix, butter and 1 egg. Using floured hands, pat mixture in bottom of greased 9" × 13" pan.
2. Combine powdered sugar and cream cheese. Add remaining eggs. Mix thoroughly. Pour over first mixture. Sprinkle with nuts.
3. Bake in 350° oven for 30-40 minutes.

Temperature: **350 °**
Time: 30-40 minutes

BOURBON CHOCOLATE PIE

Yields: **6-8 servings**

1   *cup sugar*
2   *eggs*
4   *tablespoons cornstarch*
½   *cup butter, melted*
3   *tablespoons bourbon*
1   *cup semi-sweet chocolate chips*
1   *cup pecans, chopped*
1   *9-inch unbaked pie shell*
½   *pint heavy cream*
2   *tablespoons powdered sugar*
½   *teaspoon bourbon*

Do not freeze.

1. Combine sugar, eggs, cornstarch, butter, and 3 tablespoons bourbon. Stir in chocolate chips and pecans.
2. Pour into pie shell and bake in 350° oven 30-35 minutes or until puffy and brown. Cool completely.
3. Whip cream with powdered sugar and bourbon to form stiff peaks. Serve over individual pieces of pie.

Temperature: **350 °**
Time: 30-35 minutes

BUTTERMILK PECAN PIE

Yields: **8 servings**
Preparation Time: 1 hour,
15 minutes

½   cup butter, softened
2   cups sugar
2   teaspoons vanilla
3   eggs
3   tablespoons flour
¼   teaspoon salt
1   cup buttermilk
1   9-inch pie shell, unbaked
½   cup pecans

1. Cream butter and sugar. Blend in vanilla. Add eggs. Combine flour, salt, and buttermilk. Add to remainder of ingredients and mix well.
2. Sprinkle pecans in bottom of crust, then pour mixture over.
3. Bake in 300° oven for 1½ hours. Cool. Serve at room temperature.

Temperature: **300** °
Time: 1½ hours

LEMON PIE BARS

Yields: **24 bars**
Preparation Time: 1 hour

¾   cup butter, softened
1½   cups plus 3 tablespoons flour
½   cup powdered sugar
     juice of 1 lemon
1½   cups sugar
3   eggs, slightly beaten

1. Mix butter and 1½ cup flour and powdered sugar. Press into a 9″× 13″ greased pan. Bake in 350° oven for 20 minutes.
2. Mix remaining flour, sugar, lemon juice, and eggs until well blended. Pour over crust and bake 20 minutes longer.
3. Sprinkle top with powdered sugar. Cut into squares.

Temperature: **350** °
Time: 20 minutes
Temperature: **350** °
Time: 20 minutes

PERFECT PIE CRUST

Yields: **1 9-inch pie crust**
Preparation Time: 45 minutes

¼   cup unsalted butter, chilled
      and cut into 1 inch cubes
¼   cup shortening, chilled
1½   cups instant flour (Wondra)
¼   teaspoon salt
¼   cup cold liquid (water,
      orange or lemon juice, or
      boullion combined with
      water)

1. Cut the butter and shortening into flour and salt using a pastry blender or food processor until the mixture is crumbly and pieces are the size of small peas.

2. Add liquid a small amount at a time, tossing the mixture with two cold forks until mixture comes clean from the bowl. (You may add a small amount of extra liquid if necessary).

3. Quickly form into a ball and flatten into an 8-inch circle, wrap in plastic wrap and refrigerate for 30 minutes.

4. Place dough on lightly floured surface and roll to 12-inch circle. Gently transfer pastry to a greased pie pan, being careful not to stretch. Flute edges.

5. If the pie crust is to be baked before filling, prick sides and bottom with tines of fork. Bake in the center of a preheated 400° oven for 10 minutes until lightly browned.

Temperature: **400** °
Time: 10 minutes

LOUISIANA PECAN PIE

Yields: **8 servings**
Preparation Time: 15 minutes

3	*eggs*
1½	*tablespoons flour*
½	*cup sugar*
1	*cup dark corn syrup*
3	*tablespoons butter, melted*
2	*teaspoons vanilla*
1	*dash of salt*
1	*cup pecans, chopped*
1	*9-inch pie shell, unbaked*

1. Beat eggs. Mix flour and sugar and add to eggs. Stir in remaining ingredients. Pour into pie shell.
2. Bake in 325° oven for 45 minutes.

Temperature: **325 °**
Time: **45 minutes**

Pie should not be real firm when removed from oven but the center should be set. Also if you prefer a less sweet pie, use 4 eggs and ¾ cup corn syrup.

PECAN LIME PIE
"Quick and Easy"

Yields: **6-8 servings**
Preparation Time: 10 minutes plus 1 hour set time

1	*13-ounce can condensed milk*
1	*6-ounce can frozen limeade*
1	*tablespoon fresh lime juice*
1	*8-ounce container frozen whipped topping*
2-3	*drops green food coloring*
½	*cup pecans, chopped, divided*
1	*9-inch baked pie shell*

1. Combine milk, limeade, and lime juice. Fold in whipped topping, food coloring, and ¼ cup pecans. Mix thoroughly.
2. Pour into pie shell and decorate with rest of pecans. Chill at least one hour before serving.

Lemonade and lemon juice may be substituted for the lime.

CHOCOLATE BAR PIE
Must Make Ahead Of Time

Yields: **6 servings**
Preparation Time: 10 minutes

20	*marshmallows*
6	*small chocolate almond bars*
²/₃	*cup milk*
1	*cup heavy cream, whipped*
1	*baked 9-inch pie shell*

1. Combine marshmallows, chocolate bars, and milk in top of double boiler. Heat until melted. Cool.
2. Fold in whipped cream. Pour into pie shell. Chill at least overnight.

PINEY WOODS FUDGE PIE

Yields: **6-8 servings**

²/₃	*stick butter or margarine, melted*
2½-3	*squares unsweetened chocolate (or 1 cup semi-sweet chocolate chips)*
4	*large eggs, at room temperature*
2	*cups sugar*
¼	*teaspoon salt*
1	*teaspoon Mexican vanilla*
²/₃	*cup pecans, chopped*
1	*9½-inch pie crust (deep, prepared crust)*

1. Melt butter. Beat eggs until light and fluffy. Add sugar, salt, and vanilla. Stir in chocolate chips and pecans. (If using squares of unsweetened chocolate, melt with butter over low heat, cool, then add with pecans.)
2. Pour filling into unbaked pie shell. Bake in 350° oven for 40-45 minutes. Pie will be soft inside, crusty, and filling set. Do not overcook.
3. Best if served warm, but can be made the day ahead and served cold.

Temperature: 350°
Time: 40-45 minutes

Garnish with a dollop of whipped cream and a bit of shaved chocolate, a scoop of coffee or good quality vanilla ice cream with chocolate sauce, or pour on a small amount of liquor (Kahlua, Creme de Cacao, or Choclair). It is great plain too!

GLAZED PEACH PIE

Must Make Ahead Of Time

Yields: 6-8 servings
Preparation Time: 30 minutes

Pie:

1	*9-inch pie shell, baked*
1½	*cups fresh sliced peaches*

Glaze:

1	*cup sugar*
3	*tablespoons cornstarch*
½	*cup water*
1	*cup crushed fresh peaches*
2	*tablespoons butter*
	heavy cream, whipped

1. Fill baked pie shell with 1½ cup peaches.

Glaze:

1. Mix all ingredients except butter.
2. Cook in 1 quart saucepan until clear and thick. Add butter and cool.
3. Top pie shell with mixture. Refrigerate several hours.
4. Top with whipped cream.

BUTTERMILK PIE

Yields: 8 servings
Preparation Time: 20 minutes

1½	*cups sugar*
⅛	*teaspoon salt*
6	*tablespoons butter or margarine*
½	*cup buttermilk*
⅛	*tablespoons flour*
⅛	*teaspoon nutmeg*
1	*teaspoon vanilla*
3	*eggs, well beaten unbaked 8-inch or 9-inch shell*

1. Mix all ingredients together except eggs.
2. Beat eggs in a small bowl. Add eggs to mixture.
3. Pour into an unbaked pie shell. Bake in 350° oven for 50 minutes.

Temperature: 350 °
Time: 50 minutes

BRANDY ALEXANDER PIE

Yields: 6-8 servings
Preparation Time: 15 minutes

1	*14-ounce can condensed milk*
2	*tablespoons Creme de Cacao*
2	*tablespoons brandy*
1	*cup heavy cream, whipped*
1	*prepared or homemade 9-inch cookie crumb crust*

1. Mix milk, Creme de Cacao, and brandy.
2. Fold in whipped cream until mixture is well blended.
3. Pour into pie shell. Sprinkle with shaved chocolate. Freeze 4-6 hours.

PUMPKIN CHIFFON PIE

Yields: 12 servings
Preparation Time: ½ hour

3	*egg yolks*
½	*cup sugar*
1¼	*cups pumpkin*
½	*cup milk*
½	*teaspoon salt*
½	*teaspoon ginger*
½	*teaspoon cinnamon*
½	*teaspoon nutmeg*
1	*envelope Knox gelatin*
¼	*cup cold water*
3	*egg whites, stiffly beaten*
½	*cup sugar*
1	*9-inch pastry shell, baked heavy cream, whipped (optional)*

1. Beat egg yolks and ½ cup sugar until thick. Add pumpkin, milk, salt, and spices. Cook in double boiler until thick.
2. Soften gelatin in cold water until dissolved and add to pumpkin mixture. Add egg whites (beaten) with remaining ½ cup sugar. Pour into cooled pie shell and chill.
3. Top with whipped cream, if desired.

GRAHAM CRACKER CRUST PIE

Yields: 9 servings
Preparation Time: 1 hour

3	*egg whites, stiffly beaten*
1	*cup sugar*
1	*cup graham cracker crumbs*
1	*cup pecans, chopped*
1	*teaspoon vanilla extract*

Topping:

½	*pint heavy cream*
2	*tablespoons powdered sugar*
1	*teaspoon vanilla extract*
	Baker's sweet chocolate, shaved

1. Gradually add sugar, graham cracker crumbs, nuts and vanilla to stiffly beaten egg whites. Place mixture into a lightly greased 10-inch pie pan. Bake in 350° oven for 30 minutes. Cool thoroughly.

Topping:

1. Mix topping ingredients, beating until fairly stiff.
2. Spread topping over pie and shave chocolate on top to garnish.

Temperature: 350 °
Time: 30 minutes

Keep refrigerated. Best if made several hours before serving.

RICHER LEMON PIE

Yields: **10 servings**
Preparation Time: 20 minutes

1	8-inch pie shell, baked
6	tablespoons butter or margarine
1	cup sugar
2	lemons, juice and rind grated rind
3	egg yolks
1	egg, whole
2	slices white bread, cubed and crusts removed

Topping:

6	tablespoons sugar
1	teaspoon vanilla
3	egg whites

1. Heat butter, sugar, lemon juice, and grated rind over medium heat until sugar dissolves. Heat egg yolks in a separate pan, add to sugar mixture, then cook until thick. Do not boil.

2. Scatter bread over crust. Pour hot pie fillings into crust.

3. Beat topping ingredients together until fairly stiff. Pour on top of pie and seal edges to crust.

4. Bake in 350° oven until topping is lightly brown. Cool.

Temperature: **350 °**
Time: approximately 3-5 minutes

Cream of Tartar (¼ teaspoon) may be added to topping for stiffer peaks.

RUM CREAM PIE

Yields: **10 servings**
Preparation Time: 30 minutes

1	prepared or home made graham cracker or cookie crust
½	cup dark rum
1	cup sugar
7	egg yolks
1	pint heavy cream
1	envelope Knox unflavored gelatin
¼	cup water chocolate shavings (Bakers' or Hershey's chocolate)

1. Beat egg yolks and sugar until stiff. Dissolve gelatin in water over medium heat, stirring constantly.

2. Add rum and gelatin to creamed mixture.

3. Whip cream until stiff, then fold into yolk mixture. Pour into pie shell and freeze. Sprinkle with chocolate shavings if desired.

CAROLYN'S LEMON LOG

Must Make Ahead Of Time

*Yields: **12-14 servings***
Preparation Time: 1 hour

1	*Angel food cake recipe or Angel food cake mix*
1	*3¾ box lemon pudding (not instant)*
1	*3-ounce package cream cheese, room temperature*
2	*tablespoons light cream*
½	*cup butter or margarine, room temperature*
4	*cups powdered sugar, sifted*
1	*teaspoon vanilla lemon slices fresh mint sprigs*

1. Prepare your favorite angel food cake recipe or use a mix. Pour one half plus one cup of the batter into an ungreased jelly roll pan (pan should be full). Pour the rest into an ungreased round layer cake pan to be used as you wish. Bake jelly roll pan in 375° oven for 15-20 minutes or until done.

2. Remove pan from oven and hang upside down by corners until cool.

3. To remove from pan, gently loosen one end with metal spatula and pull cake out onto a cup towel. Roll short end of cake and towel into a roll. Make certain cake is covered.

4. Prepare lemon pudding mix. When pudding is cooled and several hours before serving time, unroll cake and remove towel. Spread the pudding over the cake. Reroll cake carefully and transfer to a serving platter.

5. Combine rest of ingredients in a large bowl and beat until light and fluffy. Spread frosting on log, covering the ends also. Take back of teaspoon and make log marks.

6. Decorate with thin lemon slices and fresh mint sprigs. Cut into slices. Keep in refrigerator until serving time.

*Temperature: **375** °*
Time: 15-20 minutes

BUTTERSCOTCH CRUNCH SQUARES

*Yields: **8-10 servings***
Preparation Time: 25 minutes

1   cup flour
½   cup quick cooking oats
¼   cup brown sugar
½   cup butter or margarine
½   cup nuts, chopped (either
     pecans or almonds)
1   jar butterscotch or caramel
     ice cream topping
1   quart vanilla ice cream

1. Mix flour, oats, and brown sugar. Cut in butter or margarine until mixture is crumbly.
2. Stir in chopped nuts. Pat mixture into a 9" × 13" pan. Bake in 400° oven for 15 minutes. Stir several times while baking to form a crumbly mixture. Cool crumbs.
3. Pat about ¾ of the crumbs in a 11" × 7" or 9-inch square pan. Drizzle half of the ice cream topping over crumbs. Spoon ice cream over this mixture. Drizzle with remaining ice cream sauce. Sprinkle with remaining crumbs. Freeze until firm.
4. Cut into squares to serve.

*Temperature: **400** °*
Time: 15 minutes

Other ice cream may be substituted for the vanilla, such as pralines and cream, butterscotch, butter pecan.

'TWAS THE DINNER BEFORE CHRISTMAS

Egg Nog   page 36
Chutney Cheese Ball   page 31
French Onion Soup   page 46
Strawberry/Cranberry Salad   page 64
Rice Mushroom Medley   page 207
Holiday Glazed Carrots   page 195
George Gourley's Stuffed Chicken Breasts   page 138
Marr Family Christmas Cake   page 241

LEMON FROMAGE
Must Make Ahead Of Time

Yields: 12 servings
Preparation Time: 20-25 minutes

2	envelopes unflavored gelatin
½	cup cold water
6	eggs, separated
1	cup sugar
2	large lemons (juice of)
1	lemon rind, grated

Sauce:

1	cup bing cherries, pitted
2	cups bing cherry juice
2	teaspoons cornstarch
	salt
	almond flavoring

1. Soften gelatin in cold water and dissolve over hot water in double boiler. Set aside to cool until lukewarm.

2. Beat egg yolks with sugar until very light. Add lemon juice, rind, and cooled gelatin.

3. Fold in stiffly beaten egg whites. When fromage holds its shape, pour into a 1½-quart mold.

4. Chill and unmold. Garnish with candied cherries if desired. Serve with sauce.

Sauce:

1. Thicken cherry juice with cornstarch and a dash of salt. Add 1 cup of cherries and a dash of almond flavoring.

Have all ingredients ready as this sets quickly.

FROZEN MINT DREAM
Must Make Ahead Of Time

Yields: **20 servings**
Preparation Time: **45 minutes**

1	*pound Oreo cookies*
½	*cup melted butter*
1	*13-ounce can evaporated milk*
1	*cup sugar*
½	*cup butter*
2	*squares baking chocolate*
3	*quarts vanilla ice cream*
2	*cups whipped topping*
	chopped almonds or pecans
	Creme de Menthe

1. Crust: Crush cookies, combine with ½ cup melted butter. Put in 9" × 13" pan and 8" × 8" cake pan. Chill.

2. Filling: Combine evaporated milk, 1 cup sugar, ½ cup butter, and 2 squares chocolate. Cook in heavy sauce pan 15-20 minutes, stirring until thick. Watch closely.

3. While filling is cooling, put 3 quarts softened vanilla ice cream on crust, dividing between pans. Freeze again, then spread with cooled filling. Freeze once more, then top with 2 cups whipped topping and sprinkle with chopped nuts. Add a spat of Creme de Menthe over each slice.

HOT FUDGE PUDDING

*Yields: **6-8 servings***
Preparation Time: 15 minutes

1	*cup flour*
½	*teaspoon baking soda*
¼	*teaspoon salt*
¾	*cup sugar*
6	*tablespoons cocoa, divided*
½	*cup buttermilk*
2	*tablespoons butter, melted*
1	*cup nuts, chopped*
1	*cup brown sugar*
1	*cup hot water*

1. In a medium sized mixing bowl, sift flour, baking soda, salt, sugar, and 2 tablespoons cocoa.
2. Add buttermilk, butter, and nuts. Mix thoroughly. Pour into a 3" × 7" loaf pan.
3. Combine brown sugar and 4 tablespoons of cocoa. Sprinkle over top. Pour hot water over the mixture.
4. Bake in a 350° oven for 40-45 minutes.
5. Serve hot from the oven over vanilla ice cream.

*Temperature: **350** °*
Time: 40-45 minutes

EASTER ELEGANCE

Mini Quiches   page 26
Nutty Crabmeat Spread   page 10
French Onion Soup   page 46
Vegetable Salad   page 60
Snapper Pontchartrain   page 159
"Beginner's" Rolls   page 88
Chocolate Ladyfinger Cake   page 240
Cointreau Cake   page 239

If Snapper is not available Flounder is equally as delicious in the Pontchartrain.

CHOCOLATE PECAN TORTE

*Yields: **20 servings***
Preparation Time: 45 minutes

4   *eggs, separated*
1   *cup sugar*
2   *teaspoons rum*
2   *teaspoons flour*
2   *cups pecans, ground*

Filling and Frosting:

1   *cup sour cream, divided*
¼   *cup sugar*
1   *6-ounce package semi-sweet*
     chocolate chips, melted
     whole pecans for decoration

1. Cream egg yolks and sugar. Add rum, flour, and baking powder. Fold in nuts and set aside.
2. Beat egg whites until stiff and fold into nut mixture.
3. Divide between two 9-inch greased springform pans and bake in 350° oven for 20 minutes. Allow to cool completely on cake plates.

Filling and Frosting:

1. Mix ½ cup sour cream and ¼ cup sugar well. Add melted chocolate. Add remaining sour cream.
2. Place filling between layers and then ice.

*Temperature: **350** °*
Time: 20 minutes

MCLEOD CROWD CREPES

Yields: **12 servings**
Preparation Time: 1½ hours

Crepe:

¾	cup milk
¾	cup cold water
3	egg yolks
1	tablespoon sugar
3	tablespoons rum
1½	cups flour
5	tablespoons melted butter

Custard:

1	egg
1	egg yolk
¾	cup sugar
½	cup flour
1	cup boiling milk
3	tablespoons butter
¼	teaspoon almond extract
½	cup sliced almonds
2	teaspoons vanilla extract
2	squares or ounces of semi-sweet chocolate
2	tablespoons melted butter
1	tablespoon sugar

Crepe:

1. Blend all ingredients 1 minute in blender. Refrigerate at least 2 hours.
2. Using 1½ tablespoons of butter, cook in greased crepe pan 15 seconds on one side, 10 seconds on the other side.

Custard:

1. Beat egg and egg yolk while adding the sugar. Beat in flour and boiling milk.
2. Cook slowly in a double boiler, stirring constantly, until batter becomes very thick. Beat out lumps with a mixer.
3. Add butter, vanilla, almond extract, and almonds.
4. Spread 2 tablespoons custard on each crepe, roll, and place in buttered baking dish. Grate chocolate over crepes. Top with melted butter and sprinkle with sugar.
5. Preheat oven to 350°. Warm crepes until chocolate melts. Top with whipped cream, if desired.

Temperature: **350 °**
Time: warm only

MAPLE MOUSSE
Must Make Ahead Of Time

*Yields: **4 servings***
Preparation Time: 20 minutes

1   *cup maple syrup*
4   *egg yolks, slightly beaten*
1   *pint heavy cream, whipped*
4   *egg whites, well beaten*

1. In a small pan or microwave, heat maple syrup.
2. Slowly pour hot maple syrup over beaten egg yolks, beating constantly.
3. In a double boiler, cook mixture until it coats the spoon. Chill. Fold in whipped cream and well beaten egg whites.
4. Pour mixture into mold or individual glasses. Chill or freeze.

ALINE WARDLE'S FRAICHE À LA CREME

*Yields: **4 servings***
Preparation Time: 10 minutes

1   *pint strawberries*
½   *cup heavy cream*
¼   *cup sugar*
½   *teaspoon almond extract*
½   *cup sour cream*

1. Wash and hull strawberries. Mix with "creme fraiche" (recipe below) and refrigerate until serving time.

Creme Fraiche:

1. In a chilled medium bowl, beat ½ cup heavy cream with ¼ cup sugar and ½ teaspoon almond extract until stiff.
2. Fold in ½ cup sour cream until evenly blended.
3. Refrigerate until serving time.

Looks pretty in champagne glasses or sherbert glasses with a sprig of mint.

EASY ICE CREAM

Yields: 1½ gallons
Preparation Time: 1 hour

6 *eggs*
1½ *cups sugar*
2 *13-ounce cans evaporated milk*
2 *13-ounce cans condensed milk*
1 *quart light cream*
1 *quart milk*
2 *tablespoons vanilla*
¼ *teaspoon salt*
2 *cups peaches or strawberries, drained (optional)*

1. Combine all ingredients. Mix thoroughly.
2. Pour into freezer can of ice cream maker. Turn until stiff.
3. Pack with ice or freeze and let set 1-2 hours until firm.

CITRUS SURPRISE DESSERT

Yields: 8 servings
Preparation Time: 30 minutes

1 *teaspoon lemon rind, grated*
½ *cup lemon juice*
½ *cup frozen orange juice, concentrated, defrosted, but not diluted*
1 *cup plus 6 tablespoons sugar*
1 *cup mashed avocado*
½ *pint heavy cream, whipped*

1. In a 10″ × 6″ glass dish, combine lemon rind, juices, and 1 cup sugar. Mix well.
2. Add mashed ripe avocado and blend thoroughly. Place in freezer or freezing compartment of refrigerator and freeze for 30 minutes.
3. Whip cream, gradually adding 6 tablespoons of sugar.
4. Completely fold whipped cream into avocado mixture.
5. Cover dish with foil. Return to freezer until frozen.

DIANA TORTE
Must Make Ahead Of Time

*Yields: **15-20 servings***
Preparation Time: 30 minutes

28 *good quality macaroons*
1   *quart chocolate ice cream,*
    slightly softened
4   *tablespoons chocolate sauce*
1   *quart coffee ice cream,*
    slightly softened
14 *English toffee or Heath bars,*
    crushed

1. Oil or butter an 8-inch springform pan. Crush 14 macaroons and spread on bottom of pan.
2. Slightly soften chocolate ice cream. Spread on top of macaroons. Dribble 2 tablespoons chocolate sauce over ice cream.
3. Crush 14 macaroons and spread over top of ice cream.
4. Spread coffee ice cream on top of second layer of macaroons. Dribble 2 tablespoons chocolate sauce over the coffee ice cream.
5. Crush the toffee or Heath bars and spread on top. Place torte in freezer. Freeze until hard.

To serve:

Remove torte from springform pan and place on a serving platter. Garnish and allow to sit for 30 minutes before slicing and serving. Pass bowl of fudge sauce to really indulge.

ITALIAN CREAM DESSERT
"Absolutely Wonderful"

*Yields: **4-6 servings***
Preparation Time: 15 minutes

2   *8-ounce packages cream*
     cheese
½   *cup sugar*
4   *egg yolks, beaten*
2   *tablespoons heavy cream*
2   *tablespoons cognac*
4-6 *fresh strawberries*
     whip cream, aerosol can

1. Combine cream cheese, sugar and egg yolks in blender. Add heavy cream and cognac. Blend until smooth. Let set 15 minutes before serving.
2. Pour into champagne glasses. Garnish with a dollop of whipped cream and strawberry.

Other liqueurs can be substituted for cognac such as Grand Marnier.

SUPREME PEACH COBBLER

*Yields: **6 servings***
Preparation Time: 10-15 minutes

1	*pie crust stick*
4	*cups fresh, canned, or frozen sliced peaches, drained*
1	*cup sugar*
2	*tablespoons flour*
½	*cup butter*

1. Follow instructions for pie stick listed on back of box. Cut into strips.
2. Heat together the last four ingredients until sugar is dissolved.
3. Grease a 9″ × 9″ pan. Pour in peach mixture. Top with pie crust strips.
4. Bake in 350° oven for 45 minutes.
5. Serve with whipped cream or vanilla ice cream.

*Temperature: **350** °*
Time: 45 minutes

A wonderful summer dessert. Substitute any other fruit, fresh or frozen.

ORANGES ORIENTAL
Make 24 Hours Ahead Of Time

*Yields: **6-8 servings***
Preparation Time: 15 minutes

4	*navel oranges*
1	*cup orange juice*
1	*cup sugar*
¼	*teaspoon cream of tartar*
1	*tablespoon corn starch*
¼-½	*cup orange liqueur*
¼-½	*cup pecans or almonds*
⅛	*teaspoon red food coloring*
1	*tablespoon butter*
	Vanilla ice cream

1. Grate some "zest" from skins of oranges into glass bowl. Peel and pull off white membranes.
2. Slice across to section and then into triangle bite-size pieces.
3. In a saucepan, combine orange juice, sugar, cream of tartar, and corn starch. Bring to boil; simmer about 5-6 minutes.
4. Remove from heat and add liqueur, and a dash of red food coloring. Pour over oranges in glass bowl, mix, cover, and refrigerate overnight.
5. To serve sauté nuts in butter. Put ice cream in dish, top with oranges, then sprinkle with nuts.

CHOCOLATE MOUSSE

Yields: 4-5 servings
Preparation Time: 20 minutes

1	tablespoon butter
3	1-ounce squares unsweetened chocolate
2	eggs, divided
½	cup sugar, divided
2	teaspoons rum
1	teaspoon cold strong coffee
1	cup heavy cream, whipped

1. In a small heavy saucepan, melt butter and chocolate over low heat, stirring until smooth. Set aside to cool.

2. In small bowl, beat egg whites until foamy. Gradually beat in ¼ cup sugar until stiff peaks form. Set aside.

3. In large bowl, beat egg yolks with remaining ¼ cup sugar until lemon-colored and light. Beat in rum and coffee. Fold in chocolate mixture, then gently fold in egg-white mixture and whipped cream just to blend.

4. Spoon into 4 individual serving dishes. Chill several hours or overnight.

You can reserve about 1 cup of the mousse to put in a pastry bag with a fluted top. Form rosettes on top of each serving.

APPLES AMARETTO
"Simply Scrumptious"

Yields: 6 servings
Preparation Time: 1 hour

4	tablespoons fresh orange peel, grated
1	cup orange juice
½	cup sugar
½	cup Amaretto
8	large tart apples
½	pint heavy cream, whipped
¼	cup toasted almonds

1. Core apples and slice ¼ inch thick; set aside.

2. In a large enameled saucepan, mix orange peel, orange juice, sugar, and amaretto. Heat over moderately low heat until bubbly.

3. Lay apple slices in liquid and simmer 8-10 minutes, or until tender and most of the liquid is evaporated.

4. Arrange in individual serving dishes. Top with a dollop of whipped cream and sprinkle with toasted almonds.

MY AUNT JULIA'S BUTTERMILK ICE CREAM

*Yields: **8-10 servings***
Preparation Time: 30 minutes

3	cups buttermilk
1	cup heavy cream, whipped
1	cup sugar
1	tablespoon vanilla
1	lemon (juice of)

1. Combine all ingredients.
2. Freeze in ice cream freezer or regular refrigerator freezer. If using refrigerator freezer, stir at least once while freezing.

APPLE CRANBERRY DESSERT

*Yields: **6 servings***
Preparation Time: 15 minutes

3	cups peeled apple slices
1½	cups fresh cranberries
½	cup sugar
1	teaspoon cinnamon
	lemon juice
¼	cup softened butter
½	cup flour
½	cup brown sugar

1. Mix apple slices, cranberries, sugar, and cinnamon. Place in a buttered 1½-quart casserole. Sprinkle with a few drops of lemon juice.
2. Blend butter with flour and brown sugar until mixture is crumbly. Sprinkle over apple-cranberry mixture. Sprinkle with additional cinnamon.
3. Bake in 350° oven for 1 hour. Serve warm.

*Temperature: **350 °***
Time: 1 hour

Serve warm with whipped cream or ice cream.

FROZEN GRAND MARNIER DESSERT

Yields: **4 servings**
Preparation Time: 30 minutes

2   *egg whites*
    pinch of salt
¼   *cup sugar plus 6 tablespoons*
    sugar
1   *cup heavy cream*
¼   *cup Grand Marnier*

Berry Sauce:

1   *10-ounce package frozen*
    strawberries
1   *10-ounce package frozen*
    raspberries
    Grand Marnier to taste

1. Beat egg whites with pinch of salt until soft peaks are formed.
2. Gradually add ¼ cup sugar and continue beating until stiff. Set aside.
3. In another bowl, whip cream until stiff. Beat in 6 tablespoons sugar. Gently blend in Grand Marnier. Fold in egg whites.
4. Turn into 1-quart mold. Freeze until firm. Unmold and serve with Berry Sauce.

Berry Sauce:

1. Defrost strawberries and raspberries. Drain excess juice.
2. Purée in food processor until smooth. Add Grand Marnier to taste.

HEATH BAR DESSERT
Must Make Ahead Of Time.

Yields: **6-8 servings**
Preparation Time: 20 minutes

1½ *pints heavy cream*
2   *tablespoons powdered sugar*
2   *tablespoons instant coffee*
6-8 *Heath bars, broken into*
    small pieces
2   *packages Lady Fingers*
1   *6-ounce package semisweet*
    chocolate pieces, grated

1. Whip cream until it peaks. Add powdered sugar and coffee. Fold in broken candy.
2. Line sides and bottom of a 9-inch springform pan with Lady Fingers. Alternate layers of whipped cream mixture with remaining Lady Fingers, ending with whipped cream.
3. Top with grated bitter or semisweet chocolate.
4. Refrigerate several hours before serving.

DEMITASSE or POTS DE CREME MOUSSE

Must Make Ahead

*Yields: **4-6 servings***
Preparation Time: 15 minutes

³/₄	*cup milk*
¹/₂	*teaspoon instant coffee*
1	*12-ounce package chocolate chips*
2	*eggs*
¹/₄	*cup brandy*
¹/₂	*cup heavy cream, whipped*
1	*teaspoon cocoa*
1	*teaspoon sugar*

1. Scald milk and coffee.
2. In food processor or blender, combine chocolate chips, eggs, brandy, and coffee mixture. Blend 2 minutes.
3. Pour into cups and cover with buttered wax paper. Refrigerate. Serve with whipped cream. Sprinkle top with sugar and cocoa.

CHERRY PUFF

*Yields: **6 servings***
Preparation Time: 20 minutes

1	*16-ounce can unsweetened cherries, drained (save liquid)*
1	*cup cherry juice*
¹/₂	*cup sugar*
1	*tablespoon cornstarch*
2	*eggs, separated*
¹/₈	*teaspoon salt*
¹/₈	*teaspoon cream of tartar*
¹/₃	*cup sugar*
5¹/₂	*tablespoons flour*

1. Combine cherries, juice, sugar, and cornstarch in saucepan. Simmer until it thickens. Pour into a souffle dish or deep 1½ quart casserole. Set aside.
2. Beat egg whites. Add salt and cream of tartar. Combine egg yolks and ⅓ cup of sugar. Fold egg whites gently into egg yolks. Add flour and stir well.
3. Spoon egg mixture on top of cherry mixture. Bake in 350° oven for 25-30 minutes.

*Temperature: **350°***
Time: 25-30 minutes

285

CHOCOLATE SURPRISE

Yields: **6-8 servings**
Preparation Time: 10 minutes

2   eggs
¾   cup white sugar
¾   cup light corn syrup
2   tablespoons butter or
      margarine, melted
1   teaspoon vanilla
½   cup shredded coconut
½   cup quick cooking oats
½   cup chocolate chips
1   8-inch or 9-inch pie shell,
      unbaked

1. In a small mixing bowl, beat eggs until light and fluffy. Add sugar, corn syrup, butter, and vanilla. Beat well.
2. Add next three ingredients. Mix well. Pour into the unbaked pie shell.
3. Bake in 400° oven for 10 minutes. Lower temperature to 350° and bake 40-45 minutes longer.

Temperature: **400 °**
Time: 10 minutes
Temperature: **350 °**
Time: 40-45 minutes

CHOCOLATE WALNUT DELIGHT

Yields: **6-8 servings**
Preparation Time: 30 minutes

1   9-inch unbaked pie shell,
      refrigerated
3   large eggs, beaten
1½   cups sugar
6   tablespoons butter, melted
2   teaspoons vanilla
¾   cups flour
1½   cups chocolate chips
1½   cups walnuts, chopped
      vanilla ice cream
      Creme de Cacao
      shaved chocolate

1. Mix together eggs, sugar, butter, and vanilla until lightly blended.
2. Add flour, chocolate, and walnuts, mixing well.
3. Pour into 9-inch unbaked pie shell and bake in 350° oven for 60-65 minutes. Top will be light in color and crusty.
4. Serve with vanilla ice cream topped with Creme de Cacao. Sprinkle with shaved chocolate.

Temperature: **350 °**
Time: 60-65 minutes

KATHY'S PAVLOVA
Must Make Ahead Of Time

Yields: **6-8 servings**
Preparation Time: 20 minutes

4   *egg whites, room temperature*
1   *cup sugar*
1   *teaspoon vanilla*
1½ *teaspoons cornstarch*
1   *teaspoon white vinegar*

Filling:

1   *pint heavy cream*
½   *cup sugar*
½   *teaspoon vanilla*
½   *pint strawberries*

1. Beat egg whites until they begin to hold their shape. Gradually add sugar beating constantly until egg whites are thick and glossy. Fold in vanilla, cornstarch, and vinegar.

2. Mound meringue on a cookie sheet in a circle, indenting with the back of a spoon, making it bowl-shaped. Bake in 250° oven for 1½ hours. Turn off oven and allow meringue to dry out in cooling oven.

3. Transfer meringue to a serving plate and fill with filling.

4. Whip cream in chilled bowl with chilled egg beaters. Half way through the whipping, add the sugar and vanilla. When it forms peaks, fill center of meringue. Top with fresh strawberries.

Temperature: **250 °**
Time: 1½ hours

Other fruits may be substituted for the strawberries. It is also best not to make this on a real humid day.

STRAWBERRY TRIFLE

Must Make 24 Hours Ahead

Yields: **12 servings**
Preparation Time: 1 hour

Cake:

1	*cup cake flour, sifted*
1	*teaspoon baking powder*
¼	*teaspoon salt*
1½	*cups milk*
2	*tablespoons butter or margarine*
2	*eggs*
1	*cup sugar*
1	*teaspoon vanilla*

Pudding:

⅓	*cup sugar*
1	*tablespoon cornstarch*
⅛	*teaspoon salt*
1	*cup milk*
2	*egg yolks, beaten*
1	*tablespoon butter*
1	*teaspoon vanilla*
½	*cup heavy cream, whipped*
3	*pints fresh strawberries, divided*
3	*tablespoons sugar*
⅓	*cup strawberry or orange liqueur, divided powdered sugar heavy cream, whipped*

Cake:

1. Sift together flour, baking powder, and salt. Set aside.
2. In a small saucepan, heat milk and butter until butter is melted. Keep hot.
3. In mixing bowl, beat whole eggs on high speed until thick and lemon colored, about 3 minutes. Gradually add sugar beating constantly at medium speed 4-5 minutes.
4. Add dry ingredients to egg mixture and stir just till blended. Stir in hot milk mixture and vanilla. Blend well. Pour into 2 greased and floured 8-inch round cake pans.
5. Bake in 350° oven for 20 minutes or until cake tests done. Cool in pan 10 minutes. Remove from pans. Cool on rack.

Pudding:

1. Combine sugar, cornstarch and salt in saucepan. Stir in milk. Cook and stir over medium high heat until thickened and bubbly. Stir a moderate amount of hot mixture into beaten egg yolks. Add egg yolks to mixture in saucepan, stirring constantly.
2. Cook and stir 2 minutes more. Remove from heat. Stir in butter and vanilla. Cover saucepan of pudding with wax paper or clear plastic wrap. Chill.
3. Whip ½ cup heavy cream. Fold into chilled pudding. Set aside.
4. Reserving 14 strawberries for garnish, crush remaining berries to

make 2 cups. Combine with 3 table-spoons sugar.

Assembly:

1. Split cake layers to make 4 layers. Put 1 layer into bottom of 1½ quart souffle or trifle bowl. Spread 1 cup crushed berries over layer. Top with second layer. Sprinkle half the liqueur over second layer.

2. Spread pudding over all. Place 3rd layer on top. Spread remaining berries over this. Sprinkle cut side of 4th layer with remaining liqueur. Place layer cut side down on top of berries in bowl. Cover and refrigerate overnight.

3. Just before serving, sift a heavy covering of powdered sugar over top. Garnish with whip cream rosettes and reserved strawberries, halved.

BANANA CREAM DESSERT

Yields: **15 servings**
Preparation Time: 30 minutes

½   **cup butter or margarine, softened**
1   **cup flour**
1   **cup pecans, finely chopped, divided**
1   **8-ounce package cream cheese, softened**
1   **cup powdered sugar**
1   **12-ounce carton frozen whipped topping, thawed and divided**
1   **3½-ounce can flaked coconut, optional**
2   **3¾-ounce packages instant vanilla pudding**
3   **cups cold milk**
3   **bananas, sliced**

1. Cut butter into flour until mixture resembles coarse meal. Stir in ½ cup pecans. Press flour mixture into a 9" × 13" baking dish. Bake in 350° oven for 20 minutes. Let cool completely.
2. Combine cream cheese and powdered sugar, beating until fluffy. Stir in 1 cup whipped topping. Spread over crust, and sprinkle with coconut.
3. Combine pudding and milk. Beat 2 minutes at medium speed of electric mixer. Spread over coconut layer and top with bananas. Spread remaining whipped topping over bananas. Sprinkle with remaining pecans. Store in refrigerator.

Temperature: **350 °**
Time: 20 minutes

BRIE EN CROUTE

*Yields: **12 servings***
Preparation Time: 30 minutes

1   **package frozen puff pastry**
3   **small rounds Brie cheese of very good quality**
1   **egg yolk, beaten**

1. Roll out each sheet of pastry with rolling pin.
2. Cut a piece of pastry large enough to wrap around each round of Brie. Crimp to seal edge. Brush with egg yolk.
3. Bake in 450° oven for 8-10 minutes. Check carefully not to brown too quickly. Reduce heat to 350° and bake for 20 minutes more until crust is lightly browned.
4. Cut into wedges and serve with crackers and fruit.

*Temperature: **450** °*
Time: 10 minutes
*Temperature: **350** °*
Time: 20 minutes

Can be frozen before baking. Great for an appetizer.

BELGIUM DESSERT

Make 24 Hours Ahead Of Time

*Yields: **10 servings***
Preparation Time: 20 minutes

½   **pound vanilla wafers, crushed**
¾   **cup butter or margarine**
1   **16-ounce box powdered sugar**
2   **eggs, slightly beaten**
4   **tablespoons bourbon or rum**
½   **pint heavy cream, whipped**
2½   **cups crushed pineapple, drained**
¾   **cup pecans, chopped**

1. Line bottom of buttered 9" x 13" glass dish with crushed wafers. Save ¼ cup wafers for top.
2. Cream butter and sugar well. Add eggs and mix thoroughly. Add bourbon and pour mixture over wafers.
3. Spread top with whipped cream. Dot well with pineapple. Sprinkle with pecans and top with remaining wafers.
4. Cover and refrigerate overnight.

Keeps 1 week in refrigerator.

AMARETTO COCONUT CREAM SOUFFLE
Must Make Ahead Of Time

Yields: **10 servings**
Preparation Time: 25 minutes

½   *cup butter*
⅞   *cup graham cracker crumbs*
2   *cups sugar, divided*
4   *eggs*
1¼ *cups coconut, shredded and toasted*
3   *envelopes unflavored gelatin*
¾   *cup water*
4   *ounces Amaretto liqueur*
1   *dash almond extract*
3   *cups heavy cream, whipped*

1. Melt butter. Add crumbs and ¾ cup sugar. Press in bottom of 10-inch springform pan. Bake in 350° oven for 8-10 minutes. Cool completely.
2. Beat eggs and 1¼ cups sugar until light and fluffy. Fold in coconut.
3. Dissolve gelatin in water on low heat. Combine the gelatin, amaretto, almond, and egg mixture. Fold in whipped cream. Pour into crust and chill several hours before serving.

Temperature: **350 °**
Time: 8-10 minutes

LADY MOCHA ICE CREAM CAKE
Must Make Ahead Of Time

Yields: **10 servings**
Preparation Time: 30 minutes

1   *3-ounce package lady fingers*
½   *gallon coffee ice cream, softened*
1   *quart chocolate ice cream, softened*
2   *tablespoons instant coffee granules*
½   *cup coffee flavored liqueur*
6   *Heath candy bars, crushed chocolate sauce*
1   *cup heavy cream*
½   *cup sugar*
½   *teaspoon vanilla*

Do not defrost serving.

1. Line the lady fingers around the sides of a 9-inch springform pan.
2. Combine the two ice creams. Add coffee, liqueur, and crushed Heath bars. Pour into the springform pan. Spread a thin layer of chocolate sauce on top. Freeze for 2 hours.
3. Before serving, pour heavy cream into chilled bowl. Add sugar and whip until it begins to thicken. Add vanilla.
4. When ready to serve, unmold cake. Spread whipped cream over and serve immediately.

CREAM CARAMEL FLAN

*Yields: **8 servings***
Preparation Time: 30 minutes

¼	*cup sugar*
1	*14-ounce can condensed milk*
1²/₃	*cups milk*
4	*eggs*
2	*teaspoons vanilla*
2	*teaspoons rum*
	whipping cream, optional
	strawberries, optional

1. In a small saucepan, melt sugar, stirring constantly until it turns golden brown. Quickly pour sugar over the bottom of a 9-inch ring mold that is 2-inches deep. Cover as much of the bottom as possible.

2. In a blender, pour condensed milk, milk, eggs, vanilla, and rum. Blend on high speed until all ingredients are well mixed. Pour over sugar in mold.

3. Set ring mold in a pan of water (like a double boiler effect) and bake in 350° oven for 45 minutes or until toothpick comes out clean. Let cool.

4. Separate flan from dish with a knife. Turn onto a plate upside down. Decorate with rosettes of whipping cream and strawberries or fill center with whipped cream and halve the strawberries for dipping into the cream.

*Temperature: **350** °*
Time: 45 minutes

GRASSHOPPER CREPES

Must Make Ahead Of Time

*Yields: **12 crepes***
Preparation Time: 1 hour

Chocolate Crepes:

6	*tablespoons flour*
2	*tablespoons unsweetened cocoa*
¼	*teaspoon salt*
2	*eggs*
2	*egg yolks*
1	*tablespoon sugar*
¼	*cup vegetable oil*
⅓	*cup milk*

Filling:

2	*cups miniature marshmallows*
⅓	*cup milk*
2	*tablespoons white Creme de Cacao*
3	*tablespoons green Creme de Menthe*
	green food coloring
2	*cups heavy cream, divided*
½	*ounce square semi-sweet chocolate*

1. Combine all ingredients for crepes in blender or food processor. Blend until smooth. Let the batter rest for 1 hour in refrigerator.
2. Cook crepes 1 at a time in a greased 5-inch crepe pan.

Assembly

1. Heat marshmallows and milk in saucepan over low heat, stirring constantly until mixture mounds slightly when dropped from a spoon (about 30 minutes).
2. Stir Creme de Cacao, Creme de Menthe, and several drops of food coloring into marshmallow mixture. Set aside.
3. Beat 1 cup heavy cream until stiff. Fold green mixture into whipped cream. Fill cooked crepes and fold over. Chill until firm.
4. Top with extra whipped cream if desired. Shave chocolate or make chocolate curls and sprinkle over crepes.

SINFULLY SCRUMPTIOUS ICE CREAM

*Yields: **12 servings***
Preparation Time:

¾	cup heavy cream
¾	cup milk
1½	cups sugar
½	teaspoon salt
8	egg yolks, well-beaten
5	cups peaches or strawberries, mashed
4	cups heavy cream
	ice
	rock salt

1. Scald the ¾ cup cream and milk in the top of a double boiler. Add sugar and salt.
2. Pour a small amount of milk mixture into beaten egg yolks. Gradually add the yolks to the entire milk mixture. Cook until thickened to custard consistency. Remove from heat and cool.
3. Mix fruit with the remaining 4 cups of cream. Blend with the cooled custard.
4. If using a manual freezer, fill container ¾ full. Pack ice and rock salt around the edges, using 3 parts ice to 1 part salt. When the crank gets too hard to turn and the ingredients have solidified to a soft-ice cream stage, remove the dasher and pack down the ice cream.
5. Repack fresh ice and salt around the sides, wrap in burlap or newspaper and let stand 1 hour. Freeze in proper cartons.
6. For an electric ice cream freezer, follow the directions of the manufacturer.

All About Wine

Cin! Cin!
Skål!
A sua sáude!
Kan bei!
Serefe!
Is Ijeam!
Prosit!

Using these expressions, you'll have no problem drinking to your guests' good health and future success in Italian, Swedish, Portuguese, Chinese, Turkish, Greek and German, respectively. Still, no matter what you say in a toast, there'll always be the dilemma that faces every host planning a dinner party: just which wine is appropriate for the evening's menu.

In the past people seemed to follow a set of fairly strict rules concerning specific wines being paired with certain dishes. But in recent years many people have totally abandoned the traditional couplings, insisting that decisions about food and wine should not be dictated.

Those with expertise in the culinary and oenophilic worlds have been influenced by the new liberalizing forces to a certain degree. They agree that you don't always need to drink the same wines with certain dishes and that you needn't be afraid to try new food-and-wine combinations; however they do suggest that by adhering to a few tried and true axioms, you'll find that you derive the greatest pleasure from your wine-with-dinner events:

Too many exceptions have virtually eliminated the white-wine-with-white-meat and red-wine-with-red-meat theory. After all, red wine is often the perfect accompaniment for an Italian meal even though the tomato-sauced entree may be chicken or delicate white veal. Many times a Bordeaux or Burgundy is the chosen drink with a dinner that features roast chicken or roast turkey. However as a rule, most wine aficionados still insist that dry white selections are always best with fish and red wines are the superior companions for beef and lamb.

Generally, heavier food goes with a heavier wine; that way neither tends to overpower the other. If more than one wine is planned for a meal, the white is usually served before the red, and the dry would be poured before the sweet. It's the sweet white wines, usually thought of as the fitting partner to the dessert course, that is most typically the last wine offered. Rosés are thought of as the suitable drink when a cold entree is being presented, possibly at a casual gathering like a barbecue or picnic. Of course, dry champagne is frequently described as an acceptable accompaniment for all foods, making it a beverage that can be offered before, after or during a meal.

Be careful when serving a champagne or other sparkling wine to open the bottle gently. The host should hold the bottle so that he won't endanger himself or anyone else when the wired-down cork is finally released.

Champagne is at its very best thoroughly chilled, approximately 40 degrees. The optimum temperature for dry white wines is considered to be about 50 degrees and sweet white wines, a few degrees cooler. Although everyday red wine may be cooled down just a bit, a good red wine really should be served at room temperature. Don't forget, though, that room temperature usually signifies a 72-degree reading. Breathing time varies for different red wines, but 30 minutes is considered the minimum amount of time a red wine should be uncorked and allowed to sit before it is served.

How much to pour at a time? A 6-ounce glass, which is suitable for many different varieties of wine, is most often filled halfway for white wines or champagne but only one-third of the way for dessert wines.

Weights and Measures

STANDARD MEASURES
(All measurements are level)

1 cup	=	8	fluid ounces	=	16 tablespoons
¾ cup	=	6	fluid ounces	=	12 tablespoons
⅔ cup	=	5⅓	fluid ounces	=	10 tablespoons plus 2 teaspoons
½ cup	=	4	fluid ounces	=	8 tablespoons
⅓ cup	=	2⅔	fluid ounces	=	5 tablespoons plus 1 teaspoon
¼ cup	=	2	fluid ounces	=	4 tablespoons
⅛ cup	=	1	fluid ounce	=	2 tablespoons
1 tablespoon	=	½	fluid ounce	=	3 teaspoons

TABLE OF EQUIVALENTS

1 gallon	=	128	fluid ounces	=	4 quarts
1 quart	=	32	fluid ounces	=	4 cups
1 pint	=	16	fluid ounces	=	2 cups

CONVERTING WEIGHTS TO MEASURES

Food	Weight of 1 cup		Measure in ounces			
Butter	8	ounces	1 ounce	=	2	tablespoons
Cocoa	4½	ounces	1 ounce	=	3½	tablespoons
Cornstarch			1 ounce	=	3½	tablespoons
Gelatin			1 ounce	=	3	tablespoons
Flour (all purpose, sifted)	4½	ounces	8 ounces	=	1⅞	cups
Macaroni	4	ounces	8 ounces	=	2	cups
Rice	6½	ounces	8 ounces	=	1-1/6	cups
Rolled Oats	2¾	ounces	8 ounces	=	3	cups
Sugar (brown, packed)	7	ounces	8 ounces	=	1⅛	cups
Sugar (granulated)	7	ounces	8 ounces	=	1⅛	cups
Sugar (confectioners' sifted)	4½	ounces	8 ounces	=	2	cups
Shortening	7	ounces	8 ounces	=	1⅛	cups

ESTIMATING RAW INGREDIENTS

Macaroni	1 cup uncooked	= 2¼	cups cooked
Rice	1 cup uncooked	= 3	cups cooked
	1 cup precooked	= 2	cups cooked
Confectioners' sugar	1 pound	= 3-4	cups packed
Brown sugar	1 pound	= 2¼	cups packed
Granulated sugar	1 pound	= 2¼	cups
Heavy cream	1 cup	= 2	cups, whipped
Cheese	1 pound	= 4	cups, grated
Egg Whites	1 cup	= 8	egg whites

SUBSTITUTION CHART

1 ounce chocolate	=	3 tablespoons cocoa plus 1 tablespoon fat
1 tablespoon flour (for thickening)	=	½ tablespoon cornstarch or 1 egg or 2 teaspoons quick-cooking tapioca
1 egg (in custards)	=	2 egg yolks
1 egg (in batter)	=	½ teaspoon baking powder
1 cup whole milk	=	½ cup evaporated milk plus ½ cup water or 1 cup reconstituted nonfat dry milk plus 2½ teaspoons fat
1 cup sour milk	=	1 tablespoon vinegar with sweet milk to make a total of 1 cup (let stand for 5 minutes to sour) or 1 cup buttermilk
1 cup instant flour	=	1 cup sifted all purpose flour
1 cup cake flour	=	⅞ cup all purpose flour plus 2 tablespoons cornstarch
1 cup butter or margarine	=	1 cup shortening or oil plus ½ teaspoon salt
1 cup light cream	=	3 tablespoons butter plus ⅞ cup milk
1 cup heavy cream	=	⅓ cup butter plus ¾ cup milk
1 cup granulated sugar	=	1 cup brown sugar, packed or 1 cup honey or corn syrup* (reduce other liquids in recipe by ¼ cup)
1 teaspoon baking powder	=	¼ teaspoon baking soda plus ⅝ teaspoon cream of tartar
1 cup honey	=	1-1¼ cups sugar plus ¼ cup liquid
1 tablespoon fresh herbs	=	1 teaspoon dried herbs

*Never replace more than ½ the prescribed sugar with syrup.

AVERAGE CAN SIZES

No. 1 can   = 1½ - 2 cups
No. 2 can   = 2¼ - 2½ cups
No. 2½ can = 3¼ - 3½ cups
No. 3 can   = 4 cups
No. 10 can = 12 - 13 cups

SUBSTITUTIONS

1 tablespoon cornstarch or arrowroot	= 2 tablespoons all-purpose flour or 4 teaspoons quick-cooking tapioca
1 cake compressed yeast	= 1 package or 2 teaspoons active dry yeast
1 cup commercial sour cream	= 1 tablespoon lemon juice plus evaporated milk to equal 1 cup or 3 tablespoons butter plus ⅞ cup sour milk
1 cup yogurt	= 1 cup buttermilk or sour milk
1 cup canned tomatoes	= 1⅓ cups cut-up fresh tomatoes, simmered 10 minutes
1 teaspoon onion powder	= 2 teaspoons minced fresh onions
⅛ teaspoon cayenne	= 8 drops Tabasco
1 teaspoon dry mustard	= 1 tablespoon prepared mustard

INDEX

RARE COLLECTION
210 KEMPNER STREET
GALVESTON, TX 77550

Send me _____ *copies of* **RARE COLLECTION** *at $16.95 per copy plus $2.50 for postage and handling for each book. Texas residents please add $1.31 sales tax per copy. Please charge to* _____ *Visa* _____ *Mastercard*

Expiration Date _____ *Card Number* _____ *Signature* _____

NAME _____

ADDRESS _____

CITY _____

STATE _____ ZIP _____

For gift wrapping, add 50¢. Please make checks payable to **JLGC Publications**. Proceeds from the sale of this cookbook will go to support the many worthwhile projects sponsored by the Junior League.

RARE COLLECTION
210 KEMPNER STREET
GALVESTON, TX 77550

Send me _____ *copies of* **RARE COLLECTION** *at $16.95 per copy plus $2.50 for postage and handling for each book. Texas residents please add $1.31 sales tax per copy. Please charge to* _____ *Visa* _____ *Mastercard*

Expiration Date _____ *Card Number* _____ *Signature* _____

NAME _____

ADDRESS _____

CITY _____

STATE _____ ZIP _____

For gift wrapping, add 50¢. Please make checks payable to **JLGC Publications**. Proceeds from the sale of this cookbook will go to support the many worthwhile projects sponsored by the Junior League.

RARE COLLECTION
210 KEMPNER STREET
GALVESTON, TX 77550

Send me _____ *copies of* **RARE COLLECTION** *at $16.95 per copy plus $2.50 for postage and handling for each book. Texas residents please add $1.31 sales tax per copy. Please charge to* _____ *Visa* _____ *Mastercard*

Expiration Date _____ *Card Number* _____ *Signature* _____

NAME _____

ADDRESS _____

CITY _____

STATE _____ ZIP _____

For gift wrapping, add 50¢. Please make checks payable to **JLGC Publications**. Proceeds from the sale of this cookbook will go to support the many worthwhile projects sponsored by the Junior League.